Multinational Business & Labour

PETER ENDERWICK

ST. MARTIN'S PRESS
New York

Library of Congress Cataloging in Publication Data

Enderwick, Peter.
    Multinational business and labor

    Bibliography: p. 201
    Includes index.
    1. International business enterprises – Employees.
2. Collective bargaining – International business
enterprises. 3. International division of labor.
I. Title.
HD2755.5.E53   1984   331.25   84-17771
ISBN 0-312-55252-1

CONTENTS

TABLES

PREFACE AND ACKNOWLEDGEMENTS

This book is primarily addressed to senior undergraduate and post-graduate students following courses in International Business and Industrial Relations. In addition, I hope that it will be of value to others with an interest in the multinational enterprise. For those with little or no training in economic theory, parts of Chapter 3 may appear a little formidable. Understanding of the arguments developed in this chapter will be increased if the reader consults one of the several excellent texts dealing with international trade theory.

In no way does this book offer a definitive statement of the labour market effects of multinational business. Indeed, it invariably raises more questions than it answers. This reflects both the complexity and dynamism of developments in this area. There is a need for considerably more research on many of the very fundamental issues raised by international business. In surveying the state of research at this time I hope it makes clear the need to underpin analysis of the labour market effects of multinational business with conceptual understanding of the theory of multinational enterprise.

In the course of writing this book I have incurred a number of debts. I wish to acknowledge the help of Clare McEwan of the Social Science Library at QUB who successfully tracked down a number of obscure references. Successive drafts of the manuscript were willingly typed and amended by members of the Secretarial Centre at Queen's. Jackie Wright of the Economics Department painstakingly proofread the entire script. To all these people I offer sincere thanks. I am grateful to the OECD and ILO for permission to reproduce extracts of their regulations on multinational enterprises.

Undoubtedly my greatest debt is to my family who have willingly borne my prolonged absences. The book is dedicated to my wife, Martha, who also vetted the manuscript in the interests of the non-specialist reader. Finally, my daughter Carolyn has developed, at the age of three, an almost venerate regard for the sanctuary of my study. If nothing else writing this book has procured for me the opportunity for continuing research. I am grateful to both of them for past and, I hope, future indulgences.

1 INTRODUCTION

The author of a recent book on US labour and international trade and investment (Mitchell, 1976, p. 100) concludes

> The treatment of multinational firms in this chapter will leave many readers unsatisfied. Because of the need to confine the analysis to the labor impact, many of the most interesting aspects of MNCs have been neglected. These aspects revolve around issues of national sovereignty, political influence, the impact on foreign policy, and the general area of the 'goodness' or 'badness' of bigness in business enterprises.

The theme of this book is that the labour aspects of multinational operations are just as important and interesting as the other aspects identified. Perhaps what distinguishes labour aspects from the other issues generated by multinational enterprises[1] (MNEs) is their comparative neglect in the literature. Where they are explicitly considered, analysis is often shallow and dogmatic. This book attempts to redress the situation.

There are several considerations which prompt analysis of the relationships between labour and multinational business. Firstly, there is considerable debate over the emergence of a 'new international division of labour' (NIDL) (Frobel *et al.*, 1980) within which multinational enterprises play a central role (Michalet, 1976). What distinguishes the NIDL from its predecessor, the classical international division of labour, is the part played by the developing nations. Their traditional role of providing agricultural and mineral resources and, on occasion, slave labour, has given way to the possibility of manufacturing facilities, serving the world market, being located in such countries (Castles, 1979). Such a trend has obvious implications for the growth prospects of developing nations and the adjustment process in the advanced nations.

Secondly, the impact of the changing global division of labour is compounded by its concentration by both nation (Saunders, 1981) and industry (Plant, 1981). The fact that only a handful of nations have successfully assumed an export orientation focusing on a narrow range of commodities raises issues of the differential impact of readjustment

1

in the Western nations and the long-term prospects for development by this route in underdeveloped nations (Caporaso, 1981).

Thirdly, the impact of multinational enterprises in this process has attracted criticism. There is some evidence that the longer-term effect of direct foreign investment (DFI)[2] may be to impede development (Bornschier, 1978; Mahler, 1981). Similar criticism surrounds the alleged transfer of inappropriate technologies to developing countries (Watanabe, 1980) contributing to factor underutilisation and income inequalities.

Fourthly, in the advanced nations the spectre of the export of jobs and of 'runaway' plants has generated concern about the relative stability of employment created in multinational subsidiaries. This concern is voiced in both source nations (AFL-CIO, 1971) and advanced host countries, particularly within Western Europe (Enderwick, 1982; Hood and Young, 1982). A number of forms of foreign involvement in Third World countries, particularly subcontracting, have also been identified as potentially highly unstable (Berthomieu and Hanaut, 1980).

Fifthly, a multinational organisational structure is widely equated with a relative bargaining disadvantage for labour in its collective bargaining function (Kujawa, 1979; Szakats, 1980). The sources of labour's disadvantage include the enterprises' ability to service strike-bound plants from overseas, the fact that total revenue is not halted in the face of a dispute, the threat of production switching, inaccessibility to decision-makers and the unreliability and paucity of information disclosed by multinational firms. Many of these assertions have been absorbed into the literature without serious scrutiny of their validity.

Sixthly, one of the apparent benefits of multinational production is the introduction and dissemination in the host nation of innovative and possibly superior production and management methods (Constas and Vichas, 1981; Enderwick, 1983; Globerman, 1979). Considerable public policy interest has focused on this aspect of foreign firms' operations in an attempt to develop beneficial lessons for indigenous firms (Takamiya, 1981).

Finally, the emergence of multinational production has generally been perceived as a threat by organised labour (Edwards, 1977; Gennard, 1972). This concern has prompted a variety of labour-initiated responses (Enderwick, 1979). There is a widely held view that the only effective labour response lies in the development of multinational collective bargaining (Gennard, 1972; Heise, 1973). Despite assertions of the occurrence of such bargaining, the evidence does little to support such claims (Northrup and Rowan, 1979). The prospects for the widespread development of multinational bargaining also seem unfavourable (see Chapter 6). Analysis of the driving forces behind the spread of international production may throw some light on the reasons for the lack of success of this response and the viability and effectiveness of alternative strategies.

These considerations generate a number of questions which this study seeks to address. In attempting to evaluate competing claims and positions our analysis is guided by one central conviction. That conviction is the view that understanding of the implications of multinational business can only follow from an explicit evaluation of the determinants of this form of production (Enderwick, 1982). More specifically, analysis should be firmly grounded in the theory of the multinational enterprise. Whilst a variety of such theories are available (Hymer, 1976; Vernon, 1966 and 1979) recent years have seen an attempted synthesis of several important elements of theory (Dunning, 1981). The emergent 'eclectic' model provides a basis for the evaluation of contending claims and conflicting evidence.

Chapter 2 provides an outline of the magnitude and pattern of multinational production. The industrial distribution of such investment is examined in the light of contending theories of the multinational. The source and host labour market effects of international production are the subject of Chapter 3. The labour utilisation practices and industrial relations impact of multinationals are examined in Chapters 4 and 5, respectively. Labour-initiated responses to the multinational are scrutinised in Chapter 6. Chapter 7 provides policy implications and conclusions.

Notes

1. This study adopts a simple 'threshold' definition of the multinational enterprise. Such an enterprise is one which owns or controls income-earning assets in more than one nation. A variety of alternative definitions, of varying degrees of complexity, have been proposed (Aharoni, 1971).

2. Direct foreign investment is distinguished from other forms of international investment by the fact that the investing company, (typically an MNE), retains control over the investment.

2 THE GROWTH AND PATTERN OF MULTINATIONAL BUSINESS

Introduction

Widespread internationalisation of production is primarily a post-World War II phenomenon. Whilst the origins of the MNE may be traced back to the monopoly charter trading companies of seventeenth-century Europe, the significance of modern MNE growth presents unique problems. By comparison with its historical forerunners the modern MNE is a much larger entity whose source of power is likely to be technological advantage; an advantage which bestows far greater mobility than that possessed by firms whose monopoly was based on exclusive control of agricultural or mineral resources.

This chapter profiles the phenomenon of multinational production. The following section outlines the magnitude and growth of the MNE. The major source and host nations of DFI are then discussed. The highly uneven distribution of DFI by industry is the subject of the following section. Recent trends highlighting alternative and newer forms of market servicing are then examined. Finally, theoretical explanations of these patterns are appraised. Particular emphasis is placed on the eclectic model.

The Magnitude and Growth of Multinational Production

DFI is a significant economic phenomenon both in absolute terms and relative to economic magnitudes such as visible trade, gross national product or domestic output. Estimtes of the cumulative stock of DFI for selected dates between 1914 and 1978 by aggregate area of origin and receipt are contained in Table 2.1. Whilst considerable caution must be attached to prewar estimates, the later estimates are acceptably robust.

Table 2.1 indicates that the accumulated book value of DFI in 1978 was some \$380 bn. The rise in the·value of DFI over the period 1914-78 is apparent. Particularly significant is the rapid expansion between 1960 and 1978. The table highlights the fact that the MNE is predominantly a developed country phenomenon in terms of both

Table 2.1: Estimated Stock of Accumulated Direct Foreign Investment by Area of Origin and Receipt, 1914-78

	1914 $ bn	1914 %	1938 $ bn	1938 %	1960 $ bn	1960 %	1978 $ bn	1978 %
Area of origin								
Developed countries	14.3	100.0	26.4	100.0	62.4	98.9	373.7	96.8
North America	2.8	19.5	8.0	30.4	35.3	56.0	181.7	47.0
Western Europe	11.0	76.9	16.9	63.9	25.1	39.8	158.1	41.0
Other developed countries	0.5	3.5	1.5	5.6	2.0	3.2	31.6	8.1
Developing countries	neg	neg	neg	neg	0.7	1.1	12.5	3.2
Total	14.3	100.0	26.4	100.0	63.1	100.0	386.2	100.0
Area of receipt								
Developed countries	5.2	37.3	8.4	34.3	36.7	67.3	251.7	69.6
North America	2.3	16.0	4.1	16.8	20.5	37.6	85.6	23.6
Western Europe	1.1	7.8	1.8	7.4	12.5	22.9	136.2	37.7
Other developed countries	1.9	13.3	2.5	10.0	3.7	6.8	29.9	8.3
Developing countries	8.9	62.8	16.0	65.7	17.6	32.3	100.4	27.8
International and unallocated	neg	neg	na		na		9.5	2.6
Total	14.1	100.0	24.4	100.0	54.3	100.0	361.6	100.0

Note: neg = negligible values; na = not available.
Source: Dunning (1983).

source and destination. The share of industrialised countries as a source of DFI has only declined from 100.0 per cent in 1914 to 96.8 per cent in 1978. Similarly, in 1978 nearly 70 per cent of DFI was located in developed countries. This percentage share has risen particularly since the interwar period. Thus while DFI to the less developed countries (LDCs) has increased in absolute terms ($8.9 bn in 1914 to $27.8 bn in 1978) it has fallen in relative terms (62.8 to 27.8 per cent). The relative decline, since 1960, in the importance of US investment is also apparent.

The rapid growth rate of DFI achieved during the 1960s was not sustained in the 1970s. This is highlighted in Table 2.2 which shows the number of affiliates established by the largest US MNEs for selected periods and years. Since US DFI still comprises nearly 50 per cent of the global total (Table 2.1), trends observed for US MNEs are likely to be a reasonable indicator for that of all firms.

The acceleration in US investment which occurred through the 1950s and 1960s peaked at the end of the latter decade. The increasing difficulties of the world economy during the 1970s is reflected in a fall in the rate of affiliate establishment. This is particularly marked for the 1974/5 recession.

A distinctive feature of DFI is the importance of large MNEs in the internationalisation process. Several MNEs have value added which exceeds the gross national product of certain industrialised market economies (Buckley and Casson, 1976, p. 12). On average, larger firms tend to be more multinational in orientation. Supportive evidence for this contention is provided in Tables 2.3 and 2.4.

Table 2.3 shows the propensity of US enterprises to engage in overseas production by size. There is a clear tendency for larger firms to undertake overseas production. Furthermore, larger size is associated with a propensity to invest farther afield, i.e. not just in Canada. Smaller size is also related to alternative forms of overseas involvement to majority-owned affiliates; types of involvement which include minority holdings, joint ventures, sales offices and licensing.

Table 2.4 provides an alternative measure of overseas involvement, the overseas production ratio, for a sample of the world's largest firms. Again, there is a tendency for the largest firms to place greater reliance on overseas production.

Involvement is also clearly related to parent nationality. After allowance is made for nationality and industrial distribution, size remains a significant determinant of foreign production (Buckley and Pearce, 1981).

Table 2.2: New Foreign Affiliates Established or Acquired by the 180 Largest US MNEs, 1951-75 (number of affiliates)

Host country group	1951-60	1961-65	1966	1967	1968	1969	1970	1971	1972	1973	1974	1975
	Annual average											
Developed market economies	181	444	459	636	720	677	600	636	444	454	385	235
LDCs	114	201	210	276	86	268	253	269	202	239	234	141
Total	295	645	669	912	806	945	853	905	646	693	619	376

Source: UN (1978), Table III-19, p. 233.

Table 2.3: Majority-owned Affiliates of US Manufacturing Companies with Total Sales over $20 m in 1975 (number of companies)

Sales ranking (1973)	Total companies	Manufacture in one or more countries (excluding Canada)	Manufacture in Canada only	Non-manufacturing activity abroad	Purely national companies	Not known
Over $1 bn	210	179	7	5	18	1
$500 m – $1 bn	122	93	3	11	14	1
$100 – $500 m	592	268	60	71	150	43
$50 – $100 m	328	105	30	45	113	35
$20 – $50 m	294	63	22	24	137	48
Total	1546	708	122	156	432	128

Source: UN (1978), Table III-18, p. 222.

Table 2.4: Overseas Production Ratio (Sales of overseas affiliates and associate companies as a percentage of total worldwide sales of group) for 523 of the World's Largest Enterprises by Size Group, 1977

Sales ranking $ bn	By area: US	Europe	Japan	Total
Over $5 bn	36.3	47.9	6.4	37.3
$2.5 –$5 bn	21.9	28.0	8.4	22.6
$1.5– $2.5 bn	20.2	26.9	6.8	20.5
$1 – $1.5 bn	17.6	28.8	4.6	20.1
$0.8 – $1 bn	20.2	37.0	3.9	26.5
$0.6 – $0.8 bn	10.9	24.4	7.0	17.2
Less than $0.6 bn	15.7	21.7	0.5	19.6

Source: Dunning and Pearce (1981), Table 6.7, p. 127.

Whilst Table 2.2 showed an apparent slowdown in the growth of overseas affiliates in the 1970s, this slowdown is not reflected in the sales growth record of MNEs. Tables 2.5 and 2.6 show the sales growth record of the world's largest enterprises over the 15-year period 1962-77 by nationality and by firm size in the recent period.

Table 2.5 shows that there has been no decline in the growth record of larger MNEs during the difficult economic conditions of the 1970s. Coupling this finding with the evidence of Table 2.2 leads to the tentative conclusion that the influence of the world's largest MNEs may have increased in this period. This appears to have been achieved by consolidation rather than expansion. Table 2.6 lends some support to this hypothesis in that the fastest growth rates during the 1970s were achieved by the very largest MNEs.

Table 2.5: Rate of Growth of Sales for Selected Periods for 667 of the World's Largest Enterprises

Nationality	Period 1962/67 1962=100	1967/72 1967=100	1972/77 1972=100
US	156.3	157.0	198.7
Europe	144.8	188.4	217.0
Japan	209.4	241.2	201.9
Other countries[a]	160.2	173.5	226.2
Total	155.3	169.9	204.8

Note: a. Includes Australia, Canada, South Africa, Netherlands Antilles, Argentina, Brazil, Chile, India, Mexico.
Source: Dunning and Pearce (1981), Table 5.5, p. 100.

Table 2.6: Rate of Growth of Sales 1972-7 for 667 of the World's Largest Enterprises by Firm Size (1972=100)

Nationality	Sales ranking ($bn)						
	Over $5 bn	$2.5— $5 bn	$1.5— $2.5 bn	$1— $1.5 bn	$0.8— $1 bn	$0.6— $0.8 bn	Less than $0.6 bn
US	216.7	189.8	182.1	181.3	181.2	183.7	173.3
Europe	240.8	202.2	215.0	182.2	176.4	175.0	135.5
Japan	202.1	221.4	204.0	194.9	178.9	169.9	129.7
Other countries	541.4	229.6	199.7	209.4	191.8	182.6	156.4
Total	224.1	197.6	192.3	185.0	180.1	180.2	168.9

Source: Dunning and Pearce (1981), Table 5.6, p. 101.

These tables also reveal significant differences in growth rates by nationality. The faster rates achieved by European and other MNEs confirm the relative decline in importance of US DFI (Table 2.1). The following section provides a more detailed examination of the role of particular nations as a source of DFI.

The Geographical Distribution of DFI: Major Source Nations

As indicated above, DFI is a process dominated by the industrialised economies. Table 2.7 reveals that at the end of 1975 some 11 market economies accounted for nearly 95 per cent of the global stock of DFI.

Table 2.7: The Stock of Direct Investment Abroad by Major Country of Origin

Country of origin	$bn	% distribution
United States	124.2	47.8
United Kingdom	30.8	11.9
West Germany	16.0	6.2
Japan	15.9	6.1
Switzerland	16.9	6.5
France	11.1	4.3
Canada	10.5	4.1
Netherlands	8.5	3.2
Sweden	4.4	1.7
Belgium-Luxembourg	3.2	1.2
Italy	3.3	1.3
Total above	243.8	94.3
All other (estimated)	15.1	5.7
Total	258.9	100.0

Source: UN (1978), Table III-32, p. 236.

The overwhelming importance of the US as a source nation is apparent. The significance of both the US and UK reflect the cumulative effects of DFI which has been an established feature of these economies for a very considerable period of time (Dunning, 1970; Wilkins, 1970). The importance of West Germany and Japan is a more recent phenomenon and reflects the rapid strides these nations have made in the postwar period. Table 2.8 complements the data presented in Table 2.2 and provides a comparative analysis of affiliate formation by

Table 2.8: Average Number of New Manufacturing Subsidiaries Formed per Annum for a Sample of 180 US-based MNEs and the 209 Largest Non-US Industrial Firms

Source nation	Period 1951-55	1956-60	1961-65	1966-67	1968-69	1970-71	1972-73
US (1951-75)	83.8	192.0	322.4	390.0	508.5	431.0	378.0
UK (1953-70)	18.3	31.3	111.0	106.3	153.0	243.0	
Continental Europe (1953-70)	39.0	43.7	77.3	76.3	177.3	343.3	
Japan (1953-70)	1.7	4.7	14.7	30.0	37.7	69.7	

Source: Hood and Young (1979), Table 1.5, p. 22.

Table 2.9: Variations in International Diversification of MNEs by Nationality of Parent (1973)

Country of origin	Number of parents	1 country	Percentage of parents with affiliates in: 2-9 countries	10-19 countries	20 or more countries
United States	2,567	44	39	12	5
United Kingdom	1,588	36	50	8	6
West Germany	1,222	39	53	5	3
Switzerland	756	60	35	4	1
France	565	34	51	10	5
Netherlands	467	52	38	7	3
Sweden	301	35	47	12	6
Canada	268	57	39	3	1
Belgium	252	44	44	8	4
Australia	228	55	43	1	1
Italy	213	52	40	1	7
Japan	211	42	49	7	2
Total[a]	9,481	45	44	7	4

Note: a. Includes other countries, giving total of 29 countries.

nationality.

As Table 2.8 shows, most rapid growth rates in affiliate formation occurred amongst Japanese and European MNEs.

Source nationality has also been found to be an important determinant of the degree of multinationality. UK, French and Swedish MNEs tend to be more heavily dependent on foreign production than US MNEs, Japanese firms less so (Buckley and Pearce, 1981). These differences are picked up in Table 2.9 which shows international diversification by nationality.

The Geographical Distribution of DFI: Major Host Nations

The industrialised market economies are overwhelmingly important as both a source of, and host to, DFI. As Table 2.10 illustrates, some 74 per cent of the stock of DFI is located in developed market economies.

Table 2.10: Stock of DFI by Host Country, 1975

Host country and country group	1975
Total value ($bn)	259
Distribution of stock (%)	
Developed market economies	74
of wich:	
Canada	15
US	11
UK	9
West Germany	6
Other	33
Developing countries	26
of which:	
OPEC countries	6
Tax havens	3
Other	17
Total	100

Source: UN (1978), Table III-33, p. 237.

The distribution of DFI within developed countries illustrates two important points. Firstly, the dominant proportion of DFI appears to be prompted by a desire to service local markets. Thus investment by US firms in Canada and other foreign investors into the US as well as much northern American investment in the UK, West Germany and other members of the EEC, is clearly not the result of the existence of low-cost labour. Secondly, much DFI is characterised by 'cross-investment'. Cross-investment occurs with simultaneous DFI by two (or more) nations in the economy of the other(s). Theoretical explanations of the MNE need to explain this crucial trait of DFI. Explanations which stress the cyclical nature of location decisions (Vernon, 1966) or the uniqueness of particular currency areas (Aliber, 1970) have limited power in such circumstances. We return to these considerations later in this chapter.

The comparatively limited significance of LDCs as a host to DFI appears surprising in the light of the historical importance of investment in agriculture and the extractive industries. Other motives for investment in LDCs include the desire to secure local or regional markets, the attraction of low factor, particularly labour, costs and the need for investment support in the form of financial, trade, technical and transportation services. Table 2.11 provides a breakdown by sector and region of DFI by major source nation in 1976.

Table 2.11 shows that for the three major source nations, US, UK and Germany, investment in manufacturing accounts for around half of all DFI. For Japan the corresponding figure is 32 per cent and is surpassed in importance by investment in services. Investment in extractive industries is typically less than 7 per cent, being significantly less for Germany. Investment in petroleum continues to be important, particularly for the world's principal consumer, the US. The table highlights interesting differences by region in the significance of extractive and petroleum investments. With the apparent exception of Japan, the greater proportion of holdings in these sectors is concentrated in the advanced nations. With the exception of petroleum, recent years have seen a decline in the relative importance of mining investments. Much of the decline appears to be due to increasing intervention in, and regulation of, such sectors by host governments. One MNE response has been an attempt to reduce the risk of nationalisation by increasingly concentrating on processing, generally locating processing facilities within the industrialised nations. For example, while OPEC nations account for 84 per cent of the world's exportable oil they contain only 6 per cent of the world's refining capacity (Strenger, 1980).

In contrast, foreign investment in manufacturing and services in LDCs is of increasing importance. Evidence for US affiliates in LDCs indicates a growth rate over the period 1966-7 of 6.3 per cent in mining, 11.3 per cent in petroleum, 13.6 per cent in manufacturing,

Table 2.11: The Amount and Structure of DFI of Major Source Nations by Economic Sector and Region, 1976 (%)[a]

Region	All industries	Mining	Petroleum	Manufacturing	Services	Of which trade
US						
Industrialised countries	73.8	3.4	17.3	38.2	16.8	6.5
LDCs	21.2	1.8	2.1	8.3	9.1	2.3
Total	100.0	5.2	21.6	44.5	28.7	9.8
UK						
Industrialised countries	75.6	5.6	na	47.6	22.4	12.4
LDCs	24.4	1.0	na	11.6	11.8	4.3
Total	100.0	6.6		59.6	34.2	16.8
Germany						
Industrialised countries	69.7	1.3	3.1	50.5	14.9	1.0
LDCs	30.2	0.3	1.8	18.5	9.6	0.3
Total	100.0	1.6	4.9	68.9	24.5	1.3
Japan						
Industrialised countries	45.9	10.1	8.8	27.0	11.9	
LDCs	50.9	15.7	23.6	11.3	2.0	
Total	100.0	28.4	32.4	39.2	14.2	

Note: a. Some figures do not add exactly to the total as establishment data are not disaggregated on a regional basis.
Source: OECD (1981), Table 10, p. 47.

and 13.7 per cent in trade (26.1 per cent in finance) (Howenstine, 1982). Much of the manufacturing production in LDCs appears destined for the local market and is reflective of import substitution policies pursued during the 1950s and early 1960s. There is considerable evidence that European MNEs in LDCs produce primarily for the local market (Allen, 1973; Breidenstein, 1976; Franko, 1976). Jenkins (1979) provides evidence that much MNE manufacturing production in Latin America which is destined for export is used to service the regional market. There is indirect support for the import-substitution view in the poor export performance of US MNEs in LDCs. Their export share fell between 1966 and 1972 from 8.4 to 8.3 per cent (Vaitsos, 1976). The fall was particularly marked for Latin America (Nayyar, 1978). Similarly, there is evidence for the larger LDCs, for example Brazil, that DFI may substitute for exports, implying that such investment may be, at least in part, a market-retention response (Evans, 1979). However, in recent years the picture appears to be changing. There is evidence that the increasing competitive pressure faced in industries such as electronics may be forcing MNEs to seek LDC sources principally for export to the global market (Tharakan, 1981, pp. 99-101). In addition, the proportion of local sales of manufacturing output by majority-owned US affiliates has remained remarkably steady, being 91.6 per cent in 1966, 89.4 per cent in 1974 and 90.6 per cent in 1976. These overall figures disguise the considerable variation by region. As would be expected the percentage destined for the local market is directly related to the size and development of the market, varying from 94 per cent in Latin America to 75 per cent in Asia and Africa (Nayyar, 1978).

The above figures indicate a quantitatively limited involvement of MNEs in export from LDCs. For two reasons these aggregate figures present something of an understatement of the true nature of such involvement. The first factor is the geographical concentration of DFI within LDCs. Table 2.12 gives an outline of the geographical concentration of DFI by both region and selected nation at the end of 1978. The table illustrates the extreme concentration of DFI in LDCs. Some 15 nations attract nearly 50 per cent of investment in the LDCs. These nations have been distinguished in the literature as constituting a distinct set of economic features which classify them as Newly Industrialising Countries (NICs) (OECD, 1979). The distinguishing characteristics include the adoption of export-orientated industrialisation policies, rapid growth in industrial employment and manufactured exports and a narrowing of the real income gap with industrialised market economies (OECD, 1979, p. 6). While different studies exhibit marginal differences in the economies defined as NICs (Saunders, 1981) the major contenders are identified in Table 2.12. These figures begin

Table 2.12: DAC[a] Countries' Stock of DFI in LDCs by Region and Selected Countries, End 1978 (US $m and %)

Region	Major host countries	Amount	% of total	% of region
Europe		8,170	9	
	Spain	5,700		70
	Greece	1,050		13
	Portugal	560		7
	Yugoslavia	170		2
Africa, North of Sahara		1,920	2	
Africa, South of Sahara		4,668	5	
Central America		22,860	26	
	Mexico	6,000		26
South America		27,470	31	
	Brazil	13,520		49
	Argentina	3,340		12
Middle East		1,220	1	
	Israel	1,000		82
Asia		23,000	26	
	Malaysia	2,680		12
	Hong Kong	2,100		9
	Taiwan	1,850		8
	Singapore	1,900		8
	Philippines	1,820		8
	Pakistan	790		3
	Korea	1,500		7
Total		89,308		100
Newly Industrialising Countries (NICs) as a percentage of total LDC DFI.		43,980		49

Notes: Excludes OPEC members and Off-Shore Banking.
     a. Development Assistance Committee members.
Source: OECD (1981), Table 9, p. 46.

to illustrate why there has been increasing concern in the advanced nations over the performance of NICs and in particular the role MNEs have played in this development. Whilst only some 28 per cent of DFI is situated in the LDCs (Table 2.1), 83 per cent of this total ($73,330 m) is located in Central and South America and Asia. Within these three regions some \$35,500m of investment (48 per cent of the regional total) has gravitated to just 10 countries. The less developed nations disproportionately endowed with foreign investment display a number of predictable features. Many have a plentiful supply of low-cost labour, an export-orientation which makes their limited domestic market size less of a constraint, a heavy dependence on foreign trade, political stability and often economic and political dependence on major MNE source nations (Landsberg, 1979). The geographical distribution of private investment also illustrates the isolation of certain economically non-viable regions and nations. There appear to be areas and nations (e.g. Bangladesh) which seem to be extraneous to the development of international production (Frank, 1981a).

The role MNEs play in the economic performance of NICs is of considerable interest. Unfortunately, the available data on this question is far from complete, and at best is only suggestive of the importance of international companies. The evidence for certain NICs identified in Table 2.12 is marshalled in Table 2.13. Because most of the estimates

Table 2.13: Estimated Percentage Share of Foreign-owned MNEs in Manufacturing Employment and Exports in Selected NICs

Country	Year of estimate[a]	Percentage share in employment	Percentage share in exports[d]
Argentina	1970/69	10-12[b]	30
Brazil	1970/69	20[b]	43
Hong Kong	1971	11[c]	na
Korea	1974/71	12[b]	15
Malaysia	1970	33[b]	na
Mexico	1970	21[b]	25-30
Philippines	1970	7[b]	na
Singapore	1976/70	32[b]	70
Thailand	1970	9[c]	na

Notes: Differences in the definition of MNEs mean that the estimates are not strictly comparable.
     a. Former date applies to employment share, latter date to exports.
Sources: b: ILO (1981b), Table II.3, p. 27.
     c: UN (1978), Table III. 54, p. 263.
     d: Nayyar (1978), Table I, p. 62.

are based on sample surveys of MNEs, they differ in the percentage holding defined as constituting foreign control. Whilst this means that the data are not strictly comparable they are suggestive of the importance of foreign MNEs (Blam and Hawkins, 1975). Typically foreign

MNEs provide at least 10 per cent of employment in the manufacturing sector of these nations. Interestingly, MNEs have secured a far bigger share in those nations most successful in exporting manufactures to the developed nations (Brazil, Malaysia, Singapore). These nations have also been those most open and receptive to DFI. Given that foreign-owned enterprises tend to be among the most productive and export-orientated in these nations (Freeman and Persen, 1980; Newfarmer and Marsh, 1981), their percentage employment figures tend to understate their relative importance in economic activity. This is shown by the significantly higher figures for export shares.

The concentration of DFI geographically is accompanied by a similar concentration by product type in the NICs. This is shown in Table 2.14. Table 2.14 indicates that there is a marked tendency for manufactured exports to OECD nations from the NICs to fall into the labour-intensive industries such as textiles, clothing and footwear. Indeed, these three industries dominate OECD imports in the cases of Greece, Portugal, Hong Kong, Taiwan, Philippines, Pakistan and Korea. However, several of the larger, more developed NICs, such as Argentina and Brazil, have achieved a significant share in capital-intensive, technological exports within chemicals, machinery and transport equipment.

The Industrial Distribution of DFI

DFI is distributed unevenly not only geographically, but also by industry. Table 2.15 gives the distribution by industry of assets of US parent and affiliate enterprises in 1977. Table 2.15 shows that there is a distinct tendency for certain sectors of the US economy to be disproportionately represented abroad by DFI. These sectors are mining, petroleum and trade. The financial sector and industries such as construction and agriculture are under-represented overseas. Whilst the manufacturing sector as a whole is of approximately the same relative importance in domestic and overseas production for US firms, there are considerable differences by industry within the manufacturing sector. Industries such as chemicals, non-electrical and electrical machinery display an above average propensity to multinationalisation. Further disaggregation of the manufacturing sector by commodity is a prerequisite to identifying the shared traits of those products amenable to overseas production. Existing research (Pugel, 1981) indicates that there is a distinct tendency for DFI to originate in research-intensive, capital-intensive sectors of manufacturing. Foreign-owned firms also

Table 2.14: The Relative Importance of Selected Products in OECD Imports from NICs, 1977 (% of total)

NIC	Commodity Textile yarns and fabrics	Clothing	Footwear	Chemicals	Iron and steel	Machinery and transport equipment
Spain	4.9	2.8	6.5	8.9	9.8	35.6
Greece	18.8	14.4	3.6	10.6	8.3	9.6
Portugal	22.3	16.1	3.5	7.4	2.9	21.5
Yugoslavia	6.0	6.2	5.9	9.4	5.8	36.2
Mexico	10.9	2.9	1.0	21.8	4.8	21.5
Brazil	12.5	3.3	5.6	6.0	8.6	45.2
Argentina	3.3	3.9	0.6	14.4	9.1	41.6
Israel	2.9	6.5	. . .	13.9	0.5	14.6
Malaysia	4.5	4.9	1.3	2.7	. . .	4.6
Hong Kong	9.2	33.4	1.0	3.8	0.1	17.4
Taiwan	11.6	16.6	7.8	2.7	1.3	26.5
Singapore	5.4	6.0	. . .	8.3	30.5	56.9
Philippines	5.5	15.2	. . .	5.0	1.5	4.2
Pakistan	66.2	5.4	1.8	2.1	. . .	2.6
Korea	12.7	24.2	5.7	2.7	4.6	20.4

Source: Saunders (1981), Table 1.1, p. 4.

Table 2.15: The Percentage Distribution of Total Assets by Sector and Industry of US Affiliates and US Parent Firms, 1977

Sector/Industry	US affiliates abroad		US parent firms	
	% of all industries	% of manufacturing	% of all industries	% of manufacturing
All industries	100.0		100.0	
Mining	3.7		0.5	
Petroleum	23.3		14.2	
Manufacturing, of which:	38.9	100.0	41.0	100.0
Food and related products		7.4		7.7
Chemicals and applied products		20.3		15.4
Primary and fabricated metals		11.2		13.8
Non-electrical machinery		14.9		13.1
Electrical machinery		9.0		7.4
Transport equipment		16.8		20.9
Other manufacturing		20.4		21.9
Trade	11.5		5.5	
Finance	15.7		24.6	
Other industries, e.g. services, agriculture, construction	6.9		14.2	

Source: Survey of Current Business, vol. 61, no. 4, April 1981, p. 34.

appear to be attracted to the faster growing, export-orientated sectors (Buckley and Dunning, 1976). These findings appear to hold across a variety of market economies (Deane, 1970; Gray, 1972; Steuer *et al.*, 1973; Stubenitsky, 1970). In addition, there appears to be a direct correlation between concentration and the presence of foreign investment (Buckley and Casson, 1976; Lall, 1979; Newfarmer, 1979).

Table 2.16 confirms the role of research intensity as a determinant of international production. Whilst the data refers to a sample of 866 of the world's largest enterprises, the relationship between size and multinationality (Tables 2.3 and 2.4) implies that this sample is likely

Table 2.16: The Percentage Distribution of Sales by Industry Research Intensity for a Sample of 866 of the World's Largest Enterprises, 1977

Research intensity[a]/Industry	% of sales
High research intensity	
Aerospace	2.0
Office equipment (inc. computers)	2.0
Petroleum	22.4
Measurement, scientific and photographic equipment	1.1
Electronics and electrical appliances	9.4
Chemicals and pharmaceuticals (including soaps and cosmetics)	11.1
Total	48.0
Medium research intensity	
Industrial and farm equipment	4.7
Shipbuilding, railroad and transportation equipment	1.3
Rubber	1.6
Motor vehicles (including components)	12.1
Metal manufacturing and products	12.5
Total	32.2
Low research intensity	
Building materials	1.7
Tobacco	1.4
Beverages	1.3
Food	8.4
Paper and wood products	2.8
Textiles, apparel, leather goods	1.9
Publishing and printing	0.7
Total	18.1
Other manufacturing	1.6
Total	100.0

Note: a. See text for definition.
Source: Dunning and Pearce (1981), Table 3.4, p. 43.

to include most of the major MNEs. The evidence of Table 2.16 highlights the importance of highly research-intensive industries for the
world's largest enterprises. Research intensity is classified in terms of
percentage of scientists and engineers in total employment. High
research intensity corresponds to a figure of 5 per cent or more, medium
intensity 2-5 per cent and low research intensity less than 2 per cent
(Dunning and Pearce, 1981, p. 10). Nearly 50 per cent of the sample's
sales are accounted for by the most R and D intensive industries. Industries of lower research intensity which are still important in terms of
international production include motor vehicles and food products.
Clearly, while R and D intensity is a significant determinant of foreign
production, it is only one of several important influences.

Alternative Forms of International Market Servicing

DFI is one of several possible modes for servicing overseas markets.
The major alternatives are exporting and licensing. Exporting implies
that markets can be served without the need for foreign production.
Licensing, like DFI, does involve foreign production. It differs from
DFI, however, in that control over foreign production may be surren-
dered or traded to a related or unrelated party. Recent years have also
witnessed a growth in the significance of a number of variant forms of
foreign involvement. Involvement with less than majority participation
gives rise to joint ventures where there is a sharing of ownership and
earnings. This sharing may involve an MNE and private or public corporations or even the government of the host nation and appears to be
particularly attractive when the parties involved are from more than
one LDC (Kumar and McLeod, 1981; Lecraw, 1977). Joint ventures in
the LDCs involving MNEs from the advanced nations may take the
form of 'fade-out agreements' where the share of foreign involvement
is gradually decreased. Local control may eventually be dominant or
even total. Even more closely circumscribed involvement by advanced
nation enterprises occurs in the cases of turnkey operations and
management contracts. Considerable growth has also occurred in the
form of international subcontracting (ISC) (Sharpston, 1975). ISC is
more than a manifestation of the multinationalisation of production: it
may occur between unrelated parties or 'within border' where only
indigenous firms are involved. Nevertheless MNEs have played a significant role in the development of international (cross-border) subcontracting. The distinguishing feature of ISC is that a principal (often

an MNE or multinational buying group) subcontracts production, processing or assembly of supplied inputs whilst retaining control and responsibility for the marketing of the final product.

A variety of factors are likely to account for these variants of international involvement. The rise of non-US MNEs, particularly LDC-based MNEs, has revealed a willingness on the part of these firms to operate with less than majority ownership. Such an attitude is particularly attractive in the light of rising nationalism and an increasing desire on the part of some of the developing nations to participate in the affairs of production subsidiaries. Similarly, uncertainty in the world economy coupled with the contractionary effects of recession may have increased the significance of cost considerations and a revaluation of the inevitability of expansion via internal growth (Oman, 1981).

This section concentrates on licensing and international subcontracting in a discussion of alternative forms. These modes are selected as they are likely to have the most pronounced implications for labour, affecting employment, skill diffusion and the transfer of technology.

Licensing as a form of market servicing has attracted relatively little attention in the literature on multinational production (Telesio, 1979). Under certain conditions licensing represents an attractive form of international involvement.[1] If the knowledge to be licensed can be easily identified and transfer costs are not inordinate, market structure considerations may encourage licensing. Where markets are oligopolistic, corporate strategy may be constrained by interdependencies. Entry by foreign firms in the form of DFI may serve to reduce the returns enjoyed by all participants. In addition, the lowering of returns from DFI makes licensing comparatively more attractive. Provided there exist local producers capable of exploiting licenses and informational problems of valuation do not prevent transfer, such a strategy is likely to appeal, particularly where host government policies inhibit market penetration by other means, or where the licensor lacks the resources to mount an alternative market serving strategy.

Very little is known about the relative significance of the licensing mode in international operations. Data on licensing cover receipts from, and payments for, licences. Ideally, what is required are estimates of sales generated by licensing. One, admittedly imprecise and *ad hoc*, method of generating such estimates, is to assume that licensing royalties represent some constant percentage of sales, typically 5 per cent. Sales figures can then be obtained by scaling up receipts. In the absence of reliable information such data may be indicative of the relative significance and trend of licensing. Estimates based on this procedure for the two most important international producing nations, the US and UK, for 1971 are presented in Table 2.17.

Table 2.17: The Comparative Significance of Licensing, DFI and Exports in Servicing Overseas Markets for the US and UK, 1971

	US $m	UK £m
Licensed Sales L	10,700	1,293
Direct Investment Sales I	92,604	13,334
Exports X	33,263	8,926
Foreign Production (L+I)	103,304	14,627
Total Foreign Sales (L+I+X)	136,567	23,553
Exports as a % of Total Foreign Sales $\frac{X}{(L+I+X)}$	% 24	% 38
Foreign Production as a % of Total Foreign Sales $\frac{(L+I)}{(L+I+X)}$	76	62
Licensed Sales as a % of Foreign Production $\frac{L}{(L+I)}$	10.4	9.0
Licensed Sales as a % of Total Sales $\frac{L}{(L+I+X)}$	7.8	5.5

Sources: Estimates for the UK from Buckley and Davies (1981). Estimates for the US calculated by the author from data in Kroner (1980); Belli and Maley (1974); *United Nations Yearbook of International Trade Statistics 1970-71*.

Table 2.17 shows estimates which cover licensing receipts from unrelated affiliates in manufacturing. Management fees and royalties unrelated to sales have been excluded. On the basis of the assumption that royalty rates are 5 per cent, estimated licensed sales (L) are shown in the first row. Coupling these data with estimates for DFI sales[2] and exports allows the derivation of a number of indicative measures. These measures indicate that DFI is the principal servicing mode for both nations. Exporting is of more significance for the UK than the US. The role of licensing is clearly significant. Our estimates indicate that licensed sales are some 32 per cent of the value of exports for the US and almost 15 per cent in the case of the UK. The importance of licensing in foreign production is very similar for the two nations, being 10.4 per cent for the US and 9.0 per cent for the UK. Because of the higher propensity of the UK to rely on exports, licensing is comparatively less important for the UK as a percentage to total sales, 5.5 per cent compared with 7.8 per cent for the US. Despite the problems involved in generating these estimates they do indicate the global importance of licensing in international sourcing decisions.

The central factor encouraging the growth of ISC has undoubtedly been the changing development orientation of many less developed nations. The failure of import-substitution policies promulgated during the immediate postwar years has led to the adoption of a more open, export-orientated philosophy. Development success is increasingly measured in terms of employment creation as opposed to simply GNP growth. Linked with this change has been a recognition that private organisations such as the MNE have a major role to play in the development process (Franko, 1975). These changes have coincided with increasing global competition in the world market stimulated by the expansion of non-US MNEs, a changing industrial structure in the advanced nations encouraging a decline in the most labour-intensive sectors (Aho and Rousslang, 1979) and rising real labour costs in the industrialised nations. The increasing atomisation of the labour process coupled with an ability to conduct business operations globally has led to pressures to relocate such activities in lower-cost areas of the world. These pressures have been reinforced by the enormous increase in government regulation of business which has had a disproportionate effect on labour-intensive industries. This process of relocation is facilitated by the ready availability of low-cost docile labour and generous host government incentives (Caporaso, 1981).

This changing orientation by many LDC governments has been mirrored by a recognition on the part of the government of several major source nations that the internationalisation of production may be an inevitable result of global corporate competition. This recognition finds embodiment in the provision of tariff schedules encouraging offshore assembly (Lall, 1980). Such provisions restrict duties on advanced nations' imports, which originate from those nations in the form of raw materials or components, to the value added in the exporting nation. They are widely used by the US (Finger, 1976) and European nations (Finger, 1977). These tariff provisions undoubtedly encourage the export of manufactures from LDCs as well as the subcontracting of processing activities by advanced nation enterprises.

In assessing the impact of international production on labour it is important to recognise that such production may assume a variety of forms. Their labour market effects are unlikely to be uniform and necessitate separate analysis.

Theories of DFI and the MNE

An understanding of the labour market effects of MNEs cannot proceed without an understanding of the basic driving forces of the MNE. Indeed, a failure to incorporate theoretical underpinning is likely to generate misleading and superficial analysis (Enderwick, 1982).

Whilst recent years have witnessed great strides in understanding the MNE, certain problems exist. The most important is the failure, so far, successfully to integrate theories of the MNE with those of DFI (Calvert, 1981). There would be considerable difficulties in such an integration. The MNE does not fit easily into the framework of international trade and investment theory. Such theory is hampered by its static nature, its assumptions of product homogeneity, perfect information and selection of the nation state as the relevant decision-making unit. The MNE is principally a dynamic phenomenon attracted to imperfect market structures (Erdilek, 1976). At this stage we abstract from this problem by concentrating on theories of the MNE. This is justified by the fact that this is the pertinent unit of decision-making and a suitable vehicle for analysis of labour market impacts. Clearly labour management is overwhelmingly an internal corporate function.

The genesis of theories of the MNE is the work of Hymer (1976) who put forward the simple proposition that foreign firms are able to compete with indigenous enterprises because they possess some 'advantage' which compensates for the difficulties of operating across national boundaries. The proposition ensures the central position of market imperfections in analysing the foreign operations of firms. Clearly, without such imperfections advantages could only be transitory; in the longer run they would be competed away leaving overseas firms at a competitive disadvantage. Much discussion has concerned the nature of these advantages (Caves, 1971; Johnson, 1970), given that they must be of a type easily transferable within the organisation. However, the existence or transferability of an advantage are at best only necessary, and are not sufficient conditions, for the emergence of international production. Such investment will only occur if optimum exploitation of the advantage, from the firm's point of view, calls for control. If foreign production was not the most profitable route, one would observe much more in the way of licensing others to exploit the advantage. Despite the importance of Hymer's insight in highlighting the need for compensating advantages by foreign producers, a number of weaknesses are apparent. Firstly, the theory provides no explanation of how these advantages arise, they are simply assumed to exist. Furthermore, inability to assess the costs of acquisiton seriously inhibits the ability of the profit-maximising firm to invest rationally in competing forms of advantage. Secondly, the theory fails to consider explicitly the long-run nature of the advantage necessary to the foreign firm. Since direct investment represents the long-term commitment of often considerable assets, the theory should provide an understanding of the continuing source of advantage. If, for example, knowledge is a primary advantage, it may be ability to innovate, rather than a specific innovation, which forms a continuing source of advantage (Buckley and Casson, 1976).

This short-term view of foreign operations and the primacy of US companies was reinforced by the work of Vernon (1966) in putting forward the Product Cycle thesis. The basis of the thesis is that many products undergo a number of clearly definable life stages, which largely determine international production and marketing strategies. The model is based on a number of key assumptions. Firstly, tastes are assumed to be directly related to income. Secondly, markets in knowledge, both technical and commercial, are imperfect. Thirdly, the firm incurs communication costs when operating internationally.

In the first phase of the cycle new products and production processes are typically developed in the US in response to a large affluent market, scarce labour, and extensive research and development expenditures. Overseas demand for these products and processes develops only as foreign incomes increase. In the second stage, the firm meets foreign demand through exports until both the product and its production process become standardised. The third phase is concerned with the choice between domestic and foreign production – cost considerations being a significant influence on the form of market servicing adopted.

Vernon (1974) has attempted to generalise the model to account for direct investment from other source nations such as those within Western Europe and Japan. Despite this the thesis suffers a number of deficiencies. Firstly, it remains programmatic to the extent that the timing and transition of the component stages cannot be successfully predicted. Secondly, it cannot explain cross-investment. It cannot be applied to products which do not have a particularly strong demand in the most affluent countries or where location of manufacture is tied to some particular natural resource. Thirdly, the model can only explain that investment which is export substituting.

An important step in the formulation of a more general theory of the MNE is the work of Buckley and Casson (1976). Recognition of the existence of market imperfections is clear in the work of both Hymer and Vernon. However, it is imperfections in the market for final goods which these writers stress. An important insight of Buckley and Casson is that imperfections are also likely to be significant in markets for intermediate products. Market imperfections impose costs on firms seeking to consummate transactions through such markets. The major source of costs are imperfections in the transfer of ownership or property rights in external markets (Casson, 1979). These costs may be avoided where property rights are not transferred (i.e. ownership does not change). The firm represents an institutional response to such market imperfections and the market is internalised (Arrow, 1970; Coase, 1937). The multinationality of the firm arises because many products (e.g. information) are applicable to world markets and internalisation crosses national boundaries.

Extensions to the earlier work of Hymer are apparent. Imperfections in intermediate markets are added to those of final markets and the primary role of information is stressed. It is with the transfer of such products that imperfection costs are likely to be greatest and the incentives to internalisation strongest. The long-run nature of internalisation theory is also apparent. The replacement of imperfect external markets by institutional fiat calls for a considerable commitment of resources and elaborate patterns of communication and exchange. An element of dynamism is incorporated into the theory in that there is likely to be interaction between imperfections and internalisation (Rugman, 1981). Internalisation is likely to create considerable barriers to entry thus increasing imperfections. MNEs are both a response to, and source of, such imperfections. Whilst the internalisation concept is extremely powerful in that it encompasses and subsumes a whole body of previously existing partial explanations of direct investment (Giddy, 1978; Rugman, 1981) it is not complete in itself. To it must be added elements of location theory.

Dunning (1977 and 1979) classifies inputs as being ownership-specific (and mobile) and location-specific (and immobile) in his attempt to develop an eclectic theory of international production. The market servicing and location decisions of MNEs result from the intersection of these two sets of inputs. The existence of fragmented or protected markets or the absence of suitable local producers reduce the probability of a market being serviced by exports or licensing and increase the likelihood of direct investment. The availability of raw materials and the structure of relative labour costs are likely to influence the location of overseas production facilities. Three important implications follow from the work of Dunning. Firstly, his analysis shows that country-specific characteristics are likely to be an important influence on both ownership-specific and location-specific advantages. To the extent that this is true it is invalid to try to generalise from the investment activities of one particular source nation. Secondly, the nature and distribution of these advantages is not static, they are likely to shift over time as comparative advantage changes. The declining relative importance of US MNEs since the mid-1960s reflects the increasing international competitiveness of other nations' enterprises. Thirdly, industry-specific considerations appear to be important determinants of the market servicing choice, such considerations being particularly significant in determining the net benefits of internalisation (Dunning, 1979).

The emerging eclectic model thus comprises three central elements:

1. the existence of ownership-specific advantages;
2. the existence of incentives to internalisation; and
3. the existence of location-specific inputs.

The interaction of these elements determines the enterprise's choice of market servicing mode. *Ceteris paribus*, the greater the extent of ownership-specific advantages a nation's enterprises enjoy, the more profitably the exploitation of these advantages is achieved within the firm and to the extent that such exploitation necessitates the co-operation of foreign inputs, the more likely are such enterprises to engage in DFI. The eclectic model may also be applied on a dynamic basis to the changing net investment position of a nation (Dunning, 1979) or to the dynamics of emerging source nations of MNEs (Dunning, 1981).

Whilst considerable progress has been made in understanding the distinctive nature of the MNE, substantial theoretical limitations remain. Buckley (1983) has drawn attention to deficiencies in adequately modelling the dynamic basis of ownership-specific advantages and the danger of extending the concept from the firm to the industry. Similarly, the internalisation concept remains unexplored, particularly with regard to the determinants of switches from external market servicing modes such as exporting, to internal means (Buckley and Casson, 1981), the interaction of market imperfections and corporate activity and the administrative structure of internal markets.

The major theories outlined above would all predict a distribution of DFI very similar to that highlighted earlier in this chapter. The product cycle thesis is concerned with the research-intensive, innovatory type of product typified by the high-technology growth industries so heavily patronised by MNEs. These industries are also marked by their oligopolistic structure, a trait of the MNE stressed by Vernon. Similarly, the source of the advantage advocated in the Hymer-Kindleberger model is commonly thought to include technological advantage as a result of research and development expenditures, and commercial advantages such as the ability successfully to differentiate a product. These observations lead one to expect a notable concentration of DFI in research-intensive, oligopolistic, industrial and consumer durable industries. The most explicit predictions of the likely distribution of direct investment are contained in the eclectic model. This approach stresses the public good characteristics of knowledge, particularly technology, which, coupled with market imperfections, have in the past provided inducements to internalise markets internationally. This theory can explain the industrial distribution of direct investment as well as the larger than average size and growth rates of MNEs.

Summary and Conclusions

This chapter has outlined the growth and distribution of MNEs in the world economy. The MNE is largely a postwar phenomenon, concentrated particularly in the developed countries. Quantitatively, affiliate sales exceed the value of exports for major source nations like the US and UK (Table 2.17). Whilst there has been some slowdown during the 1970s in the rate of affiliate formation (Table 2.2), the largest most multinational enterprises appear to have maintained their relative position (Table 2.5). More than 90 per cent of DFI originates from the advanced nations, the most significant being the US. Recent years have seen rapid growth of European and Japanese MNEs. The advanced nations also attract over 75 per cent of the stock of DFI (Table 2.10). DFI which is attracted to the developing nations is also heavily concentrated, particularly in a group of rapidly developing NICs. MNEs appear to have played a significant role in the trading performance of these nations (Table 2.13). The industrial distribution of DFI is also uneven. Such investment is disproportionately important in the more highly concentrated, oligopolistic, high-technology industries.

The fact that DFI is only one form of international market servicing was highlighted. The major alternatives of exporting and licensing have received inadequate attention in the literature. Similarly, uncertainty and recession coupled with changing locational influences have generated a variety of innovative forms of international involvement. The major theoretical explanations of these patterns of DFI were also examined. The eclectic model was highlighted as a powerful explanatory tool of MNE behaviour. When applied to the labour market effects of MNEs this model generates several important conclusions.

Firstly, the model isolates the relationship between exports and DFI. Both the product cycle and early advantages models see foreign operations as a direct substitute for exporting from domestic production facilities. In the product cycle thesis, once product standardisation is achieved cost considerations dictate the need to service overseas (and even home) markets from a lower (labour) cost base. In both cases foreign operations are substituted for exporting activity. Furthermore, in the case of the advantages theory overseas operations form an offensive strategy (i.e. profit maximising motive) and do not follow from some need to defend overseas (and possibly home) market shares. The defensive strategy is considered in the product cycle case but has received little attention. This point is critical in assessing the employment effects of foreign production since if DFI must be undertaken to protect market shares, domestic job losses may be even greater (i.e. many indirect positions would also be lost) if such investment did not occur. The adverse domestic employment effects of international production are overstated if the direct substitutability of foreign for domestic operations fails to hold. This important question is examined more fully in the following chapter.

Secondly, the inevitability and uniformity of the pattern of DFI implied by the product cycle model is attenuated by the eclectic model. The view of a generation of US enterprises switching production facilities to other developed nations and later to low-cost LDCs is replaced by a consideration of the interplay between country- and industry-specific characteristics. Some industries appear to be more prone to the use of low-cost centres than others and these differences may transcend national characteristics, e.g. electronics. It follows from this that the view of employment gains in some nations (e.g. the EEC) being at the expense of another nation (e.g. the US) may be an oversimplification. There is some evidence that industrial rationalisation may increasingly involve more than just the substitution of capital for labour: transnational reorganisation may now be an unavoidable part of the process. To the extent that this is true, job losses (and gains) may be more unevenly distributed between industries than between nations.

Thirdly, the eclectic view of DFI is a longer term one which recognises the considerable resource commitment involved in transplanting administrative fiat for market exchange. The investment required to internalise market imperfections implies that the investing firm may see such facilities as a long-term and continuing asset. This is in marked contrast to the conception held by organised labour in major host nations who have expressed considerable concern at the likely instability of such investments. Such a view is, again, implied by the early theories of the MNE. Exploitation and appropriation of the full return to advantages calls for the setting up of overseas facilities. No indication of the durability of such investments is offered. The product cycle model, by stressing the importance of cost considerations traces out the likelihood of an eventual siting of most overseas production in the LDCs following the initial siting of plants in lower-cost (relative to the US) advanced nations.

These and similar deductions from the eclectic model provide theoretical guidance in assessing the impact of MNEs on labour. Such guidance is particularly crucial in analysing labour market effects, the subject of Chapter 3.

Notes

1. This section draws heavily on the work of Buckley and Davies (1981). See also Rugman (1981), Ch. 3.

2. Because of data deficiencies the value of Direct Investment Sales (I) for the UK was estimated by Buckley and Davies. Sales were estimated from data on the book value of assets on the assumption that the Sales:Asset ratio was 2:1. See Buckley and Davies (1981).

3 THE LABOUR MARKET EFFECTS OF MNEs

Introduction

The impact of MNEs on employment and income in both host and source nations has been a topic of considerable debate for the past two decades. Concern has been fuelled by the shift, in a number of developing nations, towards export-led industrialisation based on the attraction of foreign capital as well as the structural imbalances experienced by a number of advanced economy industries where import penetration and plant closures have substantially reduced employment opportunities. The changing international division of labour within many MNEs is seen as a major causal factor in these developments. Attempts to quantify the importance of MNEs in this process have met with only limited success. The major reason for this failure lies in the problem of specifying underlying assumptions of the analysis. Estimates of the impact of MNEs on employment and income distribution are acutely sensitive to assumptions adopted particularly with regard to the questions of investment-substitution and export-substitution (Caves, 1982).

The following section outlines a number of theoretical models of the effects of DFI on factor income and employment. Subsequent analysis focuses on the theoretical specification most useful in examining the labour market impact of MNEs. Succeeding sections concentrate on the direct and indirect employment impact and income effects of MNEs.

Theoretical Models of the Impact of DFI on Factor Income and Employment

A theoretical framework for analysing the probable impact of direct investment on factors of production is provided by the general equilibrium model of international trade. The following outlines a number of increasingly complex variants of the model and their implications for capital and labour.

The Basic Heckscher-Ohlin Model

Assume a two-country world comprising Host (H) and Source (S)

35

nations, two commodities (A and B) produced and traded using two productive factors, Labour (L) and Capital (K). Production technology is assumed to be constant between nations, while factor intensities vary between industries. Specifically, commodity A is assumed to be proportionately more capital-intensive than B. Both factor and product markets are assumed to be perfectly competitive and transport costs negligible. In addition, we assume that factors are internationally immobile but may move within nations. Furthermore, the two nations are assumed to be price takers, that is they face commodity prices determined in the world market. A basis for trade is provided by the assumption that factor endowments differ between the two nations; specifically we assume that S is relatively well endowed with capital.

Since country S has comparative advantage in A (the capital-intensive commodity) the establishment of trade will lead to production specialisation[1] in both nations. S will shift resources from the production of B into A. The reverse will occur in H. Within S the higher international price of A (relative to domestic prices) pushes up the returns to capital (used heavily in the production of A) relative to labour income (wages). The opposite occurs in H as the relative price of B rises increasing wages relative to capital rents. The important implication of this process is that international trade brings greater equality of factor incomes between nations, i.e. wages in H and S and rents in H and S converge. In the extreme, unfettered trade will bring global equality of factor returns.

International Capital Mobility in the Absence of Trade

We now relax the assumption that factors are internationally immobile and allow overseas movement of capital. Initially we assume that such movements occur in the absence of trade. Because of the absence of trade, production in H and S depends only on domestic demand (and prices). Because of the marked differences in factor endowments relative factor incomes will diverge between the two nations. Capital will earn a higher return in H, the capital-scarce economy. The rent differential will induce capital movement from the source (S) to host (H) nation. Such a movement affects factor endowments, reducing capital in S and increasing the capital stock in H. The effect of this is to shift inwards the product transformation curve of S. An offsetting outward shift occurs in H. Rents will increase for those MNEs investing in H; in addition, all capital in S will enjoy a higher return because of its increased scarcity (higher marginal productivity). Indigenous capital in H will experience a fall in rents as a result of the capital inflow. Labour incomes are also affected. Wages will fall in S (the loss of capital reduces the demand for collaborative labour), whilst the increased demand for labour in H will bid up wages. Again, this model yields the prediction that capital movements will serve to reduce relative factor income inequalities between the two nations.[2]

International Capital Mobility and Trade

If we assume the possibility of both capital and commodity movements between nations the conclusions of preceding models are altered to the extent that partial adjustment is absorbed in the form of a change in the structure of trade.

As in the preceding model factor movements alter factor endowments inducing a shift in the allocation of resources between activities (movement along the production possibility curve). That shift tends to offset the downward wage pressure in S (where the outflow of capital releases excess labour). As resources are shifted in S from the capital-intensive export commodity A to B more capital is released than is required by the expansion in production of B. Similarly, the demand for labour in producing the increment of B exceeds the supply released from the contraction of A's production. This inter-sectoral adjustment takes some of the downward pressure off wages in S created by the outflow of capital.

In the extreme case international capital movements will have no effect on factor incomes if a country's terms of trade (price of exports relative to imports [or import-substitutes]) are unchanged by the capital movement. Such a result is most likely to hold where the nation is a price-taker in international terms. The increasing competition in world trade and correspondence between major export nations and direct investment source nations in the postwar period indicate that such adjustment may be more significant at the present than at any time in the past. If terms of trade alter income distribution will change in favour of the factor used most intensively in the sector experiencing a price rise. Thus within our model if a tariff is raised in S pushing up prices (and output) in the import-competing industry labour would benefit in S but not in H (Stolper-Samuelson Theorem). Because of the international mobility of capital a corresponding tariff raised in H will bring permanent gains to indigenous capital. By raising the return to capital (increasing price of capital- intensive import-substitute A in H) capital flows from S will occur. Capital returns will fall as total (indigenous plus overseas controlled) capital stock rises. This model demonstrates the fundamental link between trade and investment.

Obstacles to trade tend to encourage investment (Mundell, 1957).

Sectoral Specificity of Capital and International Investment

Preceding variants of the general equilibrium model have assumed inter-industry mobility within an economy of the nation's capital and labour stock. This mobility plays a fundamental role in achieving trade adjustment in the event of international capital flows. In this variant of the model we limit the sectoral mobility of capital (but not labour). The introduction of industry-specific capital is an approximation to the view that MNEs tend to operate in similar sectors in both host and source nations (horizontal investment). Of the package of assets transferred by the MNE (capital, skills, technology, etc.) management expertise and technology are likely to display sector-specificity to a considerable degree.

Assume a movement from S to H of commodity-B specific capital.[3] The inflow of capital drives down returns to B-capital in H while wages rise. A similar fall in return is also experienced by A-specific capital in H as labour is attracted from the production of B. Since the marginal product of labour in A rises the marginal product of capital must fall.

The impact of direct investment in country S is in the opposite direction. Returns to all capital rise while the wage falls. The loss of B-specific capital raises the marginal product of B-specific capital and releases labour which moves into the production of A, in turn driving up the marginal product of A-capital.

Two important conclusions emerge from this model. Firstly, movements of sector-specific capital are capable of affecting the returns enjoyed by all units of capital within an economy, irrespective of the specificity of capital. This result is brought about by inter-sectoral shifts of labour. Secondly, changes in the terms of trade have an ambiguous impact on welfare in this variant of the general equilibrium model. Since a change in the terms of trade will have a differential impact on capital returns in the export and import-substitution industries, it is unclear *a priori* whether the economy's real wage will rise or fall. If, for example, S's terms of trade improve, the return to A-specific capital (S's export commodity) will rise while that of B-specific capital falls. Conversely, labour income falls in the production of A but rises in the production of B. Whether, overall, consumers benefit from this change depends on the pattern of demand.

The implications of the foregoing general equilibrium analysis rest on a number of crucial assumptions adopted and the operation of adjustment processes. In the case of foreign investment two are of

particular significance. The first concerns the effect of capital movements on the capital stock of the two nations S and H. It is generally
assumed that such a flow augments the capital stock of the recipient
nation (H) by an amount exactly similar to that lost by S, the donor
economy. This may or may not be the case and constitutes the
investment-substitution question. Secondly, while the above analysis
allows for trade adjustment in the event of capital transfers the extent
to which exports from S to H can be displaced by capital flows (and
overseas production in H) constitutes the export-substitution question.
It is these questions that we now consider.

The Investment-Substitution Problem

The question here relates to the possibility that capital transfers from S
to H may not correspond to the change that occurs in the two nations'
capital stocks. Ignoring the case where overseas investment funds are
raised in the host nation capital market (i.e. capital is not transferred
between nations), the non-correspondence may be brought about
through crowding out and capital rationing effects. Direct investment
by one MNE may preclude market entry by other MNEs or local
firms. Capital constraints (rising marginal cost of borrowing) mean that
for the individual MNE overseas and domestic investments may be
competitive. Local firms in both H and S, facing lower capital costs,
may fulfil investment opportunities foregone by the MNE.

Three major alternative situations have been analysed by Hufbauer
and Adler (1968). Classical case assumptions (perfectly competitive
product and capital markets) lead to a situation where international
capital transfers correspond exactly to changes in the capital stock of S
and H. The global capital stock is unchanged; only its geographical
distribution is altered.

The reverse classical case incorporates both crowding-out effects in
H and capital rationing in S. Foreign investment is assumed to preclude
indigenous investment in H which would have occurred in the absence
of the MNE. Overseas investment coupled with a rising marginal cost of
funds means that the MNE is unable to invest in S. This investment is
undertaken by another firm. As a result neither S nor H experience a
change in the size of their capital stock, merely a change in its ownership. The global capital stock is also unchanged.

The anti-classical case recognises the heterogeneity of enterprises
and products. Here a distinctive MNE undertakes overseas investment
which could not be made by any other enterprises (either indigenous
or other MNEs). Domestic investments in S are maintained by the MNE.

Because of heterogeneity crowding-out does not occur; similarly, equilibrium differences in capital costs are possible in the long run. In this case the capital stock of S is unchanged while that of H expands.

The Export-Substitution Problem

This question centres on the relationship between overseas investment and commodity trade; in particular, whether or not overseas production in H displaces exports from S to H. The link is a complex one since it hinges specifically on the motives for DFI. It is also possible to show that foreign investment and exports from the parent nation may be complementary. Furthermore, the link may change over time as a result of learning effects and the accumulation of information.

A close relationship exists between the questions of investment-substitution and export-substitution. Where DFI occurs through the conduit of the MNE decisions on capital transfer, output in H and S and trade flows are interdependent. Indeed, the institutional nature of the MNE provides the crucial link that is absent in general equilibrium models which focus on the nation as the appropriate unit of analysis.

This interdependence is apparent from the assumptions of the reverse-classical and anti-classical cases. In the reverse-classical case DFI may occur for market retention motives, i.e. it may no longer be possible to service H by exports from S. In this case DFI clearly substitutes for exports in the short term. However, in the longer term these exports would have been lost even if the overseas investment had not occurred since local production is a necessary condition for the retention of market share in H. Complementarity of DFI and exports emerges in the anti-classical case where DFI expands the capital stock of H and there is no offsetting fall in S's capital. Foreign investment may induce exports from S where a foreign presence expands product demand through increased market familiarity and goodwill. Similarly, specialisation may be increased by DFI and this could encourage affiliate imports from the parent organisation.

Empirical evidence on these two issues provides the only way of isolating those assumptions most useful in analysing the employment and income effects of MNEs. The majority of evidence has sought to examine the export-substitution question. A number of simulation studies highlight the problem of sensitivity of assumptions.

An AFL-CIO study of 1971 estimated that 500,000 job opportunities were lost to US workers between 1966 and 1969 as the result of the multinational operations of US companies. This estimate was based on the assumption that foreign markets could have been serviced by the export of US production (complete substitutability between exports and overseas production). Invoking the same assumption the Tariff Commission (1973) estimated a possible net displacement of 1.3 million jobs in the US as a result of the overseas operations of US enterprises up to 1970. Relaxing the assumption of export substitutability dramatically alters estimated employment effects. The assumption that only 50 per cent of overseas sales could be achieved by US exports generated a net job loss of 400,000 on Tariff Commission estimates. Simply assuming that the US export share of world trade in manufactures remained at its 1960 level indicated that employment gains were likely to exceed losses by about 500,000 (Bergsten, Horst and Moran, 1978). Hawkins (1972) provides similar estimates ranging from a net job loss of 666,000 to a net gain of 279,000.

We may draw on three types of study to resolve these conflicting estimates. One study (Frank and Freeman, 1978) provides an attempt to quantify industry-specific estimates of a location substitutability variable. These estimates display considerable variation by industry. Overall, they support the view that DFI occurs largely for market retention motives. In the absence of overseas investment the US share of overseas markets (and hence export sales) would be seriously eroded. All estimates are below 0.5 implying that less than 50 per cent of overseas sales could be maintained through exports from the US.

Case studies provide a second source of evidence. While there is a danger of generalising from a sample of possibly unrepresentative cases they do provide further evidence of the limited substitutability of exports and overseas production. Stobaugh *et al.* (1976) in a series of nine studies found evidence of substitutability in only two cases. Similarly, a OPIC study of investments in the less developed nations concluded that overall DFI has a favourable effect on US employment (Bergsten *et al*, 1978, p. 63). Surveys of the extent of export-substitution estimated by the investors themselves reveal that substitution is far from complete. Of a sample of Belgian MNEs investing abroad 88 per cent were of the opinion that parent nation export levels were unchanged or increased by the establishment of overseas plants (van Den Bulcke and Halsberghe, 1979, p. 42). For German MNEs producing in neighbouring European nations less than 40 per cent of turnover appeared to be potentially substitutable for source nation exports. Where affiliates were servicing third markets the percentage falls to between 15 and 30 per cent (Bailey, 1979, p. 21).

A third type of study based on statistical analysis provides a more representative source of evidence. A study by Horst (1974) indicated the possibility of a non-linear relationship. Where overseas production was small (as a percentage of domestic exports) increases in affiliate output tended to draw forth increased exports (a complementary relationship). Where overseas production represented a significant proportion of international production further increases in overseas output tended to displace export sales (substitution). Horst's analysis indicated that over the range of outputs generally observed a relationship of complementarity dominated with favourable implications for domestic (US) employment. Subsequent analysis (Bergsten *et al*., 1978) confirmed the likelihood of a non-linear relationship. These results imply that the relationship between exports and overseas production may be less straightforward than is generally assumed. They question the validity of case-study evidence and analyses which fail to control for the maturity and size of overseas facilities. Furthermore, non-linearity provides an explanation of why direct tests of the degree of complementarity of substitutability based on estimates of demand cross-elasticities between exports and foreign production have failed (Adler and Stevens, 1974).

More recent statistical studies have widened the range of substitution possibilities. Lipsey and Weiss (1981) conclude that overseas production by US affiliates does not substitute for US exports, rather it tends to displace the exports of other nations to the host market. These results are reinforced by subsequent findings of substantial differences in parent-affiliate characteristics for US MNEs. The tendency within industries for low wage, low capital-intensity parents to locate affiliates in high wage, capital-intensive economies may be indicative that domestic and overseas product ranges of US MNEs are markedly dissimilar, mitigating substitution possibilities (Kravis and Lipsey, 1982).

A variety of indirect evidence is supportive of the generally favourable effects of DFI on domestic employment. The growth of world trade and intra-MNE trade (Helleiner, 1981) has occurred in a period of proliferation of overseas investment. A number of studies (Business International Corporation, 1980; Labour Research, 1980) for both the US and UK reveal that the domestic employment performance of MNEs in the 1970s exceeded that of all manufacturing industry. Whilst in the UK manufacturing employment fell by 6.7 per cent between 1973 and 1978, a sample of the largest 50 private sector MNEs reported domestic employment contraction of only 4.3 per cent. This coincided with an expansion of overseas employment of 5.5 per cent. For three firms, rapidly expanding their overseas workforce (host employment rising by over 50 per cent) was coupled with well below average domestic employment contraction (3 per cent). During the 1970s the employment performance of both UK-based and foreign-owned MNEs was superior to that of purely national enterprises (Stopford, 1979). For the US where manufacturing employment increased, on average, by 3.5 per cent in the period 1970-78, a sample of MNEs reported net employment growth of 6.4 per cent. Again, intensity of overseas investment was positively related to domestic employment growth. None of the above studies reported any evidence of export displacement by overseas production; indeed in the US case export growth rates of MNEs were nearly 50 per cent above the average for manufacturing industry. These studies need to be interpreted with considerable caution since MNEs are disproportionately represented in the technnologically most advanced industries offering enhanced opportunities for the retention or expansion of employment.

Finally, a large number of studies of the determinants of DFI have indicated the limited role played by investment incentives (OECD, 1983) which is inconsistent with the view of MNEs being highly footloose in their location decisions. The importance of market-servicing considerations in the overseas investment decision (Root and Ahmed, 1979; Scaperlanda and Balough, 1983) and the limited role played by labour costs in the establishment of export affiliates (Kravis and Lipsey, 1982) throw serious doubts on the high degree of locational flexibility imputed to MNEs.

Overall, the evidence on export-substitution summarised here offers little support for classical assumptions (increase in H's capital stock equated with a decrease in capital in S) implying the substitution of overseas production for commodity trade. These assumptions lead, in most cases to the least favourable conclusions for source nation employment and labour income in the form of a fall in employment (as export sales decline) and real wages (the overseas transfer of capital lowering the marginal product of labour). More plausible are anti-classical or reverse-classical assumptions.

Turning to the investment-substitution possiblities, empirical evidence on this question is even more sparse. One useful approach is to distinguish overseas investments by type or motive (Hood and Young, 1979). For example, resource-based investments in mining and agriculture represent cases where domestic investment is not likely to be displaced if, as is probable, the resources are not available indigenously. This case corresponds most closely to anti-classical assumptions where the technological expertise or financial resources of MNEs limit the opportunities for other enterprises to undertake the investment. Similarly, the tendency for much processing of resources or foodstuffs to take place close to final markets raises the very real possibility of source nation investment also rising. It appears that much Japanese investment takes this form[4] (Kojima, 1978, ch. 10; Sekiguchi, 1979, ch. 2). Export-oriented investments in LDCs are unlikely to have occurred in most advanced source nations at prevailing wage and productivity levels. Whilst capital rationing in the short term may have an adverse effect on domestic capital formation, the existence of offshore assembly provisions[5] (Lall, 1980) implies that some domestic capital formation will occur probably as a result of increased specialisation. Again, investments of this type, which have provided a major stimulus to criticism of job exporting, are not consistent with classical assumptions.

Studies of MNE investment rates also fail to provide any evidence of geographical investment-substitution. A number of Business International Studies (1980) reveal that the most multinational US corporations invest domestically as much or more than indigenous enterprises. Evidence that domestic investment is relatively unaffected by external factors (Helliwell, 1976) is consistent with an apparent separation of indigenous and overseas investment decisions.[6]

Whilst the evidence on the investment-substitution question is sparse, it provides, if anything, further support for reverse- and anti-classical assumptions. Choosing between these two sets of assumptions is difficult. There is much, however, to commend the anti-classical position. This model recognises the heterogeneity of MNEs and differences between MNEs and indigenous enterprises. The recent work of Kravis and Lipsey (1982) and Lipsey and Weiss (1981) provides considerable support for such heterogeneity. Furthermore, from the point of view of many host nations DFI clearly supplements domestic saving and investment. Where this investment does not displace source nation capital formation the anti-classical position of expanding global investment and employment holds.

Two important reservations should be noted. Firstly, there may exist considerable differences by source nation in the impact of MNEs on trade and investment. It is no coincidence that protest over job loss through DFI has been most forceful in the US, whereas such investment is looked upon much more favourably in Japan, for example. Differences in the sectoral distribution of overseas production may result in investments which are trade-oriented (with favourable implications for labour) or trade-destroying depending on comparative advantages and disadvantages (Kojima, 1978). Replication of the statistical analyses outlined above covering nations other than the US would be helpful in attempts to generalise the labour market impact of DFI. Secondly, there are grounds for questioning the constancy of assumptions over the life of foreign investments. Non-linearities in the export-substitution relation noted above raise the possibility of anti- (or reverse-) classical conditions (trade and investment complementarity) giving way to classical conditions of substitution where established affiliates increasingly supply their own inputs or source requirements locally. Evidence of increasing integration of affiliates in host nations over time (Cohen, 1973; Lim and Fong, 1982) is consistent with a declining significance of parent exports. Theoretically, a nonlinear relationship is attractive since there is a problem of aggregation in positioning a complementary relationship between direct investment and exports. Capital constraints stemming from simultaneous domestic and overseas investment (anti-classical position) may not apply to the individual MNE but in aggregate it will hold given the likely response elasticity of domestic savings to expected returns (Caves, 1982). The possibility of contrasting situations applying within groups of MNEs or differing over time for the individual MNE overcomes this objection.

The Employment Effects of MNEs

Direct Employment Effects

MNEs are a formidable force in the determination of worldwide employment. For the mid-1970s it has been estimated that they employed some 45 million in host and source nations. For manufacturing and service industries perhaps 40 million employees were located in the developed market economies accounting for approximately one-third of manufacturing employment in these nations. The balance of employees, over 4 million, were located in the developing nations. In percentage terms MNE employment in LDCs is far less significant; amounting to only one half of 1 per cent of the economically active population. However, the extreme concentration of foreign investment in the developing nations (Table 2.12) means that for some nations they constitute a major source of job creation (ILO, 1981b).

Table 3.1 provides a breakdown of global MNE employment by source nation. Multinationals from the industrialised nations dominate employment creation. EEC- and US-based MNEs account for over 40 million jobs (88 per cent). MNEs from the US, UK and West Germany

Table 3.1: Worldwide Employment of MNEs by Source Nation (1973)

Source nation	Global employment	Percent of global MNE employment
Belgium	491,218	1.1
Denmark	165.216	0.4
France	3,357,133	7.3
Germany (Fed. Rep.)	5,409,369	11.7
Ireland	91,217	0.2
Italy	1,626,668	3.5
Luxembourg	35,053	0.1
Netherlands	1,831,849	4.0
United Kingdom	7,937,152	17.3
Total EEC	20,962,875	45.6
Australia	415,058	0.9
Austria	152,051	0.3
Canada	755,328	1.6
Finland	164,316	0.4
Hong Kong	23,456	0.1
Japan	1,717,851	3.7
Lichtenstein	3,724	—
Malaysia	576	—
New Zealand	61,177	0.1
Norway	118,362	0.3
Philippines	28,419	0.1
Portugal	6,550	—
Singapore	3,851	—
Spain	39,806	0.1
Sweden	1,054,303	2.3
United States	19,592,054	42.6
Total other nations	25,021,039	54.4
Grand total	45,983,914	100.0

Source: ILO (1981a), Table 1.2, p. 3.

are the most important global job creators. These figures for 1973 tend to understate the progress made by Japanese MNEs and enterprises originating in the less developed nations. While it is not possible to separate exactly the host and source nation employment created directly by the MNEs totalled in Table 3.1, an estimate for a large sample of manufacturing MNEs encompassing some 20.8 million jobs indicated that 60.7 per cent of employment was created in the source nation, the balance (39.3 per cent) occurring overseas (ILO, 1981a, p. 11). For most major source nations domestic employment accounted for by indigenous manufacturing MNEs represents a significant proportion of all such employment. In a sample of eight major source nations MNEs accounted on average for some 29.4 per cent of domestic manufacturing employment (ILO, 1981a, p. 18).

Aggregate measures of the employment growth rates of MNEs have concentrated on the less developed host economies and as a result this section focuses on these nations. LDCs have experienced rapid employment growth by MNEs. Between 1960 and 1977 employment increased by more than two and a half times. For the period 1970-7 the employment increase was 75 per cent. This growth was most rapid in the regions of Latin America and South East Asia and within manufacturing and service sectors (ILO, 1981b). Over this period employment creation was particularly notable by such emerging DFI source nations as Japan and the Federal Republic of Germany. On balance, it appears that overseas employment creation by MNEs has exceeded domestic employment growth but the performance of MNEs has generally been superior to that of uninational firms (Freeman and Persen, 1980).

These estimates of gross employment creation are likely to over-represent the true employment effects of MNEs by ignoring the method of entry and possible crowding-out effects. Clearly entry through acquisition, rather than the creation of new facilities, involves little job creation.[7] Opportunities for entry through acquisition are likely to be more limited in the case of LDCs. To some extent the empirical evidence supports this expectation. Estimates for a large sample of US MNEs indicated that for the period 1951-5 approximately half of all subsidiaries established in advanced industrial economies were acquisitions, the corresponding figure for LDCs being one-third (Curhan, Davidson and Suri, 1977). For the later period 1967-75, however, 43 per cent of US affiliates established in LDCs were acquisitions (UN, 1978, p. 224). In the Belgian case employment creation by foreign-owned MNEs was dominated by the establishment of new ventures; only some 30 per cent of jobs created were due to acquisitions (Van Den Bulcke and Halsberghe, 1979). Studies of specific sectors within less developed host nations indicate that the extent of foreign takeover may be surprisingly high. For example, takeovers accounted for some 90 per cent of the increasing share of Brazil's electrical industry held by foreign-owned firms (Newfarmer, 1978). There have been very few estimates of the investment crowding-out effects of DFI. One study, covering Nigeria, revealed that while MNEs accelerated the displacement of indigenous artisans (global deskilling) they had little impact on local business within the modern sector (Biersteker, 1978). Overall, the limited evidence on these questions indicates that the gross employment creation effects of MNEs are a largely pragmatic issue. Attempts to generalise the probable magnitude of takeover and displacement effects are likely to be of little value.

In estimating the employment effects of DFI it is useful to distinguish investments by type and sector. Opportunities for export-substitution as well as the labour intensity of activities vary considerably by sector. The three major motives for undertaking foreign investment may be classified as:

(i)   Securing access to raw materials;
(ii)   the desire to retain or increase market share; and
(iii) utilising lower cost factors (particularly labour) in assembly and export operations.

The employment effects of foreign investment in extractive sectors of the LDCs have been limited. Only some 4 per cent of Third World investment is in raw materials and agriculture (ILO, 1981b). The limited employment creation effects of such investment results primarily from the capital intensity of the extractive sector, the limited amount of processing that is carried out at the point of extraction and the temporary nature of much employment created (e.g. in construction). Recent years have seen a decline in extractive investments by MNEs in many LDCs as government regulation has increased the degree of uncertainty associated with such investments. MNEs have reacted by shifting to less risky forms of international involvement (Oman, 1981).

Investments in manufacturing and service activities, primarily serving the local market, are of far more significance. Some 87 per cent of foreign investment in the LDCs is in manufacturing and a further 9 per cent in commercial and service activities. These sectors have experienced the most rapid rates of direct employment growth. Within manufacturing, MNE employment increased by some 560 per cent between 1960 and 1977. An even more dramatic increase, some sevenfold, was experienced by commercial and service industries (ILO, 1981b). Despite the magnitude and growth of employment in these areas the impact on development is likely to be comparatively limited. For most LDCs manufacturing comprises only a very small proportion of economic activity; in addition the capital intensity of manufacturing MNEs limits both job creation effects and the diffusion of production technology.

Direct job creation is most pronounced in export-oriented assembly operations by MNEs. Since such investments are prompted by the enormous wage differences between the advanced and less developed nations they tend to be of a highly labour-intensive nature;[8] furthermore, opportunities for investment by acquisition are virtually non-existent. Wage differences are very significant; average hourly wage costs in the UK are 8 to 28 times higher than those in Third World export processing zones, the differences being more pronounced (16 to 57 times higher) in the US case (Currie, 1979). These wage differences swamp differences in productivity levels wihich with the fragmentation of tasks and deskilling may be negligible (Baerresen, 1971; Sharpston, 1975; US Tariff Commission, 1970). Exact estimates of the number directly employed in export processing zones do not exist.

Frobel *et al.* (1980, p. 307) estimated that in the mid-1970s direct employment in export-oriented establishments both within and outside processing zones amounted to 725,000. Employment within such zones amounted to more than 500,000 (Currie, 1979; Frobel *et al.*, 1980). The propensity to invest in affiliates of this type varies considerably by source nationality, as Table 3.2 indicates.

Table 3.2 shows that US and Japanese MNEs have invested most heavily in export platforms. In the Japanese case government pressure to relocate labour-intensive processes, domestic labour shortages and the fear of inflationary pressure have prompted Japanese MNEs to establish a large number of subsidiaries, particularly in South East Asia (Wall, 1976). The subsequent competitive pressures faced by US MNEs and oligopolistic reaction were significant factors determining export-oriented investments by these enterprises (Moxon, 1975; Shaw and Sherk, 1976). The importance of the US market as a destination for these exports (from MNEs of most nationalities) helps to explain the concern US labour has expressed over the role of MNEs in increasing import penetration in the US.

Indirect Employment Effects

The employment effects of MNEs comprise both direct and indirect components. The indirect effects, which may be positive or negative, are likely to be experienced in both host and source nations. The most sizeable impact is likely to be observed in host economies. Following Lall (1979b), indirect employment effects may be usefully categorised as:

   (i)   macroeconomic effects;
  (ii)   horizontal effects on related and unrelated enterprises;

Table 3.2: The Use of Export-oriented Subsidiaries Within MNEs by Source Nation, 1971-2

Source nation	Number of subsidiaries	Number of export-oriented subsidiaries (50% or more sales for export)	Export-oriented subsidiaries as a % of all subsidiaries
United States (1976)	2,362	323	14.0
United Kingdom	1,844	24	1.0
West Germany	645	3	0.5
Netherlands	310	10	3.0
Switzerland	211	3	1.0
Japan	343	92	27.0
All sources	5,715	455	8.0

Source: Turner *et al.* (1980)

(iii)   vertical linkage effects to other entities in the productive chain.

Where the activities of MNEs contribute to national income, government revenue or foreign exchange reserves, potential opportunities for stimulating employment are created. Whether these opportunities are fulfilled and the extent of job creation depends crucially on state spending priorities and the consumption patterns of recipients of incremental income. Where expenditure occurs outside the host economy (e.g. on imports) indirect employment effects will be minimal.

Empirical study of the macroeconomic impact of DFI has been bedevilled by problems of tracing and measuring effects. Furthermore, there is a need with such estimates to hypothesise the alternative position, i.e. what would have occurred in the absence of DFI? Studies which fail adequately to investigate alternatives (Bos *et al.*, 1974) generate the inevitable conclusion that DFI has a positive impact on national income. More careful specification of the possible alternatives yields intuitively more appealing results. On the assumption that foreign production could·be replaced by imports, Lall and Streeten (1977), using a sample of 159 projects in six LDCs, found that in 40 per cent of cases foreign investment had a negative effect on social income. The principal reason for this was found to be the high levels of protection offered to foreign investors. Under the assumption that DFI could be replaced by indigenous producers Lall and Streeten report far less consistent effects on social income. The most favourable impact was experienced with highly complex technological projects where the skills of local entrepreneurs were weakest. Perhaps the most important finding that emerges from these studies is the degree of variation between cases. This suggests that host government policies with respect to DFI are a major explanatory factor in determining the indirect employment effects of foreign investment.

Government policy is also crucial in determining the revenue and expenditure effects of income generated by foreign investors. MNE subsidiaries in LDCs yielded something like $6.5-7.0 billion in tax revenue in 1970, approximately 2 per cent of these countries' national income. There is tentative evidence, certainly in the case of US MNEs, that average tax rates fell during the 1960s, the drop being most marked in the extractive sector where rates are generally highest (Sabolo and Trajtenberg, 1976). Offsetting the tax and export duty revenue yielded by MNEs are the inducements offered to entice such firms. Apart from case-study estimates of the concessions provided by particular LDC hosts, very little is known about the magnitude and effectiveness of incentives (Lim, 1983). The fall in average tax rates within the LDCs appears to have coincided with a general decline in profitability of investment, although rates of return display tremendous variation by both sector and nation (Sabolo and Trajtenberg, 1976). Partially offsetting the income effects of this decline is recent evidence that MNEs may have reduced the share of earnings remitted to the parent nation (Chudnovsky, 1982). On balance, the available evidence indicates that the impact of MNEs on indirect employment creation through social income effects, under the most plausible assumption that DFI would not be fully displaced by either imports or indigenous producers, is positive. The extent of job creation depends crucially on government policy towards investors.

Horizontal indirect employment effects refer to jobs created by means other than through increments in national income or within suppliers to the MNE. Horizontal effects may be classified according to the spread of impact as narrow or broad. Narrow effects are experienced by enterprises competing with the MNE. These effects operate principally through the impact of DFI on market concentration, changes in the factor intensity of production and technological progress. The effects of foreign investment on market structure in LDCs appear complex. Initially the entry of MNEs may stimulate competition, particularly where entry involves the creation of additional plant. In the longer term, widespread product differentiation and non-price forms of competition pioneered by MNEs increase the degree of effective concentration. Evidence for Malaysia (Lall, 1979) suggests a positive relationship between foreign investment and the level of market concentration. However, the crucial test is really the effect of foreign investment on *changes* in concentration. Evidence from a number of advanced nations (Fishwick, 1982) indicates a negative association between the level of inward investment and changes in concentration. In the absence of such tests for the LDCs (but see Ballance *et al.* (1982)) the impact of MNEs on structure remains questionable. A positive association between foreign penetration and level of concentration is open to alternative interpretations. Since MNEs predominate in the less competitive industries one cannot rule out the possibility of imperfections attracting foreign investment.

Discussion of the factor intensity of MNEs in LDCs is delayed at this stage since this topic has generated a great deal of concern and a huge empirical literature. Evidence of the impact of MNE subsidiaries on technological progress in LDCs offers generally unfavourable conclusions for long-term technological adaptation and job creation. The research and development (R&D) undertaken by MNE subsidiaries tends to be restricted to product adaptation. A heavy dependence on parent company inputs in the form of major advances appears widespread among affiliates (Fairchild, 1977). It is possible that the existence of foreign producers may actually discourage indigenous technological progress (Lall, 1982). This could occur where local R&D is inhibited by the absence of basic research (not performed by foreign-owned affiliates) or where local producers cannot compete with subsidiaries supplied with technology at less than full cost. The absence of systematic evidence on these questions prevents any firm conclusion.

Even more speculative are the broader horizontal employment effects of DFI. The impact of a foreign presence on government policy, management practices and consumption patterns is plausible but neither the direction nor magnitude of such impacts have been rigorously traced.

The employment effects of vertical linkages, the relationships between MNEs and indigenous entities united in the productive chain, have been subject to far greater examination. Two principal methods of investigation have been used: the construction of input-output matrices and the analysis of sourcing decisions by MNE subsidiaries.

The use of input-output matrices is subject to considerable limitations, particularly because of their static nature (Lall, 1979b). They are, nevertheless, useful in conceptualising the direction and probable impact of indirect employment creation. Studies for the LDCs based on this approach indicate that the indirect employment effects of DFI form an important proportion of all jobs created – some two-thirds in the case of South Korea (Jo, 1976) – although there is considerable variation between nations (Tyler, 1974).

Estimates based on sourcing decisions focus on the import content of overseas production by MNEs. In comparison with their indigenous competitors foreign-owned affiliates may be expected to import a larger proportion of their requirements. The product specialisation, as well as the higher quality and technology of production typical of MNEs, reduces the likelihood of suitable local suppliers existing (Baranson, 1967; Lim and Fong, 1977). In addition, the importation of inputs from related affiliates ensures higher capacity utilisation within the MNE as well as creating opportunities for the transfer of funds.

Empirical evidence provides considerable support for these expectations. Foreign-owned firms tend to import more and develop lower domestic linkages in both developed (Hood and Young, 1976; McAleese and McDonald, 1978; O'Loughlin and O'Farrell, 1980) and developing nations (Cohen, 1973; Lall and Streeten, 1977; Mason, 1973; Riedel, 1975). These generalisations obscure considerable variation. Local sourcing increases with the size and development of host nations and appears sensitive to government stipulations. Considerable variation in the extent of employment creating linkages exists between economic sectors. Linkages are underdeveloped in the extractive sector (Girvan, 1972) when compared with manufacturing. Within the manufacturing sector import-substituting investments create more local linkages than export-orientated projects (Reuber *et al.*, 1973). Indeed, in the Export Processing Zone (EPZ) of South Korea which is dominated by MNEs, some 78.3 per cent of intermediate goods were imported in 1969 (Watanabe, 1972). Study of one particularly export-oriented industry, electronics, revealed that other important influences on the degree of local sourcing by MNEs include the type of produce produced (e.g. consumer or intermediate electronic products) and source nationality (Lim and Fong, 1982).

A fundamental weakness of the criticism levelled at the MNE of its failure to develop local linkages comparable to those of indigenous plants is the implicit assumption that the two types of plant represent direct substitutes. This is unlikely to be the case in the areas of technological sophistication where MNE subsidiary linkages are least developed. Similarly, the lower incidence of local sourcing in the least advanced LDCs coincides with the lowest probability of indigenous plants being able to displace foreign-owned affiliates (Caves, 1982).

Indirect employment gains may also be experienced in DFI source nations. An increasingly rational international division of labour may yield benefits to both host and source nations in the foreign investment process (Lall, 1980). This has been confirmed for both the US and European source nations in the case of Offshore Assembly Provisions (Finger, 1976 and 1977) which encourage the siting of intermediate processes in the developing nations.

The importance of MNEs in the export performance of the advanced nations and significance of intra-corporate trade implies that the establishment of overseas affiliates may stimulate parent exports, particularly in the initial stages of investment. Purchases by affiliates from parent enterprises are significant. In 1970, US-owned affiliates purchased about 36 per cent of the manufactured exports of US MNEs with a value of some $7 billion. Subsidiaries of UK-based MNEs generated over £81 million worth of parent exports in 1972. For West German subsidiaries in the LDCs nearly 31 per cent of their import requirements were provided by parent production (Long, 1981). The significance of these magnitudes implies that source nations are likely to experience a favourable indirect employment impact with the establishment of overseas facilities, particularly in the initial stages. The durability of jobs created depends on the extent and timing of any substitution of local sources for parent exports. There are no systematic estimates of the employment implications of such substitution.

Offsetting these direct and indirect employment effects are possible job displacement effects associated with the operations of MNEs. We have discussed above the possibility that overseas production will substitute for exports thus eroding employment in the source nation. Our discussion of the available evidence indicated the limited impact of such effects in the general case.

Displacement may also occur in host economies where MNEs drive out or acquire local competitors, increase the capital intensity of production and accelerate the loss of traditional skills. While there are no numerical estimates of the magnitude of these effects it is unlikely that they outweigh the benefits of job creation. However, there is some evidence that acquisition has become an increasingly attractive form of entry for MNEs in LDCs (Sabolo and Trajtenberg, 1976, pp.11-12) and that in certain sectors MNEs have seriously affected the viability of domestic producers (ILO, 1981b, p. 69). Offsetting this is the finding that MNE exports from LDCs may be complementary to, rather than competitive with, the products of indigenous enterprises (de la Torre, 1974). Overall, the possibility of employment displacement elevates the case for appropriate government policy in assisting structural adaptation and the retention and upgrading of traditional skills.

MNEs and the Adoption of Appropriate Technology

A major criticism of MNEs in the LDCs, and a constraint on employment creation, is their alleged failure to adopt production technologies
which reflect the factor endowments of these nations. More specifically, the relative scarcity (and higher cost) of capital relative to labour
should prompt the introduction of labour-intensive technologies in
LDC hosts.

In explaining the alleged failure of MNEs to undertake such adaptation a number of reasons have been forwarded. Firstly, cost considerations may limit the development of appropriate technologies. The
fixed costs of developing new technologies may outweigh the estimated
savings they yield (Newfarmer and Marsh, 1981; Stewart, 1974). Inter-
industry differences in the opportunities for, and cost of, adaptation
may discourage the development of labour-intensive technologies
(Yeoman, 1976). Adaptation appears particularly unlikely in process
industries such as chemicals. Indeed, one study of foreign investment in
LDCs reported process technologies being transferred unchanged in 73
per cent of cases (Reuber *et al.*, 1973). Centralisation of technology
search costs to the MNE parent are likely to bias technology choices in
favour of those prevailing in the advanced nations (Langdon, 1981;
Newfarmer and Marsh, 1981). There is considerable evidence that the
limited adaptation that does take place occurs principally as a result of
decreases in the scale of production within LDCs (Hughes and You,
1969; Morley and Smith, 1977a; Reuber *et al.*, 1973). Limited market
size within the typical LDC raises the costs of developing appropriate
technology and is compatible with observed adaptation being *ad hoc*
and ephemeral.

Secondly, factor price distortions within LDCs may reduce incentives to the adoption of appropriate technologies. The access MNE subsidiaries enjoy to internal sources of funds and international capital
markets mean that they are not bound by host capital costs which may
be considerably above world levels. As a result MNEs may face lower
relative capital costs than indigenous companies and less incentives to
seek out labour-intensive technologies. These pressures may be further
attenuated by government policies which cheapen capital inputs in
relation to labour. Policies which favour an overvalued exchange rate,
ceilings on interest rates, duty exemptions on imported capital goods
and accelerated depreciation all encourage capital-intensity (Bergsten,
1976). Similar distortions may apply to labour inputs. Restriction on

labour force adjustment including dismissals and lay-offs encourage automation of production (Chudson, 1971; Frank, 1980; Hellinger and Hellinger, 1976). A further distortion may arise where labour costs exceed those indicated by wage costs. Problems of low productivity and the absence of suitable skills raise the utilisation cost of labour units (Frank, 1980). Related advantages of capital-intensive technologies are that they reduce labour supervision and co-ordination costs (Strassman, 1968) and facilitate quality control (Baranson, 1967; Daniels and Robles, 1982; Frank, 1980).

A third reason is the possibility that MNEs may be able to meet profit objectives without recourse to optimal factor-price combinations because of the sheltered market conditions they typically enjoy (Newfarmer and Marsh, 1981). There is considerable evidence that higher levels of competitive pressure do compel firms to seek increasingly appropriate technologies (Morley and Smith, 1977b; Wells, 1973; White, 1976, Yeoman, 1976).

A final explanatory factor relates to the so-called 'appropriability problem' of MNEs (Magee, 1977). Appropriability refers to the ability of the possessors of unique advantages to obtain the full social return on their assets. Production technology provides a good example. A potential loss of return occurs where technology is imitated. One method of protecting production technology is to focus on the most complex and least easily emulated forms. These are generally synonomous with capital-intensive techniques. The use of complex capital-intensive techniques by MNEs in the LDCs then emerges as a rational, profit-maximising strategy on the part of such firms (Magee, 1981).

Empirical tests of these hypotheses have met with limited success. The evidence tends to support the view that production techniques used by MNEs in the developing nations are more labour-intensive than those found in the advanced nations (Courtney and Leipziger, 1975; Lipsey, Kravis and Roldan, 1982). Similarly, MNEs originating in the LDCs tend to adapt more fully to local factor costs than MNEs based in the advanced nations (Kumar, 1982; Wells, 1983). However, the crucial test is the relative labour intensity of foreign-owned plants and their indigenous competitors in the developing nations. Here the evidence is mixed. A number of studies indicate the relative capital-intensity of foreign-owned firms (Agarwal, 1976; Biersteker, 1978, Forsyth and Solomon, 1977; Mason, 1973; Morley and Smith, 1977b; Newfarmer and Marsh, 1981; Radhu, 1973) or report no significant differences (Chen, 1983; Chung and Lee, 1980; Cohen, 1973; Pack, 1979; Riedel, 1975) between the two types of plant.

Four important factors probably account for these conflicting results. Firstly, a number of studies have failed to include adequate controls for differences in industry-mix and market orientation between foreign-owned and indigenous plants (Caves, 1982, p. 269). Although the limited evidence does not support the view that foreign-owned firms are disproportionately attracted to the capital-intensive sectors of Third World manufacturing (Meller and Mizala, 1982), export-oriented investments tend to be more labour intensive than those established to service local or regional markets. There is a need for considerable disaggregation and careful pairing of plants if comparisons are to be meaningful. Secondly, there may be differences by source nationality in the propensity to adopt appropriate technology. The differences between advanced and Third World-based MNEs have been noted. A similar difference may exist between US and Japanese MNEs (Kojimi, 1977), although part of any difference, if such differences exist (Chung and Lee, 1980), is probably due to the export-orientation of most Japanese manufacturing subsidiaries in developing nations (see Table 3.2). Thirdly, adaptation to local factor prices may occur in less easily detectable ways. For example, MNEs may use similar quantities of labour but may concentrate on the least-skilled labour groups (Forsyth and Solomon, 1977). Similarly, there is evidence of labour substitution for capital by MNEs in ancillary services such as materials handling, packaging and distribution (Stewart, 1974; Vaitsos, 1974). These sorts of adaptation may not show up in simple capital-labour ratio comparisons. Finally, the eclectic model of DFI highlights two important sources of explanation: product and host market characteristics (Chen, 1983). The production of standardised commodities and technologies in LDCs, particularly for export, helps to explain why export-oriented MNEs and Third World-based MNEs are more likely to use appropriate technologies. In addition, the expectation that the most advanced LDCs have made the greatest progress in increasing supplies of skilled and managerial labour as well as in eliminating factor price distortions is compatible with findings of similarity in factor proportions for foreign-owned and indigenous plants in nations such as Hong Kong (Chen, 1983), Taiwan (Riedel, 1975), Mexico and the Philippines (Mason, 1973) and South Korea (Chung and Lee, 1980; Cohen, 1973).

The criticisms of MNEs and empirical evidence outlined above have been confronted by a recent resurrection of arguments about what appropriate technology really means. In contrast to the above studies which are based on the implicit assumption that an appropriate technology is one that maximises employment opportunities subject to prevailing factor prices, Emmanuel (1982) argues that the most appropriate technology is the most advanced available. Under this conception it is the most modern (and by implication most capital-intensive) technologies which maximise output and social welfare thereby creating the conditions for sustained growth and development. In the longer term continuing development allows employment objectives to be achieved. The achievements of Japan as an importer of Western technology are often cited in support of this hypothesis (Child, 1982). These arguments highlight the potential conflict which exists between short- and long-term employment objectives. In the short-term labour-intensive technologies may facilitate fuller employment but in the long run the most modern technology may be a superior alternative.

MNEs and Training Investments

MNEs may create positive externalities in the labour market of host nations through their investments in human capital. These externalities arise in two ways. Firstly, MNEs may add directly to a nation's stock of human capital by providing training for employees who would not have received such training in the absence of foreign investment. Secondly, the presence of MNEs offering comparatively sophisticated employment opportunities may stimulate potential employees to invest in general training and education in an attempt to avail themselves of these opportunities. The benefits a host nation may obtain from training externalities depend on three factors. Firstly, MNEs must provide training which would not have been forthcoming in their absence. This is most likely to occur where MNE employees would have been unemployed or confined to totally unskilled tasks in the absence of foreign investment. Secondly, there must occur labour turnover whereby acquired skills are passed on or otherwise diffused in the local economy. This condition is least likely to be met when MNE skills are firm-specific (cannot be applied productively in any other organisation) or where the underdevelopment of indigenous enterprises excludes opportunities for the use of acquired skills outside the foreign-owned sector. The third condition is that training costs should be borne by the MNE and not by employees in the form of trainee wages. Where trainees receive below-average rates the positive training benefits generated by MNEs must be offset against income losses to the host economy. These factors illustrate one potential limitation to the creation of training spillovers. There is a well-established negative association between labour turnover rates and wage levels, all other things equal. Where MNEs offer competitive or above-average wage rates there may be a tendency for the 'internalisation of labour' as employees find alternative employment opportunities comparatively less attractive. A relationship of this nature illustrates the possible conflict between the conditions of employer-financed training and the diffusion of skills through job-changing. A further complication arises when one distinguishes employees by type. Even a crude distinction between managerial and production workers illustrates the possibility of differences in the extent of training, the forms of training and the probabilities of skills being passed on for different employee types. Labour turnover rates tend to be lower for managerial staff and in the LDCs a large proportion are made up of expatriates.

The empirical evidence on these questions is far from unambiguous. MNEs in both the advanced (ILO, 1976c) and developing nations (Frank, 1980; ILO, 1981c; Mason, 1973; Moll, 1967) appear to provide at least as much in the way of training as their indigenous competitors. Comparisons of training expenditures by indigenous firms and MNE subsidiaries in the LDCs are subject to two major problems. Firstly, MNE training may be of a higher quality than that generally provided in the host nation. Secondly, much training within MNEs is undertaken outside the host economy, often within the parent nation. The effect of these differences is well illustrated in the case of Nigeria where training expenditures as a percentage of sales were found to be slightly higher for a sample of MNEs when compared with indigenous enterprises. However, annual training expenditure per trainee within MNEs was some six times higher (Iyanda and Bello, 1979). This substantial discrepancy is a reflection of size differences as well as both higher quality and more overseas training within MNEs.

Research on the question of the applicability of MNE training within other enterprises reveals the importance of controlling for employee type. The most specific forms of training are typically those provided for technicians. Training in quality control and maintenance functions tends to be firm-specific and is generally provided internally. The limited spillover potential of this type of training is reinforced by the high concentration of expatriates in senior engineering and technical positions within LDCs (Pastore, 1977). This preference undoubtedly results from appropriability considerations where the use of expatriates serves to protect MNE technological advantages and slow down the diffusion of technology within the host nation. The potential for positive training externalities is much higher in the case of production workers and managerial staff. MNE training for unskilled and semi-skilled employees contains general elements in the form of orientation and safety training. In addition, a number of MNE subsidiaries have been involved in the provision of literacy courses. Programmes for skilled workers often take the form of apprenticeships which are generally supervised by host nation training bodies. Much of such training has widespread applicability (ILO, 1981c). Exceptions to these generalisations are most likely to be found in Export Processing Zones (EPZs) where the subdivision of tasks involves a general deskilling. Here, training for what are classified as skilled operations may take less than two days (ILO, 1981c, p. 5). The physical separation of EPZs and low probability of comparable indigenous enterprises existing (Currie, 1979) mean that training benefits are likely to be limited in these sectors. The management training provided in LDCs by MNEs appears to cover a broad spectrum of skills, potentially of productive value in other employing organisations (Frank, 1980; Mason, 1973). Management training within MNEs is distinguished by the importance of parent enterprise experience as an input to the training process. Whilst such training tends towards specialisation, it appears to supplement higher level management qualifications, e.g. MBAs within developing nations.

Evidence from Brazil (ILO, 1981c) reveals that the mobility of nationals in the fields of personnel and training who move freely between foreign-owned and both public and private indigenous enterprises, provide an effective vehicle for the diffusion of management ideas. The major limitation on this form of spillover arises because of the employment of expatriates in key managerial and technical posts. The importance of expatriate employees appears to vary by nationality, being characteristic of Japanese MNEs in particular (Inohara, 1982; Trevor, 1983), the maturity of investment (Reuber *et al.*, 1973) and the organisational and technical complexity of the enterprise (Hirsbrunner, 1974). There is some evidence that the period 1960-77 witnessed the increased localisation of professional and managerial staff (ILO, 1981b, p. 39), despite the general absence of host government stipulations on the employment of nationals (Howard, 1971). In addition, those multinationals who have adopted a long-term commitment to the replacement of expatriates (Hirsbrunner, 1974) do not appear to have faced an overwhelming constraint in the absence of suitably skilled locals (Desatrick and Bennett, 1977). The opportunities for increased substitution of nationals within MNE subsidiaries appear considerable.

The evidence on rates of labour turnover within MNE subsidiaries highlights the importance of wage levels. A general study of manufacturing MNEs in developing nations (Reuber *et al.*, 1973) estimated a turnover rate of 6.6 per cent. Correcting this figure for those leaving the labour force (deaths, retirements, etc.) yields a likely estimate of around 4.0 per cent, a figure which appears to hold for a variety of areas and employee types (Svedberg, 1983). Quits appear much lower when MNE wages and conditions are particularly favourable (Cohen, 1973) and much higher, approaching 50 per cent or more (Jenkins, 1982), in EPZs where conditions of work are decidedly less attractive (ICFTU, 1983). These estimates, certainly for MNE affiliates outside EPZs providing the most extensive training, indicate that the potential for training externalites is fairly low.

There has been very little study of MNE trainee wage policies. Reuber *et al.* (1973) reported no evidence of trainees receiving apprentice wage rates. Unfortunately, it is not clear that this exhausts the possibilities for MNEs seeking to avoid training costs. One study covering Brazil and Mexico found evidence of employees being encouraged to obtain training in their own time by, for example, practising other jobs (Miller and Zaidi, 1982). Evidence from EPZs reveals that training costs may be held down by the widespread employment of women typically comprising between 80 and 90 per cent of all direct workers, receiving wages of one-fifth to one-half of those offered to comparable male employees (Jenkins, 1982). This practice is also apparent in the electronics industries of Ireland (Murray and Wickham, 1982) and Scotland (Booz, Allen and Hamilton, 1979).

In conclusion, it appears that the potential contribution MNE training may make to labour market development, particularly within LDCs, exceeds that currently being achieved. Obvious limitations exist in the practice of some MNEs in poaching local trained workers and graduates by the provision of above-average levels of remuneration, the importation of inappropriate (capital-intensive) technology and the erosion of traditional skills by the growth of a modern sector dominated by foreign-owned firms. More positive government involvement in the training practices of MNEs could achieve considerable incremental benefits. A number of policies suggest themselves. A training tax, rebated to those enterprises meeting training objectives, could be used to influence both the quantity and type of training undertaken. Increased co-operation between government training bodies and MNEs could be encouraged. Finally, there is some evidence that government stipulations on the employment and training of locals by MNEs are not necessarily detrimental to the attraction of foreign investment *(Social and Labour Bulletin*, 1981).

MNEs and the Stability and Structure of Employment

As well as being a primary influence on the quantity of employment opportunities provided in source and many host nations, MNEs have implications for both the stability and structure of employment.

Analyses of the net employment benefits of MNEs make implicit assumptions about the duration and stability of jobs created by foreign investment. Generally, MNE subsidiaries are expected to operate, if not indefinitely, certainly well into the foreseeable future. These assumptions have increasingly been questioned in recent years (Enderwick, 1982) as high and rising rates of corporate failure have coincided with an increasing trend towards disinvestment and product rationalisation within MNEs (Boddewyn, 1979; Sachdev, 1975). This concern has been reinforced in advanced host and source nations by the concentration, by both area and industry, of disinvestment (Chopra *et al.*, 1978; Torneden, 1975). The selectivity of this process may be indicative of underlying structural forces which are bringing about important changes in global production patterns (OECD, 1981).

The question of disinvestment has received comparatively little research attention; indeed the role traditional influences on investment play in divestment decisions is unclear (Boddewyn, 1983). Analysis of the nature of multinational business leads to mixed expectations regarding the stability of such investments. Whilst there is evidence that MNEs display superior pre-locational adaptation (Ashcroft and Ingham, 1979) there is some doubt about the effectiveness of their analysis of commerical viability. US firms in Italy appeared to overvalue government financial assistance and underestimate the market constraints they faced when undertaking investment appraisals (Lamont, 1970). Similarly, studies of the divestment process have highlighted the views of firms that some divestments are inevitable and stem from deficient initial evaluation (Boddewyn, 1979; Torneden, 1975).

Secondly, some disinvestment may be inevitable as market patterns, cost factors and product lines change. Such changes may necessitate worldwide production restructuring as firms seek to attain optimun locations and market servicing postures. Structural adjustments raise the possibility that for some firms divestment may form one element of corporate strategy. The evidence does not support this hypothesis. Despite the fact that many MNEs appear to be well informed as to what constitutes, for them, an optimal location pattern (Hood and Young, 1980), disinvestment decisions are generally seen as responses to specific, often organisational, problems (Sachdev, 1975; Torneden, 1975). These findings are supported by evidence that the divested operations had generally been run on a relatively autonomous basis and were often barely integrated with other corporate activities (Hood and Young, 1980; Sachdev, 1975; Torneden, 1975).

A third consideration relates to the underdevelopment of local linkages by MNEs in many host economies. There is evidence that the degree of marketing autonomy a subsidiary enjoys is positively related to stability over the business cycle (McAleese and Counahan, 1978). This finding may reflect the ability of plants to redirect excess supplies and exploit untapped market segments. The level of autonomy is particularly low in processing activities where backward and forward linkages in the host economy are comparatively undeveloped. This holds for both peripheral regions of advanced host nations (Hood and Young, 1976; O'Loughlin and O'Farrell, 1980) and in Third World EPZs (ILO, 1981b). Traditional criticisms of the underdevelopment of such linkages (outlined earlier in this chapter) focus on the loss of growth potential associated with branch plant investments and the danger of the emergence of a 'dualistic' economy. The above analysis indicates that a further cost of underdeveloped linkages, particularly forward linkages, may be a greater instability of subsidiaries.

The instability of investments in EPZs and subcontracting relations are compounded by other factors. Their existence depends on the continuation of favourable import policies in the developed nations which account for the major proportion of such exports. The disproportionate concentration in a handful of sectors of exports from the newly industrialising countries raises the possibility of selective import controls being introduced in the major markets of the advanced industrialised economies. The repression of trade union rights and absence of effective government regulation of working conditions in EPZs means that little opposition is likely to be faced by MNEs planning divestment. There is some evidence that rising labour costs and bottlenecks in the supply of low-cost female labour have prompted disengagement in a number of cases (ICFTU, 1983). In contrast, union action in source nations may ensure that the largest share of output cuts in the face of downturns in demand is borne by subsidiaries and subcontractors in the LDCs (Helleiner, 1973; Sharpston, 1975). These issues are discussed again in subsequent chapters where the labour segmentation and adjustment policies of MNEs are examined.

The impact of MNEs on the structure of employment is felt most strongly in source nations. These effects manifest themselves in two major ways. Firstly, foreign investment may lead to a change in source nation skill-mix as production activities increasingly take place overseas while higher-level functions are retained in the parent nation. Secondly, to the extent that DFI increases international specialisation and import competition a change in sectoral-mix may occur as the competitiveness of certain source nation industries declines.

There is considerable evidence that multinationalisation does lead to a change in skill-mix within the investing industries. Jobs lost tend to be production-related and often encompass heavily unionised occupations. The employment created in the source nation is primarily for skilled professional and managerial activities (de la Torre *et al.*, 1973; Hawkins and Jedel, 1975; Jordan and Vahlne, 1981). This process may be seen as a result of the international concentration and centralisation of economic activity (Hymer, 1972). A corresponding change in skill-mix is likely to be experienced in host economies. For advanced host nations the skills demanded by foreign investors are likely to exist already; this is unlikely to be true in the case of less developed countries. Unfortunately, there has been very little study of the effects of inward investment on skill-mix (ILO, 1981a).

Overseas investment is one contributory factor in the increasing specialisation of global production. Within this process the developing nations have dramatically increased their share of output of selected, particularly labour-intensive, commodities. One result of this has been increased competition and structural problems in the traditional sectors of many advanced nations (Plant, 1981). A problem of skill mismatch may occur in these sectors as employment opportunities are denied to new labour market entrants unqualified to compete for the type of jobs created. This applies particularly to the young unskilled and members of minority groups. This problem may be exacerbated by the existence of minimum wage laws which prevent wage competition (McMullan, 1982). A further erosion of employment may occur as advanced nations pursue strategies of capital deepening and the upgrading of labour skills in an attempt to regain competitiveness (Dixon *et al.*, 1983).

The sectoral concentration of vigorous import competition is particularly marked. A US study revealed 79 domestic industries which produced products in import-sensitive groups. Employment declines were experienced in 38 of these industries over the period 1972-9. More than half of these industries were involved in the production of textile, clothing and leather goods (Schoepfle, 1982). To these industries might be added footwear and consumer electronics as areas where import competition is of major significance (Plant, 1981).

The importance of MNEs in this process is unclear. Two factors suggest that their role has been limited. Firstly, import competition appears to have been only one, and not the most important, source of job loss in the traditional sectors. Secondly, MNEs are not the only producers of LDC exports (see Table 2.13). A considerable degree of import competition is likely to have been experienced by these sectors in the absence of DFI.

Table 3.3 presents an analysis of the first question: the extent to which import competition has contributed to job losses. The table covers four import-sensitive UK industries for the period 1970-75. Whilst the experience of these four sectors displayed some variability, they do reveal that import competition, particularly from LDCs, has been a minor source of job loss. Of the 176,000 jobs lost by these sectors over the period 1970-75, 105,700 (60 per cent) were the result of productivity enhancing technological change. Import competition from other advanced nations accounted for a further 17.5 per cent, while the residual 23,600 jobs lost (13.5 per cent) could be attributed to LDC imports. Even in the clothing sector, the most import-sensitive of those considered, only 17.3 per cent of lost jobs were displaced by LDC imports. Estimates for nations such as West Germany (Plant, 1981) confirm the limited role played by LDC exports in the decline of employment in traditional sectors of the advanced nations.

Table 2.13 provided estimates of the MNE share of manufactured exports from a number of newly industrialising countries. It is apparent that the advanced nations would have faced a significant degree of competition from these nations even in the absence of foreign investment. While exact estimates of the value of MNE exports from the LDCs are not available, US evidence indicates that in aggregate they represent a relatively small proportion of all trade.

Non-petroleum exports from US majority-owned affiliates in the developing countries comprised about 11 per cent of US merchandise imports in 1975. This figure represents a steady decline over the preceding 10 years (Helleiner, 1981, p. 39). Widending this to encompass related-party trade (defined as where one transactor owns 5 per cent or more of the voting stock of the other) as opposed to majority-owned affiliates, the 1977 percentage figure is 28.1 per cent (Helleiner and Lavergne, 1979, p. 298). Taking manufactured products, some 37.0 per cent of US imports in 1977 were from related parties in the LDCs. To this figure should be added the imports supplied under subcontracting arrangements. An estimate of these imports (based on items entering the US under tariff provisions 806.30 and 807.00) would be an additional 5 per cent in 1977 (Helleiner, 1981, p. 52). Overall, then,

Table 3.3: Estimates of the Direct Causes of Job Loss in Selected UK Industries, 1970-5

	Years	Footwear	Clothing	Cotton textiles (fabrics)	Textile yarns
Employment	1970	97,100	364,000	61,200	83,000
Employment	1975	75,300	320,500	47,400	57,500
Job change due to:					
(a) productivity change	1970-75	-8,100	-81,900	-4,700	-11,000
(b) consumption change	1970-75	-5,700	+54,600	+ 300	-10,200
(c) net import penetration	1970-75	-8,100	-30,800	-8,400	- 7,100
(d) of which LDCs	1970-75	-1,710	-19,450	-2,225	- 215
(e) unexplained residual	1970-75	+ 100	+14,600	-1,000	+ 2,800
Average annual loss of employment due to LDC trade (%)		0.4	1.7	0.8	0.05

Source: Cable (1977).

some 33 per cent of US non-petroleum imports in 1977 were from a related party in the LDCs. Taking only manufactured imports the figure is around 47.0 per cent. These aggregate estimates tend to obscure the considerable variation of experience by both nation and industry (on the latter see Helleiner and Lavergne, 1979, pp. 309-10). Little is known about the importance of such trade for non-US enterprises.

These figures highlight the likelihood of an adjustment problem existing in the labour markets for most advanced economies. Macroanalysis tends to obscure the microeconomic costs of import penetration. In aggregate, employment generated by US export industries supplying the LDCs plus the reduction in inflationary pressure achieved through importation outweighs the number of jobs that imports destroy (Sewell, 1978). This discounts the micro problem of adjustment which arises because workers displaced tend to be largely unskilled, often older, located in declining regions and, as a result, immobile (McMullan, 1982). The difficulties of adjustment are compounded by the economic stagnation experienced in recent years. These problems indicate the case for government intervention and assistance in facilitating the necessary restructuring. In conclusion, it is likely that many of the sectors under pressure from LDC exports would have experienced difficulties even in the absence of DFI although MNEs have probably worked to strengthen the processes of change.

Income Effects of MNEs

The general equilibrium model of international trade and investment provides a useful framework for analysing the income effects of MNEs. Within source nations the major focus of attention has been the effects of DFI on the functional distribution of income, that is the relative shares of capital and labour. Concern in host nations, particularly the LDCs, has concentrated on the impact of DFI on the inequality of personal income distribution, that is the distribution of income between individuals or groups in the labour market.

The most significant effects occur in a model of international capital movements in the absence of commodity trade. Factor income differences between nations will result from differences in factor endowments. Capital's share of national income will be proportionately greater in the capital-scarce nation (H in our analysis). Rent differentials will trigger capital outflows from S. The effect on incomes in S will be twofold. Capital rents will increase as the marginal productivity of indigenous capital rises (with the decrease in capital stock). In addition, S-based MNEs will enjoy higher income flows from their investments in H. Capital's increased share of income in S is achieved at the expense of labour. Wages will be subject to downward pressure as the demand for labour in S declines (the loss of capital reducing the demand for attendant labour). The opposite occurs in H where the inflow of capital pushes down returns for all units of capital (both indigenous and foreign-owned) and increases the demand for labour and wage share of national income. These conclusions lead to an expectation of opposition to outward capital flows on the part of labour in S and indigenous capital in H since these are likely to be the losers in income distribution terms. In the absence of trade adjustment the greater equalisation of factor shares between S and H may lead to significant shifts in income shares within H and S.

Using a simple model of the US economy, assuming capital movements but not commodity trade, Thurow (1973) estimated that labour's real income would fall by 8 per cent while the real return on capital would rise by over 22 per cent if unfettered capital movements occurred. A similar magnitude of redistribution has been estimated by Musgrave (1975). Her analysis indicated that if the 1968 stock of $80 billion US overseas investment had been invested domestically labour would have gained 7.2 per cent of national income (giving a share of 79.4 per cent) while capital's share would have fallen from 22.8 per cent to 20.6 per cent. These movements involve a redistribution of some $25 billion. A more sophisticated model incorporating savings effects was proposed by Frank and Freeman (1978). They assume S to be a single commodity economy while H contains two sectors, one a foreign enclave the other employing only indigenous capital. S-based capital is assumed to enjoy a higher return in H and enjoy an advantage over H-based capital. Allowing saving in S to respond to potential returns implies that the repatriation of MNE capital could actually reduce S's capital stock (through a fall in saving as potential investment returns decline). The effect on income distribution of repatriation is thus similar to capital outflow; relative wages fall in S.

While the endogeneity of savings behaviour represents an extension of early models these analyses suffer a number of fundamental problems. Firstly, the estimates are based on classical assumptions, the most important of which implies that capital flows correspond to offsetting gains and losses in the capital stocks of H and S. Not only are the alternative situations of reverse-classical and anti-classical assumptions ignored, the analysis fails to consider the possibility of inward capital flows to S. These may occur as the marginal productivity of capital rises or because of competitive pressures triggering oligopolistic reaction (Knickerbocker, 1973). Secondly, they generally ignore the productivity impact in H of the transfer of technology. Where these are considered (Thurow, 1973) the benefits are seen to be shared by both foreign and domestic capital. The eclectic theory of DFI highlights the benefits offered by internalisation in protecting firm-specific advantages, including technology. The widespread adoption of the MNE as a vehicle for transfer implies that appropriability is likely to be enjoyed by the originators of technology. The resultant income flows have important implications for both the level and distribution of national income. The third, and most significant, weakness relates to the omission of trade adjustment mechanisms. As indicated earlier in this chapter trade adjustment may offset some or all of the income impact of outward investment. As capital leaves S factors will be moved from the production of capital-intensive exports (A) towards labour-favouring commodity B. At the same time the fall in national income would work to stem the importation of labour-intensive products. With sufficient adjustment the terms of trade and functional distribution of income would be unchanged.

Casual interpretation of trends in the functional distribution of income for both the US and UK indicates that the trade adjustment mechanism has been significant. Neither nation experienced a significant decline in labour's share of national income as outward investment accelerated in the postwar period; indeed if anything the opposite has occurred.[9]

There has been little investigation of the impact of DFI on functional income shares in H. The general equilibrium model predicts a tendency towards equalisation as capital inflows lead to net job creation and increase the demand for labour. Rising wage rates coincide with a decline in the marginal productivity of capital. Any equalisation in factor shares depends crucially on classical assumptions that DFI represents a net addition to H's capital stock and that production technologies introduced by foreign investors are similar to those prevailing in the host economy. The first condition will be violated where MNEs raise investment funds in the host capital market or where DFI captures the most attractive investment projects driving out indigenous producers. Similarly, competitive pressures may force host-based enterprises to penetrate the economy of the source nation. These conditions may apply in the case of cross-investment between the US and Europe where rivalistic reaction appears to be an important motive behind

foreign investment (Graham, 1978). In addition, the existence of offshore funds (e.g. the Euro-currency market) raises the possibility of
US investment being funded from outside the US.

An implicit assumption of the perfectly competitive general equilibrium model is the existence of full employment. Inward investment,
particularly in capital-favouring projects, releases scarce labour resources which may be more effectively deployed elsewhere in the economy. Adjustment of this form is unlikely to be observed in many host
nations where unemployment or underemployment of labour is
endemic. Differentiation of the labour force in terms of skills or geographical location reduces the likelihood of orderly labour market
adjustment occurring. A more likely result is an increased demand for
an already scarce skilled labour elite. This possibility and the attendant
implications of a more unequal personal distribution of income, partic-
'ularly within the LDCs, have received considerable research attention.

MNEs may influence income inequality at a number of levels. Differences by sector in the degree of MNE penetration raise the possibility
of uneven development within host economies with adverse effects for
equality of income distribution (Chase-Dunn, 1975). Similarly, differences emerge by sector in the extent to which MNE activity affects
inequality. The most significant effects are associated with mining investments where wage gains may be made at the expense of workers
outside the mining enclave (Girvan, 1976, p. 44). By contrast foreign
ownership has little influence on income distribution within agriculture.

A second source of inequality relates to the gains made by selective
groups of indigenous employees at the expense of other members of the
labour force. Dualism of this form may arise because of the practice of
'credentialism' associated with MNEs in less developed host nations
(Lloyd, 1982; Miller and Zaida, 1982). Credentialism occurs when
hiring decisions are based on the possession of qualifications in preference to intensive investigation of the attributes of individual appli-
cants. Often the qualifications in question are unrelated to the tasks
concerned. A primary result of this form of screening is an increase in
occupational and economic stratification. These practices may contribute to the emergence of Third World labour aristocracies comprising
key employees of large-scale modern sector plants (Arrighi, 1970; Saul,
1975). These developments not only increase income inequality, they
may also reduce possibilities for positive redistribution. Where elites
seek to protect individual interests they may develop links with their
counterparts in the major source nations, weakening the strength of the
host state (Rubinson, 1976) and lowering the probability of concerted

labour opposition emerging. A number of studies indicate that MNEs have contributed to inequality in this way (Langdon, 1981). Over time, income inequality may be worsened where dualism slows down capital formation or growth by affecting savings rates and consumption patterns (Sabolo and Trajtenberg, 1976).

The tendency for MNE subsidiaries to pay above average rates (ILO, 1975), even where skill levels and qualifications are comparable to those of indigenous employees (Mason, 1973), increases income inequality between enterprises. Within MNEs, remuneration levels for expatriates, with generous overseas allowances and skill premiums (Sabolo and Trajtenberg, 1976), reinforce the likelihood that MNE penetration will be associated with a deterioration in equality of income.

These studies of the impact of multinational business on host nation income distribution are subject to two major weaknesses. Firstly, as indicated earlier in this chapter, economic growth, particularly in the early stages, is frequently correlated with an increase in inequality. The growth of inequality may occur independently of the extent of foreign ownership. There is a need then to separate out any contributing role played by MNEs in this process. Secondly, the static cross-section nature of many of the studies cited raises the possibility of misinterpretation of the causal process. It may be that MNEs are unduly attracted to economies characterised by considerable income disparities. Even low *per capita* income economies may support a feasible market for MNE output where inequality is high. A good example is provided by the cases of Mexico and Brazil. Both economies are characterised by tremendous inequality. In Mexico the economically poorest 40 per cent of the population enjoy only 10.5 per cent of income whereas the top 20 per cent receive 64.0 per cent of national product. The respective figures for Brazil are 10.0 per cent and 61.5 per cent. In both of these economies US MNE subsidiaries are important producers and they channel 95 per cent of manufacturing output to the host economy. Inequality sustains this market.[10] In the face of these problems a suitable test for causation would involve time-series analysis of MNE penetration and income inequality.

This section on the income effects of MNEs has revealed little systematic understanding of the magnitude of such effects. In source economies the adjustment of trade patterns and questionable applicability of classical assumptions implies that income distribution may be relatively unaffected by outward investment. In host nations, particularly LDCs, the possibility of a correlation betwen MNE penetration and inequality of income must be conceded. However, the causal nature of these processes and the distinct role played by MNEs is more controversial. Clearly, further research on these topics is urgently required.

Conclusions

The foregoing analysis indicates that the labour market impacts of MNEs are complex and multifarious. One result of this has been limited understanding of the magnitude of such effects. A useful starting point for analysis of these questions is provided by the general equilibrium model of international trade. Coupling this framework with the institutional dimension of the MNE stressed by the eclectic model, provides a way of examining competing claims. Considerable reservations must attach to employment estimates of DFI which are based on classical assumptions. The available evidence on MNE behaviour does not lend support to these assumptions. It is under classical assumptions that the most sizeable employment losses are experienced in source nations. Little credibility should be attached to these estimates.

Similarly, the eclectic approach reveals why concern over the labour market effects of MNEs varies considerably between source nations. Japanese overseas investment which has focused on extractive and export-oriented projects has generally complemented domestic resource endowments, particularly labour. The issue of job loss through foreign investment has not really arisen. At the other extreme stands the US where critics of DFI have overemphasised the substitutability between overseas production and source nation exports. Inter-industry variability in the propensity to internationalisation has compounded the problem of adjustment in major source nations. Differences by nationality in corporate responses to the competitive conditions of the 1970s and 1980s are a further contributory factor. The emphasis placed by many European and American MNEs on domestic rationalisation and restructuring have heightened links between domestic and overseas production in an unfortunate way (Franko and Stephenson, 1982). The failure of many Western MNEs to anticipate changing comparative cost conditions has led to a surge in divestment and rationalisation in a number of sectors. The likelihood that overseas production is increasingly a requirement for market retention should serve to emphasise the complementarity of domestic and overseas production. The reaction towards lobbying for selective protection of domestic markets or controls on outward investment is an understandable development.

At a number of places in this chapter the importance of government policy in influencing employment and income effects of DFI has been highlighted. Such policies are likely to be particularly effective in determining indirect job creation, the technology of production, as well as training investments and the recruitment of nationals. MNEs have generally been both willing and able to respond positively to host nation directive policies (Frank, 1980; Sachdev, 1978). More research is required to understand the role and limitations of government policy, particularly in LDC host economies (see, for example, the contrasting analyses of Lall (1980) and of Hill (1982) and Lim and Fong (1982)). Furthermore, the assumption that government policy is an exogenous variable may be violated where foreign investment creates or exacerbates a relationship of dependency (Bornschier, 1982).

In source nations there may be a case for government intervention in the form of adjustment assistance. Trade adjustment represents a major mechanism within the general equilibrium model for absorbing the impact of capital flows. Whre inter-sectoral labour mobility is impaired there may be a case for government assistance in retraining and fostering geographical mobility to facilitate adjustment. Similarly, the sectoral concentration of the adjustment burden implies that government policies may be required to ensure the more equal distribution of restructuring costs. We return to these issues in the final chapter.

Finally, more research is required on a number of topics considered in this chapter. Perhaps the most pressing are those relating to the questions of export-substitution and investment-substitution. Replication of the statistical analysis pioneered in the US for European and other major source nations would be of value. There remains a role for careful cast-study analysis of the effects of DFI decisions. One advantage of analysis at this level is that the questions of export-substitution and investment-substitution can be handled at the appropriate unit of analysis, i.e. the MNE, rather than at the national level characteristic of general equilibrium models.

Notes

1. Specialisation will be less than complete in the probable case of increasing cost conditions, i.e. concave product transformation curves.

2. An important qualification to this conclusion occurs where capital movements affect patterns of demand. A number of studies (Sunkel and Feunzalida, 1979) cite the demonstration effect of MNEs in altering indigenous demand patterns in favour of sophisticated consumer goods, particularly in less developed nations.

3. An exogenous change is required to trigger the capital movement. Given

perfect mobility of labour nationally and capital internationally, the marginal products of factors by sector will be identical for H and S but will diverge between A and B within H and S.

4. To some extent the assumption of domestic investment being maintained in resource-based DFI may be increasingly tenuous in the Japanese case as processing is located closer to source. See Ozawa (1982).

5. Offshore assembly provisions encourage global specialisation by inducing the overseas processing of domestic components. Upon importation to the source nation tariff liability is based only on the overseas value added.

6. Such separation is much less likely in the case of an MNE where international organisation provides a mechanism linking domestic and overseas investment.

7. Job creation effects could be negative in such a case where acquisition is followed by rationalisation or even closure (ILO, 1981a, p. 14), although the limited evidence available (van den Bulcke and Halsberghe, 1979) indicates that job losses are similar for newly created and acquired foreign affiliates. It is possible that after acquisition employment growth may be above average (Lipsey, 1982).

8. There is evidence that the export processing activities dominated by MNEs are up to 100 per cent more labour-intensive than the average for all manufacturing industry in Third World host economies (Helleiner, 1976; Watanabe, 1972).

9. In the case of the US see Bergsten *et al.* (1978), ch. 4. For the UK representative trends are examined in King and Regan (1976).

10. Figures on income distribution were drawn from Ahluwalia (1974). The estimates of local sales by MNEs were calculated from data in Chung (1978).

4 THE LABOUR UTILISATION PRACTICES OF MNEs

Introduction

In addition to having a significant impact on the external labour market, as highlighted in Chapter 3, the MNE is likely to enjoy considerable discretion in the management of labour within the firm. Indeed, a remarkable feature of the modern corporation is the extent to which the pricing and allocation of labour has become an internalised function (Doeringer and Piore, 1971) greatly attenuating the role of market forces.

This chapter provides an examination of the labour utilisation practices of MNEs. The following section on productivity performance indicates that foreign-owned firms tend to outperform their indigenous competitors. Part of the productivity differential appears to be the result of differences in labour utilisation. The sources of variability in labour contracts and alternative approaches to labour utilisation are then discussed. In the light of this discussion empirical evidence on the practices of MNEs is examined. The chapter concludes with a number of important implications of the analysis.

The Productivity Performance of MNEs

There is considerable evidence that MNE subsidiaries enjoy a productivity advantage over their domestic competitors in many advanced host nations (see, for example, Dunning, 1966; Fishwick, 1982). Table 4.1 presents productivity comparisons for foreign-owned and indigenous plants by industry order for UK manufacturing in 1979. As the table shows the overall productivity advantage of foreign-owned firms as measured by net output per head, was around 55 per cent. To some extent this figure reflects the disproportionate concentration of foreign plants in the more productive, technologically progressive sectors (Dunning, 1976). Disaggregation to the industry order still conceals considerable differences in intra-industry location. Some of the bias can be eliminated by exclusion of coal and petroleum products and ship-building, marine engineering and vehicles. In both cases foreign invest-

Table 4.1: A Comparative Analysis of Productivity Levels and Growth for Foreign-owned and Indigenous Plants in UK Manufacturing, 1979 and 1971-9

Industry	Net output per head 1979 (£)			Change in net output per head 1979-1971 (%) 1971		
	Foreign-owned plants	Domestic-owned plants	Foreign ÷ Domestic	Foreign-owned plants	Domestic-owned plants	Foreign ÷ Domestic
Food, drink and tobacco	16,039	10,849	1.48	239.9	269.4	0.89
Coal and petroleum products	169,043	29,005	5.83	870.9	455.5	1.96
Chemicals and allied industries	16,730	16,040	1.04	241.0	272.3	0.89
Metal manufacture	13,172	7,482	1.76	396.9	224.2	1.77
Mechanical engineering	10,978	9,169	1.20	241.6	272.9	0.89
Instrument engineering	7,668	7,829	0.98	228.4	271.4	0.84
Electrical engineering	9,694	8,438	1.15	227.7	268.8	0.85
Shipbuilding and vehicles	12,152	7,470	1.63	518.1	235.4	2.20
Metal goods	10,178	7,954	1.28	253.9	257.8	0.99
Textiles	8,812	6,309	1.40	130.6	231.7	0.56
Leather, fur, clothing and footwear	8,581	5,308	1.62	272.0	263.3	1.03
Bricks, pottery, glass and cement	11,426	10,982	1.04	170.6	302.4	0.56
Timber and furniture	9,739	8,471	1.15	238.2	255.8	0.93
Paper, printing and publishing	12,037	10,391	1.16	241.6	288.0	0.84
Other manufacturing industry	11,377	8,026	1.42	215.2	258.0	0.83
All manufacturing	13,792	8,891	1.55	318.7	262.9	1.21
All manufacturing (excluding coal and petroleum and shipbuilding and vehicles)	11,919	9,002	1.32	239.1	265.3	0.90

Source: Business Monitor PA1002, Report on the Census of Production 1979, Summary Tables.

ment is heavily concentrated, into petroleum products and vehicles, respectively. The effect of this is to lower the differential to 32 per cent.

This is likely to represent the upper limit of the true difference if matched sample data were available. The trend of productivity growth over the period 1971-9 is also shown in Table 4.1. Here industry disaggregation is crucial. Overall, it appears that over the period foreign-owned firms were increasing their productivity advantage despite the superior productivity growth performance of domestic firms in 11 of the 15 cases. Exclusion of the high 'growth' industries reveals that the real trend is a narrowing of the differential. This phenomenon has been observed in other nations such as Australia (ILO, 1981a). Analysis of the reasons for this narrowing cannot be separated from an examination of the factors likely to endow foreign-owned firms with superior productivity performance.

A multitude of factors have been proposed in explaining productivity differences (Nelson, 1981; Prais, 1981). The importance of economies of scale may be reflected in differences in plant and firm sizes. A comparison of size by ownership for UK manufacturing is presented in Table 4.2.

Table 4.2: A Comparative Analysis of Enterprise and Establishment Sizes of Foreign-owned and Indigenous Entities in UK Manufacturing, 1979

Nationality	Average enterprise size (employees)	Average establishment size (employees)
US-owned	536	431
EEC-owned	367	279
Other	409	281
Average: All foreign-owned enterprises and establishments	477	368

Source: Business Monitor PA1002, Report on the Census of Production 1979, Summary Tables.

As Table 4.2 shows foreign-owned firms enjoy a considerable size advantage over indigenous firms. This advantage is apparent in many other advanced host nations (Deane, 1971; Gray, 1972; Horst, 1972). The advantage is particularly marked in the case of US firms (Dunning, 1976). To some extent the data in Table 4.2 represent an overstatement of the size advantage of foreign-owned firms. Since most MNE affiliates are attracted to oligopolistic industries their competitors are likely to be represented by the largest UK firms. There is evidence (Prais, 1976) that the larger UK plants are probably of a size comparable to that of foreign-owned plants. Nevertheless, the size differential of foreign-owned plants is not simply a reflection of their disproportionate concentration in industries characterised by extensive economies of scale, as Table 4.3 illustrates. Foreign-owned plants enjoy a size advantage over domestic competitors in all the industries examined; on average they are some six times larger.

Table 4.3: A Comparative Analysis of Size by Industry for Foreign-owned and Indigenous Plants in UK Manufacturing, 1979

Industry	Average plant size (employees)		
	Foreign-owned plants	Domestically-owned plants	Foreign ÷ Domestic
Food, drink and tobacco	559	97	5.8
Coal and petroleum products	365	115	3.2
Chemicals and allied industries	339	101	3.4
Metal manufacture	274	130	2.1
Mechanical engineering	305	48	6.4
Instrument engineering	295	41	7.2
Electrical engineering	477	109	4.4
Shipbuilding and vehicles	1656	191	8.7
Metal goods nes	229	31	7.4
Textiles	271	84	3.2
Leather, fur, clothing and footwear	282	41	6.9
Bricks, pottery, glass and cement	214	52	4.1
Timber and furniture	88	20	4.4
Paper, printing and publishing	161	36	4.5
Other manufacturing industry	320	48	6.7
All manufacturing	368	57	6.5
All manufacturing (excluding coal and petroleum and shipbuilding and vehicles)	308	52	5.9

Source: Business Monitor PA1002, Report on the Census of Production 1979, Summary Tables.

The productivity advantage of foreign-owned firms may be the result of their use of more highly qualified labour or simply that they are more capital-intensive. What direct evidence there is on labour skills by nationality is not supportive of the hypothesis that foreign-owned firms utilise comparatively more skilled labour, certainly in the case of advanced nations. The employment of graduate and professional labour does not appear to be influenced by ownership nationality differences (ILO, 1981a). There do appear to be systematic differences by nationality in the use of indirect (administrative, technical and clerical) labour. In the UK manufacturing sector, for example, indirect workers make up some 51.2 per cent of the labour force for foreign-owned firms but only 38.9 per cent for domestic firms. At first this may appear suprising. Since the affiliates of MNEs are likely to enjoy access to parent company research and development and overhead functions such as information processing and financial control, they might be expected to employ a smaller percentage of non-operatives. The reverse finding may be indicative of relative managerial inefficiency (Stopford, 1979). While the research of Pratten is supportive of the view that the UK management of subsidiaries of the same company is generally rated below that of management in other host nations (Pratten, 1976), the relevant comparison is between foreign-owned and domestically-owned plants in the UK. The fact that the share of research and development expenditures and employment of foreign-owned firms in the UK exceeds their output share may be indicative of the superior application of knowledge (ILO, 1981a; Scriberras, 1977). The deficiencies of indigenous UK firms in this area have been noted before (Pavitt, 1979).

There is little systematic evidence of differences in the quantity and quality of capital between foreign-owned and domestic companies, certainly for the industrialised nations. Comparison of US plants in the UK with indigenous establishments indicates that there are little or no differences in capital-output ratios if allowance is made for industrial distribution (Dunning, 1976). Since there appears to be very little difference in the age of capital between the UK and US (Bacon and Eltis, 1974), the fact that UK affiliates of international companies may have less sophisticated technology than related affiliates (Pratten, 1976) reinforces the view that quality and quantity differences in capital do not provide an explanation of the productivity advantage of foreign-owned firms.

Considerable insight into the probable causes of the productivity differential has been provided by comparative studies of a number of subsidiaries, located in various nations, sharing a common parent enterprise (Pratten, 1976). When UK operations were compared with similar plants in North America, Germany and France, the respective percentage productivity differentials were +50, +27 and +15. It was also reported that the pattern of higher overseas productivity was true for both UK and non-UK firms. Coupling this finding with the fact that these intra-firm productivity differences are only about half of the overall productivity differences between the countries concerned, allows the tentative conclusion that there are location-specific impediments to productivity operating within the UK. Consideration of some of the major determinants of productivity in terms of their international mobility helps to clarify this point. Clearly, technology and management skills are two influences which may be transferred, fairly readily and at low cost, internationally within the enterprise. The same argument does not apply to labour, particularly labour attitudes and practices, which are highly location-specific. Similar locational constraints apply to considerations such as scale of production and the length of production runs which are likely to reflect the size of markets served. There is considerable evidence that it is just these sorts of factors which are cited by MNEs as constraining their UK operations (Lincoln, 1975). The fact that overseas plants are more productive than their domestic rivals implies that either foreign-owned firms are more, (but not completely) successful in overcoming these environmental impediments, or that domestic plants have inferior management or technology.

For the UK there is evidence to support the view that domestic plants may be comparatively poorly managed (Pratten and Atkinson, 1976; Swords-Isherwood, 1979) and that this failing may be partially responsible for the underutilisation of capital in UK plants (Pratten, 1977). Evidence consistently reports the significance of union restrictions on the utilisation and deployment of labour as being a major contributory factor in the poor productivity performance of UK industry (Prais, 1981; Pratten and Atkinson, 1976). Such union job regulation practices may result not only in overmanning, fractious labour relations and resistance to technical change, but may also encourage the design of smaller plants or shorter production runs since difficulties in labour relations appear to be positively correlated with size (Jones and Prais, 1978; Prais, 1981).

The Nature of Labour Contracts and Choice of Labour Control Strategies

The labour contract is notable for both its scope and imprecision. Typically the contract covers not only a range of price and utilisation combinations but also the rights of both the individual concerned and the position of institutional parties to the agreement such as unions and management. Additional terms may specify institutional arrangements for administration, interpretation and enforcement of the agreement.

The sources of incompleteness in the labour contract derive from informational problems. Problems arise either because information does not exist or is costly to collect and process. Contract specification difficulties are likely to be positively related to the existence of multiple objectives, the degree of complexity of the organisation and its activities and the extent of uncertainty. Clearly, specification of requisite labour activities is made more difficult by poor definition of, or conflict between, objectives. Similarly, complex activities necessitate the collation and evaluation of large amounts of information. Uncertainty generates the need for contingent labour contracts which provide for a future performance contingent upon the occurrence of some previously defined event. The sheer complexity of writing contingent claims contracts is a major constraint on their use. Further problems arise in defining *ex ante* the appropriate adaptation in the light of a given change and agreeing on the state of the world that comes to pass. Specification costs are only one part of the problem information deficiencies create. Even if labour contracts were fully specified there are positive costs of monitoring and enforcing contracts (Jackson, 1982).

The incompleteness of labour contracts because of specification and transactions (monitoring and compliance) costs provides scope for discretionary behaviour by organisation members (managers, workers). The implication of discretionary choice is that effort becomes a variable input to the productive process. Individuals are likely to exercise some discretion over a number of dimensions of their work, principally:

   (i)   the activities carried out;
  (ii)   the pace at which activities are carried out;
 (iii)   the quality of activities; and
 (iv)   the time spent on activities.

For Leibenstein (1976) the discretion individuals enjoy in selecting a particular activity-pace-quality-time (APQT) combination presents management with a choice of two basic strategies for labour control. The first strategy involves the pre-setting of APQT bundles: the specification of the nature of each task coupled with the direction and evaluation of effort. The alternative approach necessitates granting individuals considerable discretion in the choice of an appropriate APQT bundle.

Such choice may be bound by basic constraints (minimum quality standards, attendance during a specified period particularly if tasks are interrelated). A number of considerations influence the choice of optimal strategy. The pre-setting of APQT bundles is likely to be extremely difficult where organisation goals are unclear or subject to change, where tasks are complex and task- or job-specific knowledge is important. Such a strategy also requires considerable resource commitments in the form of information inputs as well as supervisory and quality-control expenditures. Furthermore, application of such a strategy is likely to display diminishing returns at a comparatively early stage where individuals are subject to close supervision in the performance of repetitive tasks. Organisation of work based on the pre-setting of effort is likely to be correlated with problems of low employee morale and high rates of labour turnover.

Multinational enterprises have played an important role in the development and dissemination of both types of labour management strategy. Strategies of direct control (Friedman, 1977) are epitomised by the scientific management movement associated with F.W. Taylor. For Taylor the scope for enhanced profitability lay in the intensification of work rather than in any increase in the apparent duration of work. Such intensification could be achieved by the elimination of porosity in the labour relation. The origins of porosity were inefficient organisation of tasks and the discretion individuals enjoyed in the carrying out of tasks. Taylor offered three principles for achieving more efficient production: the separation of design from execution; the subdivision of tasks; and the scientific study of movements. The embodiment of these ideas in a strategy for labour management found their earliest expression at the Ford Motor Company in Michigan in 1913. 'Fordism' coupled the principles of scientific management with flow-line operation and methods of remuneration based on generous daily rates which ensured an adequate supply of labour (Palloix, 1976). The US origins of assembly line production are not coincidental. Even by the early 1900s the large domestic US market and labour shortages (coupled with high wages) created an environment conducive to the adoption of large-scale labour-saving production methods.

The impact of these practices outside the US is unclear. Whilst the principles of scientific management were to be found in England in 1905 and other European nations in the next few years (Pichierri, 1978), the incidence of such schemes was comparatively low. Indeed, even in the United States it appears that Taylorism was largely confined to smaller non-union plants (Edwards, 1979. p. 101). The principles of assembly line production were diffused in the UK partly through the setting up of overseas affiliates by US-based companies. Ford established a plant in Manchester in 1911. Dunning (1969) estimated that UK employment in US-owned affiliates increased from between 12,000-15,000 in 1914 to 90,000 in 1939. This expansion appears to have been concentrated in England; certainly it did not occur to the same extent in Scotland (Forsyth, 1972). The increased penetration of US-owned firms in England is correlated with a marked increase in the use of flow production methods in the 1920s and 1930s, particularly within motor vehicles and textiles (Friedman, 1977).

The ideological underpinning of Taylorism (and Fordism) indicate its limitations in the face of probable union opposition. Such practices assume absolute management control over all aspects of the workplace environment; employees are seen as simply responding to a structure of incentives. Similarly, the individualistic orientation of schemes of this type ignore the social and group context of much work (Pichierri, 1978). However, more significant than the probable opposition strategies of direct control are likely to encounter, are the inflexibilities they create.

Direct control strategies, particularly when coupled with assembly line production, are widely equated with high levels of job dissatisfaction (George, McNabb and Shorey, 1977). This dissatisfaction may manifest itself in the forms of labour turnover or absenteeism. In the US, Ford experienced annual rates of labour turnover approaching 400 per cent and daily absentee rates of 10 per cent, even in 1914 (Gartman, 1979). Attempts to encourage labour tenure through high wage policies or bureaucratic institutionalisation tend to increase costs and rigidity. If dissatisfaction materialises in the workplace the adoption of direct control strategies is likely to alter its form and impact. The deskilling which occurs with an extensive division of labour is likely to increase the homogeneity of perception of those involved. Similarly, the concentration of employees in large units as characterised by assembly line production facilitates mobilisation for collective protest. At the same time deskilling eases opportunities for substituting employees (or even capital) in the event of industrial action. Under such circumstances there are likely to be strong incentives for localised, sectionalised forms of action or even modes less prone to detection (sabotage, poor-quality work, etc). The economics of selective action are fostered by the considerable interdependencies extensive job fragmentation and assembly line co-ordination bring (Gartman, 1979, p. 204; Friedman, 1977, p. 94). Further sources of rigidity stem from technical change which necessitates a flexible and responsive labour force and changes in product range which entail alterations in the length of production runs or quality (Wood and Kelly, 1982).

The limitations of direct control strategies have led to a search for alternative methods of organising work. Information problems provide a key to the forms of incentive structure within organisations. If presetting of APQT combinations is not feasible incentives are likely to be geared towards ensuring efficient levels of effort and quality. Similarly, capitalising on employee knowledge may be facilitated by non-preset work schemes. Forms of bureaucratic control derive from attempts to embody control of the labour process within the hierarchical social structure of organisations (Edwards, 1979). They appear to emerge in two distinct situations. Firstly, large enterprises such as IBM and Polaroid have installed forms of paternalistic management prompted by a desire to forestall unionism. Secondly, attempts to impose direct control practices in the face of effective union organisation have evolved into bureaucratic control structures where unions have sought to institutionalise jointly negotiated procedures. The advantage to management of such arrangements is to contain and partially regularise workplace conflict. Given the vulnerability of modern productive processes to selective disruption this may be a significant consideration.

Bureaucratic control coupled with a degree of employee autonomy may be an optimal strategy when tasks are non-homogeneous. In terms of the labour market such idiosyncrasies arise from non-standardisation of plant and equipment, individual adaptations of processes, economies of team production where group structures and membership are maintained, and firm-specific informational idiosyncrasies. The general problem such tasks create is that of small numbers exchange as transactions are negotiated and executed. These problems are compounded in uncertain and complex situations when one recognises the existence of bounded rationality (Simon, 1961) and the possibilities for opportunistic behaviour in the light of information impactedness (Williamson, 1975). The latter two terms require some clarification. Opportunistic behaviour extends the concept of self-interest to encompass the use of guile. Such behaviour arises primarily from partial or distorted information disclosure and misrepresentation of intentions. Information impactedness is a derivative condition arising from the conjunction of uncertainty, bounded rationality and opportunism. It refers to differences in awareness and knowledge that cannot be costlessly reduced.

The modern corporation attempts to overcome these difficulties through a judicious combination of bureaucratic control and individual autonomy. The emergent form is the employment relationship within an internal labour market (ILM) (Doeringer and Piore, 1971). The ILM evolves when the allocation and pricing of labour occur primarily within the organisation; incumbents are differentiated from labour in the external market. Such an arrangement represents a far more effective way of ensuring efficient team production. The rigidity of the authority relationship is reduced where individual contracts are replaced by a general collective agreement. Furthermore, peer group involvement increases the likelihood of a constructive reponse to change. The substitution of a collective agreement for a series of individual contracts stresses the importance of organisational interests over individual concerns and reduces the incentives for opportunistic behaviour. The assignment of wage rates to tasks as opposed to individuals serves to increase flexibility. Such flexibility is achieved by ensuring more certain income flows in exchange for a surrender or relaxation of property rights in jobs.

The incentive structure of the ILM serves to facilitate efficient internal transactions. A promotional reward system based on seniority fosters co-operation and the sharing of task-specific knowledge. Screening can be achieved at lower cost and risk when entry occurs at lower-level positions. Such a system also discourages labour turnover. The loss of seniority and other pecuniary rights serve to reduce the mobility of incumbents. This reduces the high cost of turnover which the firm faces in the case of labour endowed with firm-specific (and task-specific) training. The viability of the system is enhanced when self-monitoring is encouraged and methods of internal conflict resolution are set up.

The Labour Utilisation Practices of MNEs

There are several reasons to expect the labour utilisation practices of MNEs to differ from those of indigenous firms.

Firstly, such practices are invariably subject to the influence of source nation values. Differences in the scope of collective bargaining lead to differences by nation in the role of self-financing bargains. Shearer (1970) argues that the predominantly economic bargaining motives of US unions have forced US employers continuously to seek more efficient forms of labour utilisation. Furthermore, differences by nation in managerial discretion to utilise labour (Shearer, 1970; Blanpain, 1970), coupled with the role of tradition and union opposition (Flanders, 1970), generate probable differences in experience and approach.

Secondly, multinational structure may influence labour utilisation practices. The centralisation of certain key decisions may generate response rigidities within subsidiaries. Similarly, a decentralised structure may be conducive to greater flexibility and antagonistic to pressures for multinational collective bargaining. MNEs operating globally-integrated production systems may adopt decentralised structures in recognition of their vulnerability to such bargaining overtures (Roberts, 1973). The existence of productive operations in several nations may generate comparative data instrumental in the imposition of labour utilisation practices unrepresentative of host nation practices in general (Steuer and Gennard, 1971).

Thirdly, foreignness may lead to differences in the perception and discounting of risk and information imperfections. Such informational deficiencies are likely to be particularly marked in the case of labour. This follows from both the locational specificity of labour and the importance of non-economic considerations in the successful management of labour. These factors mean that foreignness may be a considerable disadvantage. It is interesting that this disadvantage is one likely to apply to foreign entrants regardless of their international experience. Locational specificity and uniqueness implies that this type of problem is unlikely to be significantly attenuated in the case of established MNEs, any more so than for first time or 'naive' entrants.

Fourthly, as the eclectic model highlights, ownership-specific advantages may differ significantly by nation. Whilst US MNEs appear to have comparative advantage in concentrated market structures (Buckley and Dunning, 1976), MNEs from LDCs appear to operate most successfully in small-scale, labour-intensive processes (Kumar and McLeod, 1981). This phenomenon of national differences in ownership-specific advantages is complicated by evidence which indicates that the profitable exploitation of certain advantages appears to depend crucially on where such exploitation occurs. Thus while Japanese MNEs appear to enjoy successful labour relations in advanced host nations such as the UK (Takamiya, 1981) and the US (Negandhi and Baliga, 1981), application of their techniques in less developed host nations has resulted in considerable conflict (Negandhi and Baliga, 1979).

Fifthly, the eclectic model predicts that there may be significant differences in labour force structure between multinational and uninational firms.

Market imperfections are the major stimulus to internalisation; the nature of such imperfections have important implications for the composition of administrative substitutes to the market mechanism. Casson (1982) argues that imperfections exist in both market-making and market-servicing functions. The imperfections which prompt internalisation of market-servicing activities were discussed in Chapter 2. Market-making activities encompass contact-making and the specifications, negotiation, monitoring and enforcement of contracts. The underdevelopment of markets and high costs of conducting external transactions in market-making activities encourage internalisation.

This process has an important implication for employment structure within MNEs. It implies that MNEs will seek to operate at the premium or high quality end of the market spectrum. Such a desire follows partly from the high costs market-making pioneering firms (MNEs) incur. The recovery of these costs is facilitated by premium pricing of an innovative service. In addition, concentration on higher quality output encourages non-price forms of competition and product differentiation. Competitive strategies of this type are compatible with the oligopolistic market structures within which MNEs are predominantly found.

One result of this difference in average product quality is that MNEs are likely to devote considerably more resources to market-making activities. Activities such as contact-making and contract negotiation are best undertaken by skilled clerical workers. This hypothesis is consistent with the finding that indirect employees are proportionately more important in MNEs than in domestic enterprises. Indeed, the interpretation of this finding becomes much more plausible in the light of market-making activities (Stopford, 1979).

A second implication is that a competitive strategy based on higher quality calls for considerable investments in quality control. Strict control may be easier to achieve where training is undertaken within the enterprise. The desire to maintain quality provides a strong incentive for the internalisation of both specific and general training programmes. For specific training, which has productive application within a single organisation, the demands of strict quality maintenance plus the non-proprietary nature of such training lead to the prediction that firms incurring training expenditures are likely to provide considerable incentives for trainees to remain within the organisation. Where quality is paramount firms may even seek to provide general training: training which is normally obtained prior to employment and which is typically financed by the trainee. In this case competitive requirements may dictate the need to amend traditional training programmes.

The above hypotheses enable a provisional sketch of the likely labour utilisation practices of MNEs to be attempted. The importance of US-based multinationals in the world economy implies that the exporting of domestic practices is likely to display a marked American bias. The case for such practices is reinforced by their apparent success in the highly productive US economy. The analysis is facilitated by distinguishing those types of industries within which MNEs predominantely operate. They are characterised by two major forms of production technology: assembly line production (electrical and electronic products, motor vehicles) and continuous flow processes (chemicals, selected foodstuffs). Whilst labour requirements and management strategies pursued display systematic variation according to production technology both technologies are compatible with the existence of a 'dualistic' labour force characterised by a large number of unskilled operatives and a small number of semi- or highly-skilled employees performing supervisory, regulatory and planning functions.

Continuous flow processes are generally characterised by high capital intensity and the use of a limited number of unskilled operatives. Planning, regulatory and co-ordinatory tasks are performed by a comparatively small core of highly skilled technicians. Labour control problems are minimal: output rates and quality are primarily machine-controlled. Industries based on flow production tend to be located in the major advanced economies and have been relatively immune to the processes of international relocation. The major explanatory factors accounting for this are the advantages of locating processing facilities close to the market served (petrochemicals) and the comparative absence of labour control problems within such industries. Establishments tend to offer above average levels of remuneration and working conditions. Such policies foster employment stability and the acquisition of firm-specific skills. Incorporation of key employees within ILMs and systems of bureaucratic control serve to contain and regulate potential conflict. The ILMs within this type of industry are characterised by vertical stratification, high degrees of unionisation and procedures based on seniority. Incorporation of key employees increases the dichotomisation of operatives from skilled technicians. Segmentation of plant-level employees is reinforced by enterprise-level stratification based on centralisation of management, planning and innovation functions at the level of regional or global management centres (Hymer, 1972).

The more interesting examples of labour utilisation practices of MNEs are afforded by those industries based on assembly line production. This form of production process remains the most important for the majority of MNEs. As indicated above assembly line production is synonomous with extensive deskilling. Traditionally, the demand for unskilled labour in these industries has been met in the advanced nations by the attraction of immigrants (both in the US in the early twentieth century and European nations such as Britain, France, West Germany and Switzerland in the post-1945 period) or the incorporation of marginal sectors of the labour force (racial minority groups, women). While the processes of rural exodus and marginalisation were assured, production remained in the major market economies of North America and Europe. Overseas markets were served primarily by export. Within this process the less developed nations were limited to their traditional role of supplying raw materials and, occasionally, labour.

The unique conjunction of a variety of developments in the immediate post-World War II period considerably enhanced opportunities for the global pursuit of profit through direct investment. The opening of world markets, falling communication and transport costs and increased US involvement in European recovery resulted in a rapid expansion of multinational, particularly US, business. The largest 187 US enterprises established 2,009 overseas subsidiaries between 1946 and 1961 (Vaupel and Curhan, 1973). This investment was undoubtedly prompted by local market-servicing considerations. Paradoxically, the expansion of overseas production in the postwar period reinforced the limitations of direct control strategies within the context of assembly line production. The concentration of relatively homogeneous workers within large-scale units increases the probability of collective forms of protest materialising. Deskilling and the subdivision of work foster the development of a collective perception of workplace relations; the conditions for conflict materialising are exacerbated by a combination of repetitive tasks and close supervision.

This paradox is illuminated by distinguishing between labour's market bargaining power (MBP) and its workplace bargaining power (WBP) (Arrighi, 1982). The former refers to the relative power of labour as a factor in supply; the latter relates to labour's bargaining power within the workplace. Deskilling and assembly line methods have reduced labour's MBP. This decline has occurred as alternative employment opportunities are limited for employees with increasingly specific and fragmented skills. Similarly, where work is machine-paced and controlled the returns to traditional skills of organising work and quality control have declined. At the same time the inflexibilities of assembly line production (task interdependency, rising burden of indirect labour costs) serve to raise labour's relative WBP.

These inflexibilities are reinforced in the case of vertically- or horizontally-integrated MNEs. For such enterprises disruption of production may generate considerable 'external' costs in that intra-enterprise trade flows may be fractured. Empirically, the significance of intra-firm trade indicates that such considerations are likely to influence a large number of MNEs. In 1977, 48 per cent of US imports were supplied by a party related by ownership (5 per cent of more stock holding) (Helleiner, 1981). Using a sample of 329 of the world's largest firms, Dunning and Pearce (1981) report that, on average in 1977, one-third of parent company exports were destined for affiliates. Indeed, such figures probably understate the dependence of MNEs on internalised trade flows. There is a case for including trade flows stemming from subcontracting arrangements, the magnitude of which was examined in Chapter 3. Whilst formal ownership links may not cover such trade the dependence of subcontractors on principals for technology and marketing assistance indicates the degree of mutual dependence.

In the light of these rigidities and potential weaknesses management are likely to devise a number of strategies to ensure the continued profitable utilisation of labour. We may distinguish four such strategies. The first is the further internationalisation of production. Overseas operations offer a means of segmenting a firm's labour force by state boundaries. They provide a method for tapping new sources of labour if investment occurs in areas where labour is unemployed or underemployed. Similarly, the international segmentation of production allows management to pursue a variety of labour control strategies under conditions of comparative disjunction. This may ameliorate inflexibilities and facilitate policy application and adaptation. For MNEs labour market dualism may be achieved at an international level. Investments, particularly in the LDCs, provide access to a large pool of unemployed labour. This is not to argue as some writers (e.g. Arrighi, 1982) that internationalisation of business is prompted solely by a desire to obtain lower cost or more docile labour.[1] Such an explanation of DFI ignores the demand (market) factors triggering investment. Similarly, it is incompatible with cross-investment, e.g. Japanese and European investment in the US. Access to previously untapped labour supplies is, in most cases, an attractive by-product of the investment process.

A second strategy relies on stratification of the workforce. Stratification may be achieved at both the national and international levels. Within the individual enterprise stratification is an inevitable outcome of the operation of ILMs. Since perfect substitutability in administrative capability between all members of an organisation is unlikely to exist, efficiency considerations dictate task specialisation with respect to decision-making. The emergence of hierarchy is then inevitable. The separation of functions of conception and execution initiatives a process of stratification apparent at both the national and the international level. At the international level MNEs are associated with the development of a new international class structure comprising a transnational managerial class, an established labour class and social marginals (Cox, 1976). These groups are increasingly formed at the international level as MNEs centralise control and innovatory functions within the advanced (core) nations and assign production and assembly operations to the less developed (peripheral) economies (Hymer, 1972). Stratification, like segmentation, provides an effective means of increasing workforce heterogeneity.

Subcontracting is a third managerial strategy which can be identified. Subcontracting has traditionally been associated with large-scale companies, particularly those faced by cyclical or volatile patterns of demand (Friedman, 1977). It offers benefits of flexibility as a low-cost method of dual sourcing of inputs and means of insulating employees from the adverse effects of a downturn in demand. A distinction is often made between cross-border and within-border subcontracting (Berthomieu and Hanaut, 1980). MNEs play an important role in both types of subcontracting. Where overseas subsidiaries are established subcontracting may occur to host nation suppliers. Indeed, in many cases investments may be subject to government stipulation of a certain minimum percentage of local value added in production. MNEs have accelerated[2] cross-border subcontracting particularly in electronics, textiles, toys and sports goods.

The fourth category encompasses a variety of strategies management may apply in source and advanced host nations where there exist considerable obstacles to flexible labour adjustment. Such obstacles arise primarily from effective union opposition and government regulation in the form of employment protection. Within-border subcontracting is a traditional method of pursuing profitable labour control. A related strategy is the use of outwork or homework. The major advantages of outwork include zero labour supervision costs, the ability to purchase discrete and variable amounts of labour and payment related directly to output (Rubery and Wilkinson, 1981). Since processes of assembly line production do not readily lend themselves to the use of outwork this form of labour process may be confined to ancillary or service functions within the industry. Outwork may also be used to extend product ranges, particularly for limited volumes of output or where technology is subject to rapid change or has yet to reach standardisation. Like subcontracting, outwork has the effect of segmenting labour and may forestall the development of cohesive labour opposition.

A number of enterprises operate in industries or areas where the retention of employment is a major concern to government. This is particularly true of industries such as automobiles which tend to be geographically concentrated and to generate considerable indirect employment. Where plants are located in declining areas or enjoy a monopsonistic position, flexibility to relocate internationally may be curtailed by government intervention. In situations of his nature employers may seek to engage in concession or give-back bargaining. Such bargaining is based on the concession by employees of controls on work practices, the acceptance of wage freezes or even cuts in exchange for employment assurances or guarantees. It is prompted by a desire to reduce labour costs. Concession bargaining may be related to government financial aid to companies experiencing difficulties or attempting to restructure their operations.

A final component of this strategy group which appears, superficially, to tackle the problem of worker alienation inherent in mass assembly production is job recomposition. Job recomposition refers to a variety of practices, variously termed job enrichment, enlargement, etc., involving the reversing of the detailed division of labour. Typically the work cycle and number of tasks performed by an individual is greatly increased. Job recomposition in the automobile industry, particularly within Scandinavia, has received a great deal of publicity. The motives for recomposition are unlikely to grant a paramount role to problems of worker alienation. More significance is likely to be placed on the dictates of achieving efficient production with expanding product ranges in accordance with growing market demand (Kelly, (1982). The shortening of production runs and role for employee initiative in product adaptation are incompatible with traditional assembly line techniques. Unlike self-financing methods of reorganising labour processes such as productivity bargaining, the future of job recomposition is uncertain. Increasing international competition, particularly from Japan where exploitation of the benefits of assembly line production appears to be carried to an extreme (Kamata, 1983), has prompted management to seek alternative solutions to the problem of assembly line inflexibilities. Increasingly, in the advanced nations that solution appears to lie in the adoption of 'new technology' rather than profit-eroding humanist moves such as job recomposition. Furthermore, recomposition should be seen as a manifestation of neo-Fordism since the hierarchical stratification of functions of conception and execution is unaffected (Palloix, 1976). We may derive a number of testable hypotheses from the above discussion which can be usefully compared with existing empirical evidence.

Empirical Evidence on the Labour Utilisation Practices of MNEs

The preceding analysis provides a plausible rationale for the finding that MNEs are generally characterised by a workforce exhibiting a high ratio of indirect to direct employees. More specifically, problems of ensuring efficient control of labour inputs implies that MNEs are likely to devote comparatively more resources to supervision. The finding of Chapter 3, that MNEs in LDCs tend to adopt comparatively more capital-intensive technologies, is compatible with a desire to minimise problems of labour (and quality) control (Strassman, 1968). Studies covering a number of LDCs (summarised in ILO, 1981b) reveal that indirect employees (managerial, clerical, etc.) generally form a greater proportion of all employees for MNE affiliates. Furthermore, there is evidence that the importance of such employees has increased over time.

Secondly, the locational-specificity of labour as a factor of production and the importance of local knowledge in its efficient management implies that labour management within MNEs will be one of the most decentralised functions. The use of local personnel is likely to be more pronounced at the operational level and will be directly related to cultural differences ('psychic distance') between source and host nation.

A large number of studies have indicated that labour management is one of the most decentralised functions within MNEs (Bomers and Peterson, 1977; Hedlund, 1981). Decentralisation appears to be positively related, although non-linearly, to increasing subsidiary size and the degree of local uncertainty. Similarly, the method of foreign entry appears to affect decentralisation, being greater in the case of acquisition of an existing enterprise. A concomitant of decentralisation is likely to be an emphasis on plant or company-based bargaining. For Britain, where there has been a significant trend within private sector manufacturing to localise collective bargaining (Brown, 1981), foreign-owned firms appear to have adopted such patterns both earlier (Steuer and Gennard, 1971) and more fully (Buckley and Enderwick, 1984). Single-employer bargaining necessitates more extensive and specialised personnel functions. Labour relations managers within foreign-owned firms, certainly in the case of Britain, are more likely to be better qualified and to undergo formal training within the firm than their counterparts in domestically-owned plants.

Thirdly, our analysis implies that there are likely to be observable differences in labour utilisation practices between MNE affiliates and indigenous firms in the advanced nations as well as differences between the advanced and less developed nations. In the latter case we might expect a more intensive utilisation of labour in the advanced nations while the LDCs provide opportunities for both extensive and intensive utilisation of labour resources.

Turning first to the comparative labour utilisation practices of MNEs within the developed nations, we draw on the findings of Brown (1981). This study revealed that foreign-owned firms do display a more intensive utilisation of labour. This intensity of utilisation is mirrored in a higher propensity to operate shift production. Labour deployment was found to be more systematic within foreign-owned plants where job evaluation procedures were widely employed.

Direct investment in the LDCs provides opportunities for increasing both extensive and intensive labour utilisation. Changes in the number of hours worked represents the major method of increasing the extensive utilsation of labour. Legislation and effective union opposition curtail the use of this strategy in the industrialised nations. In the less developed nations MNEs (and indigenous employers) appear to exploit this strategy. Average annual hours worked in South East Asia tend to be about 50 per cent greater than in Western Europe (Frank, 1981b). The intensity of work in the less developed nations is attested to by work-related accident rates which may affect more than 20 per cent of the labour force and the detrimental health impact of repetitive tasks performed under largely unregulated conditions (Frank, 1981a). The ability to impose such an intense utilisation of labour appears to result from both a lack of effective opposition and, in some cases, implicit government support. Union organisation in LDCs, certainly within large foreign-owned establishments, is primarily based on company unions. Several factors account for this. Firstly, such unions are often an outgrowth of paternalistic consultative procedures. Secondly, government impetus to the spread of unionisation may operate through dominant employing units. Thirdly, dualistic divergence with the coexistence of large-scale modern plants and a traditional sector impedes the development of craft- or industry-based unions. The ineffectiveness of these unions as a counterbalance in the workplace is reinforced by internal schisms between white-collar and blue-collar employees and between local and national organisations (Lloyd, 1982). In many cases employer strategies are legitimised by supportive government policy in the form of anti-strike legislation, wage controls (Frank, 1981a) and impediments to viable collective bargaining (ILO, 1981b).

Fourthly, the analysis generates the prediction that MNE wage levels will be comparatively higher than those offered by indigenous establishments. The higher productivity levels achieved by MNEs provide the means to offer higher rates. The motivation to pass such rents on in the form of higher wage levels stems from a desire to attract and retain labour of a particular quality and, in many cases, to forestall industrial action (Enderwick and Buckley, 1983) or unionisation (Hamill, 1982). For the developed nations there is an overwhelming volume of evidence that MNE subsidiaries do pay comparatively higher wages (ILO, 1976). The only study presenting conflicting results (Tariff Commission, 1983) is seriously flawed. The magnitude of the wage differential appears to vary between nations (ILO, 1976) and type of employee. Overall, these studies indicate that MNEs adjust their wage levels to take account of local circumstances, subject to at least equalling remuneration rates provided by comparable indigenous plants.

The problems of wage comparability, principally differences in plant size and workforce composition, are compounded in the case of the less developed nations. Nonetheless, a similar differential in favour of MNEs has been widely reported (ILO, 1976). There is some evidence (Lim, 1977) that much of this differential derives from a generous provision of fringe benefits. Whilst there is agreement between the more and less developed nations on the existence of an MNE wage differential, there is less consensus on its cause. Within the LDCs the existence of an inverse relationship between the size of the differential and the level of economic development (Taira and Standing, 1973) has been interpreted as a means of attracting a suitable supply of labour in terms of skill and dependability.Within the advanced nations where such a supply is generally forthcoming the differential is consistent with a desire to discourage unionisation or union action. Whilst this area has received insufficient attention there is tentative evidence of a positive relationship between intra-firm trade (and vulnerability to production disruption) and MNE comparative wage differential (Enderwick and Buckley, 1983).

A fifth hypothesis relates to the likely pattern of industrial conflict within MNEs. As the analysis of this chapter would suggest MNE subsidiaries incur a comparatively greater proportion of disputes apparently triggered by labour utilisation issues (manning levels, working conditions, dismissals, etc.). The collective and perishable nature of these aspects of workplace relations is compatible with a pattern of frequent short stoppages. Similarly, the lower percentage of employees involved in strike action and higher proportion of disputes encompassing a single section of employees within subsidiaries (Buckley and Enderwick, 1984) is in line with our expectations.

Sixthly, a number of studies focusing on company rationalisation strategies within the major source nations provide extensive support for the hypotheses derived in this chapter. Whilst there is considerable evidence that, overall, employment stability in foreign-owned affiliates is similar to that within indigenous firms (Killick, 1982; McAleese and Counahan, 1979; Van den Bulcke, 1983) there is a tendency for disinvestment by MNEs to be concentrated within the less prosperous regions of advanced host nations. Although this result is questionable in the case of UK studies (Townsend, 1983), which fail to recognise the overrepresentation of foreign investment in the peripheral regions (Watts, 1980), more careful analyses confirm this finding for the North of England (Smith, 1982), Scotland (Hood and Yound, 1982) and Northern Ireland (Harrison, 1982).

Whilst the regional bias of disinvestment is likely to be affected by historical location patterns and the sectoral distribution of industry, it is probable that opposition to closure or contraction is likely to be less effective in such areas. Regional economies are often characterised by structural weaknesses, above average levels of unemployment and a predominance of disadvantaged groups such as women or immigrants within the labour force (Anell, 1981; Kreye, Frobel and Heinrichs, 1980). In the case of Northern Ireland employment loss in foreign-owned affiliates has been comparatively greater in those sectors where overall employment stability has been lowest (Harrison, 1982). Furthermore, there is evidence that protection offered to domestically weak industries provides insulation from neither import competition nor pressures to relocate to lower cost areas of the world economy (Juhl, 1979).

There is evidence that both direct foreign investment and international subcontracting have been used to shelter source nation employees from the full effects of downturns in demand (Helleiner, 1976). The cushioning effects of direct investment on source nation employees is well illustrated in the case of Belgium. In the recessionary years of 1975-6 while foreign-owned firms in Belgium experienced a plant closure rate in excess of that for indigenous enterprises the differential was accounted for by divestment by European, and particularly Dutch, enterprises (Van den Bulcke, 1983). Substitutability between exports from the parent nation and DFI is likely to be high in a case such as this characterised by cost comparability and geographical proximity.

The use of international subcontracting is well developed in industries such as clothing and electronics. It has been estimated that between 1965 and 1970 almost half of the increase in clothing imports into Western Europe was accounted for by goods supplied by subcontractors. Almost half of Western European electronics industry expendiure goes on external purchases excluding inter-affiliate trade (Plant, 1981). Fluctuations in final demand appear to be magnified by subcontracting relationships. Thus in the one-year period 1974-5, employment in the Free Trade Zones of the Mexican border fell by 19.4 per cent to 83,000. Employment in the electronics industry of Singapore experienced a fall of 29.2 per cent in the same year (ILO, 1981b, p. 82). The durability of employment created by subcontracting appears to depend on the motives behind such arrangements. A desire to enjoy access to lower costs of production is likely to generate more stable employment than where domestic supply constraints necessitate overseas capacity (Sharpston, 1975).

Enterprises and sectors unable to participate in the benefits afforded by foreign investment or international subcontracting have resorted to restructuring based on capital investment and technical change, an intensification of work practices or simply rationalisation (Massey and Meegan, 1982). MNEs subject to constraints on their ability to restructure internationally have turned to investment in new technology and concession bargaining in an attempt to increase competitiveness. Indeed, some employers see the two processes of international relocation and restructing as imperfect substitutes (Moxon, 1975).

The adoption of new technology is well illustrated in the case of the Western European motor industry. The short-lived experiments in job recomposition have given way to substantial investments in robot technology and increased automation as global overcapacity and import competition have eroded profitability. The employment losses connected with the closure of vehicle assembly plants in the major source nations have prompted government intervention and subvention (e.g. British Leyland in the UK, Chrysler in the US). State subsidies have

been tied to reforms in working practices, acceptance of new technology or wage concessions. The adoption of robot technology has been
fastest in nations such as Japan, Sweden, West Germany and the United
States, all major source nations of MNEs (Whitehill and Takezawa,
1978). The limited studies of the introduction of such technology
(Zermens, Moseley and Braun, 1980) demonstrate that problems of
labour supervision provide a major impetus to robotisation. In the UK
where there has been opposition[3] to the introduction of such technology in some sectors (Benson and Lloyd, 1983; Central Policy
Review Staff, 1975) MNEs have resorted to unilateral imposition
(British Leyland) or the bypassing of traditional union channels of consultation (Ford, UK).

Concession bargaining in the current recession has been most prevalent in the US occurring in sectors suffering global overcapacity (automobiles, tyres) and low-cost foreign competition (steel, automobiles).
It has been most intense in those industries characterised by substantial
employment stability and effective union organisation (McKersie and
Cappelli, 1982). The best known case in the UK concerned the
American-owned Hyster fork-lift truck subsidiary in Scotland. The
company successfully imposed a 10 per cent wage cut on its non-
union workforce in exchange for guarantees of job security. The wage
concessions appeared as part of a restructuring process involving the
closure of related affiliates in other European nations including Holland
and Belgium. In other cases of reorganisation Scottish plants have been
less fortunate in retaining jobs (Hood and Young, 1982).

Finally, we examine empirical evidence on the labour force stratification and segmentation effects of MNEs. Stratification occurs at three
levels:

  (i)   within plants;
 (ii)   within nations; and
(iii)   within the world economy.

As outlined above, within plants, the growth of ILMS has brought
formalisation of economic stratification.

Within nations stratification appears in the concentration by industry of DFI (see Table 2.15). MNEs tend to gravitate towards the
more dynamic sectors and avoid areas subject to structural problems in
the advanced nations (ILO, 1981a, p. 74). This sectoral distribution
creates stratification where the employees of foreign-owned affiliates
enjoy faster wage growth and enhanced employment stability. Within

many advanced nations a further source of stratification arises from the spatial separation of corporate functions. The concentration of white-collar employment in core regions of both the US and UK is well documented (Armstrong, 1979; Gudgin, Crum and Bailey, 1979). The intra-nation spatial separation of production and control functions is characteristic of both national and multinational multiplant enterprises (Crum and Gudgin, 1978; Leigh and North, 1978). In the case of multi-nationals, however, separation is increasingly assuming an international form (Hood and Young, 1977).

The international stratification of functions emerges most clearly in the case of research and development (R&D). Only some 15 per cent of US corporate expendiure on R&D is devoted to research undertaken outside the US (Behrman and Fischer, 1980). The propensity to under-take overseas R&D appears to be positively related to enterprise mat-urity, global organisation (Hewitt, 1980) and the extent to which affiliates service local markets (Hirschey and Caves, 1981). The R&D that does occur abroad tends to focus more on product development and adaptation than basic research. Similarly, such research is heavily concentrated into major host nations such as Canada, the UK and West Germany offering adequate local facilities (US Senate Committee, 1973).

The centralisation of R&D within MNEs creates a system of inter-national dependency and stratification in the generation and diffusion of new products and processes. It is not clear that the resulting stratifi-cation is the result of deliberate corporate intentions. Empirical evidence indicates that both positive and negative host country induce-ments to attract R&D have little impact in the absence of an adequate local scientific and technical infrastructure (Behrman and Fischer, 1980). Indeed, there is considerable controversy as to whether host nations, particularly the less developed nations, benefit from the decen-tralisation of R&D (Lall, 1982). The presence of an MNE-financed research base may stifle local creative efforts or bias the type of work undertaken where the foundation of basic research is absent. Irrespec-tive of the motives for international stratification its effect is to create a global centralisation of critical functions in the major source nations (Hymer, 1972), mirroring a similar centralisation within such nations. The resulting stratification in employment opportunities and rewards both within and between nations creates major divisions in the work-force of an MNE.

Similar divisions may emerge as a result of the labour segmentation effects of MNEs. Again these effects are observable at three distinct levels:

(i)   within plants;
(ii) within source nations; and
(iii) within host nations.

Labour force segmentation within MNE plants may be pursued on a racial basis or through segregation of employees by the use, for example, of homeworking. Segmentation on a racial basis is an accusation levelled at a number of MNEs through the collection of case-study material. A good example is provided by the case of International Harvester where there is some evidence that minority workers are overrepresented in the least desirable jobs and have been subject to a lower degree of job security (Barrera, 1979). More contentious is the assertion that the subordinate position of minority group employees has been consciously created and maintained. Clearly, occupational crowding and lower job security is at least partially determined by differences in skill acquisition and seniority. Similarly, pre-market discrimination (access to schooling, etc.) accounts for a significant proportion of the relative disadvantage of minority employees in the US (Addison and Siebert, 1979, ch. 6).

The internationalisation of production is likely to provide a degree of segmentation within DFI source nations. Segmentation occurs as internationalisation affects employment structure within the source nation. Jobs lost tend to be production-related and, in the US, union organised (Preston, 1980). The sectors most affected by the internationalisation of business, electronics, clothing, etc., tend to be those employing some of the weakest groups within the labour force such as women and migrant workers (Ansell, 1981; Hancock, 1983; Jenkins, 1982). Similarly, the affected industries are often located in the less prosperous and accessible regions (Kreye, Frobel and Heinrichs, 1980). In contrast, the source nation employment creation effects of the process fall principally on skilled and professional clerical and managerial occupations (de la Torre, 1973; Hawkins and Jedel, 1975; Jordon and Valhne, 1981). The discrepancy between the characteristics of those adversely affected by outward investment and the type of jobs created highlights the low probability of those displaced being able to take advantage of employment opportunities.

MNEs may introduce a further source of segmentation within the parent nation. There is some evidence that the degree of multinationality of an industry's principal enterprises is negatively related to the strength of protective pressure sought by that industry (Franko and Stephenson, 1982). This implies that in those industries where opportunities for multinational relocation are limited, e.g. steel, protective measures are more likely to be adopted. This serves to create a further discrepancy in the prospects for employees of industries characterised by MNEs and those in purely national industries. The lower probability of protection and skill mismatch between jobs lost and those created in sectors dominated by MNEs contributes to inter-industry labour market segmentation.

At the international level foreign investment has long been associated with dualistic development, particularly within LDCs. Dualism appears both between and within host economies. The marked geographical concentration of DFI in the LDCs was highlighted in Chapter 2 (see Table 2.12). A handful of countries, including Brazil, Mexico, Argentina, Singapore and Hong Kong, account for the dominant proportion of Third World investment undertaken by major source nations such as the US, West Germany, Switzerland, Japan and the Netherlands (ILO, 1981b, p. 24). Whilst there is some recent evidence that investments are increasingly being attracted to a second wave of rapidly growing export-orientated economies (OECD, 1982), a number of nations (e.g. Bangladesh) and regions (e.g. Central Africa) appear to be completely unaffected by the internationalisation of production. The highly unequal distribution of foreign investment in LDCs raises the likelihood that any development effects of MNEs will be enjoyed by only a minority of potential recipients.

Recent research on the impact of MNEs on the Third World has questioned the extent to which DFI generates a dualistic structure by propelling development within major recipient economies (for a representative summary see Bornschier, 1982). According to this school of thought foreign investment may have an initial positive impact on development (accentuating dualism between host nations) but the longer-term effect is to create structural imbalances retardant to development (stabilising or reducing inter-nation dualism). The mechanisms of underdevelopment include a slowing down of domestic investment as foreign investment accentuates income inequalities, the crowding out of indigenous investment opportunities (Bornschier, 1980), and increased technological dependence and social and economic instability (Ballmer-Cao, 1979). While these results question the extent to which DFI is likely to contribute to dualistic development between Third World host nations, they do highlight the likelihood of internal dualism, i.e. differential sectoral development within nations.

It is the processes of internal dualism associated with MNEs which have attracted most interest. A number of studies have identified a positive relationship between the penetration of MNEs and high levels of income inequality and unemployment (Mahler, 1981). One short-coming of these studies is a failure to isolate the distinct impact of MNEs within the general process of development. That growth is likely to increase inequality, particularly in its initial stages, is a well estab-lished finding (Lecaillon, Paukert, Morrisson and Germidis, 1983). The independent role played by MNEs within a process of increasing inequality must be isolated from the comparable effects of develop-ment.

Two practices of MNEs have been particularly closely associated with dualism: high wage policies and inappropriate technology. Whilst there is little doubt that affiliates in LDCs pay above average wages (ILO, 1976; Sabolo and Trajtenberg, 1976), the differential appears to have a firm economic rationale. Comparatively higher skill levels and productivity are likely to be reflected in wage premiums. The finding that much of the differential comes in the form of fringe benefits (Lim, 1977) may indicate a desire by employers to attract and retain better quality employees. Evidence to support this hypothesis comes from Taira and Standing (1973), who report that the US-owned affiliate wage differential is negatively related to *per capita* income in ten Latin American host nations. This result is compatible with a wage policy designed to draw out a suitable supply of labour, that supply being least forthcoming in the most undeveloped nations.

Inappropriate technology (see Chapter 3) provides a basis for dualism resulting in technological unemployment (Singer, 1970). Such dualism is particularly likely where the spillover of benefits from the foreign-owned sector are limited or are accompanied by the erosion of traditional skills (global deskilling) (Frank, 1981b, p. 104).

These labour force schisms which are created by the operations of MNEs are replicated in other areas of economic life, particularly the consumption sphere. It is likely, for example, that on average indivi-duals in the advanced nations gain more in consumption welfare than they lose through adverse employment effects associated with foreign investment and international subcontracting (Sharpston, 1975). This serves to reduce the degree of opposition within such nations to the growth of multinational business. Developments within MNE plants in source and advanced host nations work to reinforce the international segmentation of labour. Most notable are the development of single staff status and single union representation (Hamill, 1982; Takamiya,

1981) within MNE plants. One effect of such developments is to increase employee homogeneity within plants at the expense of inter-plant cohesion.

The processes of segmentation outlined above require qualification on two counts. Firstly, it is not apparent that overseas investment is primarily prompted by a desire effectively to segregate employees. Rather, this seems to be a consequence of a process initiated mainly by market-servicing considerations. This is not to deny that MNEs take advantage of, and even exacerbate, existing divisions in the labour force (Michel, 1983) but it is difficult to lay the blame for sexual and racial divisions on the operations of MNEs; indeed such divisions predate capitalism (Friedman, 1977, p. 113). Secondly, there is less inevitability and predictability in the patterns of internationalisation than some writers recognise (see Hymer, 1972). There is evidence of reverse movements of production facilities from periphery to core nations as technological developments have reduced unit labour costs (Castles, 1979; ILO, 1981a, p. 76). The dynamism of the determinants of international production is likely to exacerbate further the disjunction of global labour.

Conclusions

Firstly, the foregoing analysis has important implications for labour's relative bargaining power and the prospects for multinational collective bargaining. Unlike conventional discussions of the obstacles to multi-national bargaining (Ulman, 1975) which focus on the structural impediments to such a development (e.g. conflicting union ideologies, differing industrial relations practices and legislation, etc.), our analysis highlights the positive role management action plays in discouraging international union activity. Such action serves to raise the costs to labour of operating across borders. In addition, the increase in relative bargaining power of labour (WBP) has occurred as a by-product of structural transformations in the world economy and not as the result of any rise in international class consciousness or formation (Arrighi, 1982). Labour organisations appear to have played a very limited part in any alteration in the balance of relative bargaining power. We return to this theme in chapter 6.

Secondly, while the above analysis highlights the opportunities MNEs enjoy in LDCs for the intensive (and extensive) exploitation of labour, little attention has been paid to the methods by which surpluses are appropriated. Appropriation could ocur through the terms of trade (unequal exchange) (Emmanuel, 1972) if equilibrium wage differences exist between the trading nations. Appropriation through unequal exchange depends on product differences between trading partners. The growth of Third World export platforms serving the global economy implies that in the absence of protective tariffs in the advanced economies such production may usurp opportunities for trade and hence opportunities for unequal exchange (for a further discussion see Brewer, 1980). One response within certain sectors of the advanced economies has been restructuring with a movement towards higher value added commodities (Franko and Stephenson, 1982). Such movements across branches of industry have important implications for adjustment in core economies to structural changes in the world economy. Appropriation might also occur through the weak bargaining position of Third World host economies *vis-à-vis* MNEs (Trajtenberg, 1976). These weaknesses may be difficult to overcome where MNEs develop increasingly sophisticated methods of appropriation (Hoogvelt, 1982). These arguments are examined more fully in Chapter 7.

Thirdly, the analysis throws into question whether or not the 'nation-state is just about through as an economic unit' (Kindleberger, 1969, p. 207). Whilst this may be true of tariff policy, the institution of the nation-state provides a basis for labour segmentation by MNEs. It is apparent that national boundaries will continue to provide a major arena for labour strategies in the foreseeable future.

Finally, further research is required in a number of areas discussed above. One important topic which has received scant attention is the extent to which labour segmentation is a primary strategy of MNEs. Empirical testing of this hypothesis is urgently required.

Notes

1. Clearly investments in some worldwide export platforms are prompted primarily by the availability of low-cost labour. However, such investments are a small, but growing, aspect of international production.

2. Cross-border subcontracting also occurs between uninational enterprises in the advanced nations and suppliers in the LDCs. Large retailers and buying houses are a good example (Hone, 1974).

3. Union opposition led to the closure in 1979 of a Goodyear Tyre plant with the loss of 700 jobs.

5 THE LABOUR RELATIONS PRACTICES OF MNEs

Introduction

Preceding chapters have investigated the welfare effects of MNEs through both their impact on the labour market and labour utilisation practices. This chapter investigates MNE industrial relations practices which provide bounds within which labour utilisation and management occurs.

On theoretical grounds there are a number of characteristics of MNEs which lead to an expectation that they will pursue labour relations practices that differ in type or degree from those associated with indigenous enterprises. Several of the factors were outlined in Chapter 4. The influence of source nation values is just as likely in labour relations management, particularly where expatriate staff play a central role (Trevor, 1983). The informational deficiencies faced by foreign affiliates in the successful managment of labour is a major source of start-up problems (Negandhi, 1983, p. 35; Newbould et al., 1978, p. 172). The possession by MNEs of income generating firm-specific assets provides an attractive target for the bargaining overtures of organised labour. Attempts to protect rents may manifest themselves as anti-union practices or a reluctance to disclose information on corporate performance. Bargaining intransigence by multinational management may be reinforced by the multi-plant nature of MNEs which has the effect of increasing the elasticity of demand for labour and reducing the relative bargaining power of employees (Caves, 1982).

The labour relations practices of MNEs are widely perceived by labour organisations as a source of friction in the maintenance of union-management accord (Edwards, 1977; Gennard, 1972). Whilst there is some tendency to confuse size effects with those resulting from multi-nationality, two sources of labour concern are the claimed bargaining advantage of MNEs and their tendency to impute source nation values and ideologies to the often markedly different industrial relations systems prevailing in host economies.

The bargaining advantage of MNEs is thought to stem from their ability to relocate production facilities in the face of fractious labour relations or rising labour costs and the possibility of servicing strike-bound plants from duplicate facilities located at alternative sites. In addition, multinational structure has been equated with a centralisation of expertise by management bargainers familiar with a variety of environments and armed with information on corporate performance which may be obscured from local employee representatives. The charges relating to transplantation of source nation practices and values have been levelled most vigorously at US and Japanese MNEs and centre on policies of union recognition, bargaining practices and the pioneering of novel management techniques. This charge is not regarded with disquiet by all. The innovatory practices of foreign-owned firms may generate considerable spillover benefits in the form of superior business practices (Constas and Vichas, 1981; Globerman, 1979) or more rapid productivity growth (Caves, 1980, p. 178).

The difficulties of analysing the labour relations practices of MNEs in host nations are compounded by the problem of disentangling size effects from those related to ownership nationality. There is considerable evidence that MNE subsidiaries enjoy a size advantage over their indigenous competitors in most host economies (Deane, 1971; Rosenbluth, 1970; Steuer, 1973). Size is a major influence on many facets of industrial relations. It is an important determinant of union recognition, bargaining arrangements (Brown, 1981), management characteristics (Turner, Roberts and Roberts, 1977) and patterns of industrial conflict (Prais, 1981). The influence of size is made more complex by the possible existence of firm size and plant size interaction effects (Shorey, 1980), as well as an indirect impact via income levels and market concentration. Clearly, size effects must be controlled in comparative analysis of labour relations practices.

The intention of this chapter is to evaluate labour concern over the industrial relations practices of MNEs. The following section examines comparative data on union organisation within MNEs. The bargaining and management practices of MNEs are the subjects of the following two sections. A number of the innovatory labour relations practices pioneered by MNEs are then analysed. The incidence of industrial conflict within MNEs is also examined. In the light of the evidence an attempt is made to evaluate the two major charges against MNEs outlined in the preceding paragraphs. Finally, a number of concluding comments are offered.

Union Organisation Within MNEs

Introduction

The importance of union organisation within an enterprise lies in both the direct and indirect impact such organisation has on industrial relations practices. Unionisation has a direct effect on the bargaining power and cohesion of employees. In addition, collective organisation of employees is likely to modify labour relations practices in a number of ways. Unionisation has been associated with a lowering of labour turnover rates (Medoff, 1979), an increased likelihood of grievance and arbitration procedures being incorporated in contacts and a more effective exchange of information within the workplace (Freeman, 1980). Considerable controversy surrounds the likely effects of union-isation on productivity. Advocates argue that unionisation has potential productivity-enhancing effects within the organisation as labour turnover and subsequently recruitment and training costs are lowered (Freeman and Medoff, 1979). Critics have questioned the empirical significance of such effects (Addison, 1982), emphasising the detri-mental impact of union wage and non-wage provisions achieved through the exercise of monopoly power (Addison and Barnett, 1982). These considerations raise the possibility that MNEs may pursue a selective unionisation policy focusing on attempts to capitalise on the benefits of union organisation whilst minimising any attendant disadvantages.

Union Acceptance and Recognition

Organised labour has expressed considerable concern over the union recognition policies of MNEs. The anti-union attitude of a number of large, particularly US, MNEs is well documented (Gennard, 1972). Whilst such an attitude is not confined to MNEs, indeed size appears to be a more persuasive influence than multinationality *per se* (Warner, 1973), the size of, and determination displayed by, these MNEs has ensured the attraction of a great deal of interest.

Empirical evidence from a number of nations tends to support the crucial role played by size and nature of the work group concerned in the formulation of anti-union policy. Such an attitude has been displayed by a number of significant foreign investors in the US (Greer and Shearer, 1981). However, there is no evidence that foreign investors are disproportionately attracted to US regions or states where unionisa-tion is poorly established (Little, 1978). In the UK survey evidence from the Trades Union Congress (Sopford, 1979) suggests that foreign-owned affiliates are more resistant to union acceptance, particularly in industries such as chemicals, vehicles, electronics, engineering and finance. An analysis covering the chemical, electrical and mechanical engineering industries (Hamill, 1982) revealed that non-recognition was a feature of 31 per cent of foreign-owned plants compared with only 4 per cent of indigenous establishments in the case of manual employees. The corresponding figures for non-manuals were 48 per cent and 32 per cent, respectively. These findings tend to highlight the role of size as an influence on union acceptance policies. Industries such as chemicals, engineering and vehicles are characterised by above average establishment and enterprise size.

Union Rationalisation

There is some evidence that certain MNEs have attempted to select the benefits of unionisation whilst simultaneously avoiding one of the difficulties, inter-union disputes, associated with the craft-based union system characteristic of the UK and certain sectors in the US. More specifically, these MNEs attempt to circumvent or rationalise multi-union structures. In the UK a number of foreign-owned firms, and in particular US and Japanese firms, granting union recognition rights display a marked preference for dealing with one rather than a number of unions (Hamill, 1982; Takamiya, 1981). A similar desire, including the by-passing of existing unions, is evident in the strategies of recent Japanese investors in the US (*The Economist*, 1982). Survey evidence of inward investors in the US reveals that they are reluctant to accept union security clauses (Greer and Shearer, 1981).

There is mounting evidence that these practices are not representative of all MNEs. In the UK where multi-union structures are widespread, there is little evidnce that MNE affiliates actively seek to rationalise these arrangements. Rather, they appear to object to certain, particularly white-collar, unions in their workplace (Buckley and Enderwick, 1984; Enderwick, 1984). This evidence suggests that a rationalisation policy may be one confined to particular sectors (Hamill, 1982) or MNEs of a particular nationality (Takamiya, 1981). One might expect such a policy to be displayed by those MNEs preferring entry in the form of majority ownership (US and Japanese MNEs) and in the establishment of new facilities rather than through acquisition. Similarly, the present recession has provided conditions where changes in union representation may be implemented fairly readily. These changes have coincided with the acceleration of inward investment into the US, and the rise of Japanese investment in particular.

Union Security

Chapter 3 indicated that the job restructuring effects of multinational production may have an adverse impact on union security in source nations such as the US. As heavily unionised production jobs are lost and replaced by less well organised white-collar occupations, overall union density rates may be expected to fall. Similarly, union power may fall as the average size of bargaining units declines (Kujawa, 1979b). In host nations the available evidence indicates that union security is at least as good within MNE subsidiaries as that of indigenous enterprises. While union density rates appear comparable for foreign-owned and indigenous manufacturing plants in the UK (Buckley and Enderwick, 1984) (but see Warner (1973) and Hamill (1982)), the picture for other nations, such as Belgium, is a little less clear (Blanpain, 1977; Liebhaberg, 1980). Part of the differences between these studies may lie in the geographical dispersion of DFI within host nations. MNEs tend to be overrepresented in the peripheral regions of the UK (Watts, 1980) where union recognition may be more difficult to achieve (Forsyth, 1973). However, the UK experience stands in contrast to that of other European nations where inward investors are disproportionately attracted to core regions (Hamilton, 1976). Where overseas investors have located in the less developed regions of Continental Europe unions have sometimes experienced difficulty in establishing collective organisation (ILO, 1976a, p. 5).

Bargaining Practices Within MNEs

Introduction

Whilst there has been little research on the determinants of bargaining practices, there is some evidence to indicate that industrial structure may play a significant role (Deaton and Beaumont, 1980; Hendricks and Kahn, 1982). Single-employer bargaining arrangements tend to be correlated with large plant size, product market concentration, above average expenditure on labour relations management, multi-plant structure and foreign ownership. The industrial distribution of MNEs tends to favour sectors with just these characteristics. For some host nations, such as Britain, the tendency of foreign-owned manufacturing firms to engage in company or plant-based bargaining was an early source of concern (Steuer and Gennard, 1971). Interestingly, the intervening period has seen a dramatic increase in the adoption of bargaining at these levels; they are now the most important bargaining levels in

British manufacturing (Brown, 1981; Daniel and Millward, 1983).

The independence company-based bargaining provides brings a number of apparent advantages. Employers enjoy an increased discretion in the utilisation of labour as well as closer control over labour costs. In addition, initiatives in tackling restrictive practices, unconstitutional disputes and the introduction of new technology are easier to achieve at this level (Enderwick, 1983). These benefits of independence in collective negotiation help explain the attitude of some MNEs towards bargaining federations (ILO, 1976a).

Bargaining Levels Within MNEs

There is considerable evidence that MNE subsidiaries adopt bargaining arrangements which are generally compatible with local conditions. This compatibility is achieved by extensive decentralisation of responsibility for collective bargaining (ILO, 1976b). However, where considerable differences exist between source and host nation practices, and particularly where host nation practices are less than favourably regarded, incongruity may be observed. The British industrial relations system provides a revealing case. Foreign-owned firms operating in British manufacturing and service sectors display a markedly higher preference for unilateral bargaining arrangements. Plant level bargaining, over both wage and non-wage issues, appears to be particularly valued by such firms (Buckley and Enderwick, 1984; Enderwick, 1984). While size is a major influence on the adoption of plant-based bargaining structures, the preference displayed by foreign-owned subsidiaries holds even after controlling for size.

Refusal to negotiate over pay increases is evident on the part of only a very tiny percentage of MNEs. However, interesting differences in willingness to negotiate non-pay issues are revealed by MNEs. For manufacturing industry a comparatively larger proportion of foreign-owned firms refuse negotiation over issues of recruitment, manning levels, changes in production methods and capital investment. These crucial aspects of labour utilisation are regarded as managerial prerogatives and not open to joint regulation. Foreign-owned firms in British service industries tend to assert managerial control over issues of labour adjustment (redeployment, redundancy and capital investment). These practices go some way in explaining the higher labour productivity of MNE subsidiaries in Britain (Enderwick, 1983) as well as being compatible with a desire for independence in the determination of collective agreements.

Membership of Employers' Associations

The preference for unilateral bargaining displayed by MNEs is reinforced, at least in the British case, by a higher probability of non-membership of employers' associations (Buckley and Enderwick, 1984; Hamill, 1983). Whilst non-membership is not a universal feature of MNEs, two major reasons for non-federation are widely cited. For many MNEs, for example Massey Ferguson and Chrysler in the UK, non-membership reflects a desire to gain more direct control over both the scope and localisation of negotiations (Kujawa, 1971). This motive appears particularly powerful in the engineering sector (Hamill, 1983) where craft-based unions have been associated with above-average rates of industrial conflict. Secondly, for MNEs pursuing an anti-union policy involvement in federation bargaining arrangements implies an unacceptable tacit recognition of union negotiators (Hamill, 1983; ILO, 1976a).

The precise relationship between unilateral bargaining arrangements and non-membership of employers' associations appears to be complex. For most less developed nations where such associations tend to be underdeveloped plant-bargaining is a widespread feature of MNEs. In those European nations where collective joint negotiation is well entrenched, MNEs play a far more active role in the actions of employers' associations. For example, in Belgium collective agreements reached through federated bargaining may encompass non-member firms as well as attaining legality. The powerful position such associations fill explains their attraction for foreign-owned MNEs. In 1974, 42 per cent of the delegates to the influential industrial relations committee of the Belgian metalworkers employers' association were provided by the 25 per cent of their membership composed of foreign-owned firms (Liebhaberg, 1980, p. 33). Where federated bargaining provides a floor to the determination of wages and working conditions a number of MNEs superimpose upon this structure company-based bargaining as a supplement to industry-wide agreements (ILO, 1976b). On balance, it appears that the non-affiliation of certain large, particularly US-based, MNEs to employers' association has been influential in furthering the decentralisation of bargaining in both Britain (Hamill, 1983) and European nations such as Denmark (Liebhaberg, 1980).

Bargaining Procedures

Comparative research of bargaining procedures reveals that MNEs couple their preference for independent company-based negotiations with extensive formalised provisions for handling bargaining disagreements. These developments have been reinforced within several MNEs by the adoption of single staff status and harmonisation (IRRR, 1981). The use of enterprise-based disputes procedures reflects the avoidance of industry-wide procedures encapsulated within the activities of employers' associations. Similarly, MNEs reveal a higher probability of using third party intervention in the settlement of disputes.

An examination of the consultation practices of MNEs within the bargaining process reveals a source of potential union concern. Management negotiators within MNE subsidiaries are much more likely to engage in extensive upward consultation with higher-level management within the organisation in the course of bargaining. Similarly, within multi-plant MNEs management displays a high probability of engaging in consultation with their colleagues in related plants. These findings are consistent with the concern of organised labour that a multinational structure may be associated with insensitivites or obstacles in the bargaining process. A major source of such insensitivity appears to lie in the extensive provisions for upward consultation introduced by such firms. A further cause of frustration to union bargainers may lie in the preference MNEs manifest for conducting separate negotiations where manual employees are represented by more than one union. As well as weakening labour cohesion such a procedure may lead to difficulties in settlement as key groups set bargaining precedents or initiate imitative processes.

Labour Relations Management Within MNEs

Introduction

Analysis of the labour management practices of MNEs is compounded by the interaction of size and ownership effects. The development of specialist personnel functions and systematic management practices as well as decision-making structures are all heavily influenced by establishment and enterprise size. Labour concern with the management practices of MNEs focuses on the degree of centralisation of decision-making processes and information disclosure practices.

Centralisation of Decision-making

Multinational structure provides opportunities for the centralisation of key decision-making processes. Centralisation, which is widely held by union officials to have occurred (Blake, 1972), may lengthen and obfuscate bargaining processes. Empirical analysis of this question yields two major conclusions. Firstly, labour relations appears to be the most decentralised functional area within MNEs (Bomers and Peterson, 1977; Hedlund, 1981; Newbould *et al.*, 1978). Secondly, the degree of decision-making centralisation is generally higher within multinational than multi-plant uninational enterprises (Buckley and Enderwick, 1984; Greer and Shearer, 1981).

These generalisations are, however, subject to a number of limitations. The extent of decentralisation within MNEs appears to be related to enterprise nationality (Hershfield, 1975), the issue being considered and structural characteristics of the enterprise. Centralisation of decision-making is a trait more characteristic of US and Japanese MNEs than those based in Europe (Negandhi and Baliga, 1981). Centralisation and parental involvement appear more likely to occur over issues of dispute settlement (Blake, 1973; Peccei and Warner, 1981) or deteriorations in performance (Aslegg, 1971; Welge, 1981) although ownership nationality is, again, an important influence on the probability of such involvement (Roberts and May, 1974). The degree of autonomy subsidiaries enjoy in decision-making is negatively related to the importance of intra-enterprise trade (Hamill, 1982; Hedlund, 1981) and majority ownership (Otterbeck, 1981). These structural characteristics help to explain the comparatively higher degree of centralisation of decision-making within US-based MNEs which favour majority ownership and conduct a very high degree of intra-enterprise trade. Isolation of the determining role played by these considerations is made more difficult by the possibility of nonlinear relationships varying over time (Peccei and Warner, 1976).

Comparative analysis of reporting patterns within foreign-owned and indigenous enterprises confirms the more hierarchical decision-making structures adopted by MNEs. Such firms tend to make more extensive resource commitments to the personnel function. Personnel managers within MNE subsidiaries tend to be more specialised and both more highly and relevantly qualified. Despite such qualification, considerable decentralisation of decision-making authority within MNEs tends to be coupled with extensive provisions for upward consultation. In comparison with their domestic competitors MNE subsidiaries are more likely to require personnel managers to report to a higher management tier with primary responsibility for industrial relations matters. Similarly, within MNEs the industrial relations function is more likely to be represented at the level of the corporate board. The specialisation and upward consultation procedures characteristic of MNEs are likely to result in management structures that are both broader and more hierarchical. Such structures are clearly compatible with the charges of protracted and secluded decision-making raised by labour organisations. Offsetting these charges is the higher probability of utilising external sources of advice displayed by foreign-owned firms. Outside intervention reflects the value of local knowledge as an input in successful labour management and may facilitate the achievement of management-labour accord. On balance, the evidence reviewed does lend some support to labour concerns. Part of the problem may lie not simply in the degree of centralisation-decentralisation of decision-making authority, but as a result of the additional layers of communication imposed on organisational structure by the requirements of elaborate internal management consultation channels. This problem is considered further in the following chapter where the question of labour's access to key management decision-makers is discussed.

Information Disclsoure

An area of consistent labour concern has been the information disclosure practices of MNEs. In many host nations majority-owned subsidiaries are not bound by the same legal provisions on information disclosure as indigenous firms. Labour's concern focuses on four aspects of information disclosure; the level of corporate aggregation information covers e.g. plant, regional or global level; the type of information disclosed, e.g. financial, operational; the timing of information disclosure, e.g. prior consultation; and finally the reliability of such information.

The corporate level is the usual one for the publication of external information such as company accounts. However, for many MNEs a preference for plant-based bargaining questions the usefulness of external information sources to union negotiators. Thus the finding that MNEs in Britain tend to provide as much information as their indigenous competitors (Buckley and Enderwick, 1984) may disguise the real problem of the relevance and applicability of information rather than merely the quantity provided. MNEs display a preference for disclosing financial and operational data (ILO, 1976a) and a greater reluctance in providing information on manpower needs and related issues (Enderwick, 1984). Concern over the timing of information disclosure focuses on the fact that often events precede the provision of information on those events. This is of particular concern in the case of lay-offs, plant closures, rationalisation and product changes. For union representatives enjoying access to high-level decision-making processes, e.g. West German union representatives on supervisory boards, these concerns are far less pressing (ILO, 1976b). The reliability of information is likely to depend on a number of factors.

The primary internal influence is undoubtedly the practice of transfer pricing (Plasschaert, 1979). Transfer pricing refers to the process whereby prices are imputed to transactions conducted within the MNE. In the absence of comparable market transactions, accurate (arm's length) prices may not exist. Intra-corporate pricing then offers opportunities for price setting influenced by objectives such as a desire to transfer funds, to reduce tax liabilities or import duties. These practices, the incidence of which is likely to be positively correlated with the importance of internal trade, erode the validity of financial and operational data. Evidence on the extent of transfer pricing is inadequate to enable generalisations to be made. The practice appears to be particularly significant in the chemical (pharmaceutical) industry (Lall, 1973; Vaitsos, 1974b), although practices vary significantly by both host and source nation (Tang, 1979 and 1981). Reliability of information is also influenced by national differences in the standard of reporting as well as problems of accounting comparability.

The major source of information for union negotiators within MNEs is probably internal sources. There is some evidence that the plant and corporate bargaining practices adopted by many MNEs increase the exchange of information principally through consultation processes (Buckley and Enderwick, 1984; ILO, 1976b). A great deal of information is provided within consultative committees but the refusal of many MNEs to negotiate over crucial aspects of labour utilisation (noted above) means that the content of discussion may be laid down by managerial dictate. Furthermore, the prospects for union representatives gaining access to the key decision processes appear remote. Foreign-owned firms in the UK, and US-based MNEs in general (De Vos, 1981), reveal a marked antipathy towards employee participation. A similar conception appears to be held by Japanese enterprises (Sasaki, 1981, p. 52), where decision-making structures are not conducive to participation. Some Japanese MNEs operating in West Germany have even restricted size in order to avoid German legislation on statutory works committees (Trevor, 1983, p. 160).

Innovatory Labour Relations Practices of MNEs

Introduction

MNEs have been responsible for the introduction of innovative labour relations practices in a number of host nations. These innovations have been dominated by the transference of often well-established source nations practices. Two distinct waves of innovation can be detected, corresponding in the 1950s and 1960s to the overseas expansion of North American enterprises and more recently to the dramatic rise in Japanese DFI.

The Innovatory Practices of North American MNEs

The practices pioneered by North American MNEs in the postwar period have received a mixed reception in the major recipient nations of Western Europe. The more democratic work climates associated with foreign-owned firms (Chruden and Sherman, 1972) and experiments in alternative forms of work organisation, such as job enlargement and semi-autonomous work units (Gunter, 1975), although often short-lived, have received a guarded welcome.

More concern has been expressed about practices which represent a significant departure from host nation norms. Emphasis on merit and performance as the basis for remuneration and promotion tends to eclipse the European preference for linking rewards to seniority. This emphasis translates into a higher propensity for foreign-owned firms to utilise systematic procedures of job evaluation and work study and the replacement of incentive payment systems by forms such as measured day work. These schemes enable increased management control over earnings, greater flexibility in labour deployment and reduced resistance to the introduction of new work practices. In addition, incentive schemes such as payment by results have been correlated with problems of high absenteeism and turnover (White, 1981). Many of these aspects have subsequently been absorbed in large measure into the industrial relations system of host nations such as Britain (Brown, 1981). The same is true of the bargaining preferences of MNEs. Decentralisation of bargaining levels and the development of plant- and company-based disputes procedures have been notable trends in British industry (Daniel and Millward, 1983).

North American MNEs have experimented with the negotiation of fixed-term agreements, lasting in some cases two or three years. In Belgium, General Motors reached agreement on a three-year contract at its Antwerp factory in the late 1950s. More recently, the three-year agreement reached in Britain by the US-owned Caterpillar Company in November 1982 coincided with a spurt of similar private sector agreements. The failure of this practice to become firmly entrenched and more widely diffused probably reflects the problem of high and varying inflation rates experienced in the late 1960s and 1970s which tend to discourage long-term pay commitments.

A number of MNE innovations have been directed at specific problems. An over-arching concern has been the more effective utilisation of labour. Foreign-owned firms have been in the forefront of the reassertion of managerial prerogatives (Storey, 1983). The innovatory role of US MNEs in productivity bargaining has been widely documented (Flanders, 1964). Productivity bargaining is characterised by the provision of financial and other inducements for the acceptance of changes in work practices and an easing of union excursions into management prerogatives. The majority of agreements concluded in the 1960s concentrated on issues of the nature of work, particularly demarcation and the institutionalisation of overtime (McKersie and Hunter, 1972). Although productivity bargaining was discredited in the 1970s by its widespread identification with attempts to circumvent a variety of incomes policies, its motives have re-emerged in an alternative form.

Recent measures have focused on the use of direct financial inducements to the surrender of adverse labour sanctions, particularly the strike weapon. The experience of the Ford Motor Company in this area is illuminating. After difficulties in attempting to ensure individual adherence to agreements (wildcat stoppages), attention has turned, in both Belgium (Blanpain, 1977) and Britain (Enderwick, 1983), to the use of financial incentives to compliance, often contingent on the recognition of a number of unilateral managerial rights.

The most recent innovation associated with US-based MNEs has been the practice of concession bargaining. This form of agreement, which has been most widespread in the US, is motivated by the difficult trading conditions faced by many MNEs in the 1980s where recession, global overcapacity and competitive pressure have prompted the search for cost cutting. US agreements have displayed a number of interesting features which indicate that concession bargaining may be seen as a logical development of earlier practices such as self-financing productivity agreements. A number of agreements have made explicit the trade-off between wage and employment levels. Employment guarantees have been offered in return for pay freezes or cuts in a number of instances. The role of Ford has again been significant in this area. The recent Ford/UAW negotiations over lifetime employment security have focused on employee concessions on work rules and the merging of job classifications, both crucial influences on labour flexibility. In the UK, Ford's 'After Japan' proposals emphasise the need for greater flexibility in labour utilisation. The pay concessions obtained by Hyster at its Scottish plant involved the passing on of rationalising employment cuts to other European plants.

The Innovatory Practices of Japanese MNEs

The innovatory practices associated with recent Japanese overseas investors form part of a coherent labour strategy, in many ways distinct to these enterprises. The comparative advantage of Japanese MNEs in advanced host economies appears to lie in their ability to maintain quality of production and intensive labour utilisation (White and Trevor, 1983). Whilst Japanese MNEs have not been guilty of the wholesale transfer of home country practices they pursue a strategy emphasising union rationalisation, employee flexibility and strict workplace discipline (White and Trevor, 1983).

Their approach to union recognition is not one based on discouraging a union presence, rather efforts are made to ensure single union representation. A number of firms have attempted to harmonise conditions for manuals and non-manuals. Staff status provides opportunities for simplifying multi-union representation which in turn facilitates the acceptance of flexible working practices. Furthermore, shop stewards are provided with a very significant role, particularly in negotiation. Such an approach brings considerable benefits in reducing union rivalry and demarcation disputes and in strengthening formal union representation. These advantages may be fostered by the granting of closed shop provisions or the injection of flexibility clauses into initial agreements. Employee flexibility and high rates of labour utilisation may be encouraged by the rationalisation of wage structures. Basic rates may be assigned to a number of grades. Employee assignment to grades may be made on the basis of the number of skills an individual could exercise. Such a structure has been adopted by the Japanese Toshiba subsidiary in the UK. A distinct benefit of this structure has been the encouragement it gives to the acquisition of skills with obvious implications for flexibility, retraining and the provision of training. Acceptance of the importance of labour attitudes is also apparent in the case of many Japanese investors. They favour a 'greenfields' policy of entry in the form of new facilities (Stopford, 1979) and joint ventures have not proved very successful. Interestingly, a number of these innovations have met with difficulties when applied in the LDCs. Understaffing, used to facilitate job rotation, has generated a number of disputes (Negandhi and Baliga, 1981).

The importance of this second wave of investment is that it illustrates a significant feature of recent foreign investment trends. While the quantity of international investment has slowed down since the late 1970s the potential impact of such investments, particularly in the area of labour relations, is probably greater than ever. The increasing variety of source nation, and particularly the growth of Japanese MNEs, coupled with the present recessionary conditions, have created an environment more conducive to the acceptance by organised labour of changes in representation structures and working practices. The development of innovative agreements within indigenous plants, doubtless faciliated by depressed economic conditions, is already occurring.

MNEs and Industrial Conflict

The level and pattern of industrial conflict experienced by MNE affiliates is of importance for two major reasons. Firstly, the contribution made by DFI to host nation output and employment objectives depends on the economic performance of foreign-owned plants. That performance, and hence contribution, is likely to be impaired where a problem of management-labour conflict exists. Secondly, the labour relations experience of inward investors may influence the investment decisions of other potential investors. For example, the overseas image of Britain as a conflict-ridden economy represents a formidable obstacle to the attraction of foreign capital (Buckley *et al.*, 1983).

The expected impact of ownership nationality on industrial conflict is unclear. Unfamiliarity with host nation industrial relations practices and possible reliance on source nation methods combine to increase the probability of conflict. The well established correlation between size and likelihood of industrial action (Edwards, 1980; Prais, 1978) corresponds with higher levels of conflict within MNE subsidiaries which tend to be of above average size. The more intensive utilisation of labour evident within MNEs and their dependence on intra-firm procedures for resolving disputes implies that higher levels of industrial action may be observed within such plants. Offsetting these considerations are the union rationalisation practices of MNEs which may reduce the incidence of inter-union disputes in particular and the use of paternalistic policies of union non-recognition coupled with above average levels of remuneration. Paternalism reduces the demand for industrial action with the provision of generous wage and non-wage benefits whilst simultaneously raising costs of effective employee organisation through nonrecognition.

The ambiguity of *a priori* expectations is compounded by the structual features of MNEs. Where MNEs operate duplicate plants or practice dual sourcing, the effect of industrial action on a particular plant may be limited. If labour acknowledges its bargaining weakness, the moderation of employee demands should reduce the probability of conflict by narrowing the zone of potential disagreement. A similar, but inverted, argument may be applied to vertically integrated MNEs. Inter-plant production linkages considerably enhance the effectiveness of industrial action lowering management's relative bargaining power. As a result, management capitulation may lower both the probability of disputes and their expected mean duration.

Empirical study of the comparative strike record of MNEs has been most prolific in the British case, possibly reflecting that country's general concern with the problem of industrial stoppages. Although the existing work displays considerable diversity in coverage, data sources and methodology, a number of areas of agreement are discernible.

There is consistent evidence that strike incidence (generally measured by working days lost) is higher for foreign-owned affiliates (Davies and Thomas, 1976; Enderwick and Buckley, 1982; Forsyth, 1972; Hamill, 1982; Millward, 1979), although there is significant variation in the extent of the differential. Conflicting results emerge when strike incidence is related to output (Gennard and Steuer, 1971). Given the productivity advantage of foreign-owned firms in the UK (see Chapter 4) this result is not surprising. There is some recent evidence (Buckley and Enderwick, 1984) that the impact of stoppages may be lower in the case of overseas-based MNEs where the similarity of strike duration and employee involvement in comparison with indigenous firms is attentuated on an employee-related basis by the above average size of affiliates.

There is less consensus on comparative strike frequency rates. There is considerable debate as to whether strike frequency rates for MNEs and indigenous firms are comparable (Hamill, 1982) or higher in the case of foreign-owned firms (Davies and Thomas, 1976; Enderwick and Buckley, 1982; Forsyth, 1972; Millward, 1979). The major exception to these results is again Gennard and Steuer (1971). Because of data problems this study compared stoppage ratios with output ratios. The high productivity levels achieved by MNEs would tend to understate their share of stoppages. The considerable variation of results on comparative strike frequency results from a number of factors. Measures of strike frequency differ between the studies and data deficiencies mean that estimates leave a lot to be desired. In addition, results appear sensitive to industry coverage and time period selection. Within the set of foreign-owned firms strike frequency is related to source nationality.

A number of studies have relied on simple measures of strike frequency such as the proportion of plants affected by action. The problem of compiling robust estimates of the denominator in this measure, the set of all foreign-owned plants, has been a major cause of variation. There are severe limitations with official data (Forsyth, 1972; Millward, 1979). Lists compiled by researchers are particularly likely to omit smaller sized plants and comparisons within the smallest size bands are the least reliable (Enderwick and Buckley, 1982). Problems arise from differences in data sources. Studies that rely on official strike returns are likely to understate the frequency of stoppages within MNE subsidiaries. This occurs because MNEs suffer a large number of short stoppages, lasting less than one day. The threshold definition[1] adopted in the compilation of UK strike statistics means that such stoppages are unlikely to be recorded in official figures.

Comparative analyses of strike experience appear highly sensitive to both the period and sectors covered (Hamill, 1982). These findings raise the question of whether studies which cover a single year (Millward, 1979) or limited span (Enderwick and Buckley, 1982) provide representative results. An additional problem emerges with evidence that source nationality has an influence on stoppage activity independent of the effect of multinationality. Thus US-based MNEs have a worse strike record in Britain than other MNEs (Enderwick and Buckley, 1982). The possible existence of a regional influence on strike rates (Forsyth, 1972; Hamill, 1982) suggests the need to control for this factor also. The conceptual limitations characteristic of strike models and multifarious influences identified mean that definitive answers to these questions are not likely to be forthcoming in the near future.

One interesting finding that has been reported with reassuring consistency is the fact that MNE subsidiaries incur a larger proportion of stoppages over labour utilisation issues including manning levels, recruitment and working condition and supervision (Buckley and Enderwick, 1984; Davies and Thomas, 1976; Enderwick and Buckley, 1982; Forsyth, 1972). These findings are consistent with expectations given the intensive labour utilisation displayed by MNEs and their attempts to reassert managerial perogatives in just these areas. Although very little work has been done on comparative experience of non-strike action within MNEs, such action appears, at least in the British case, to be as significant as stoppages (Buckley and Enderwick, 1984).

MNEs and Labour's Relative Bargaining Power

In the light of the foregoing analysis we may re-evaluate the view that labour is seriously disadvantaged when bargaining with MNEs. The argument, in its most sophisticated form (Kujawa, 1980), comprises four elements.

The first concerns the possibility of relocation of production facilities by MNEs. Actual shifts reduce job security and labour demand; the threat of closure may be deployed as a bargaining tactic. The distinction between threatened and actual closure is an important one. As with all forms of threat credibility depends on its occasional exercise. There is very little documentation of cases of plant closure in the face of industrial relations problems or collective bargaining intransigence (but see Arnison, 1971). However, the threat of closure, as a bargaining tactic, has been displayed by a number of well-established MNEs.

The feasibility of production location is low, certainly in the short term (Jedel and Kujawa, 1976; Kujawa, 1971). Readily quantifiable cost considerations relate to disengagement costs such as redundancy payments,[2] transfer and set-up costs and the loss of production incurred. Furthermore, where plants are linked within an overall enterprise strategy, disengagement has serious repercussions for global production patterns and co-ordination. The significance of intra-enterprise trade within MNEs, highlighted in a number of places in this book, lends support to the importance of such costs. This constraint is likely to be particularly effective in the case of affiliates serving large local markets. The American example is a case in point. A survey of foreign-owned firms in the US revealed that the majority of sales were destined for the host (US) market and that affiliates depended heavily on the supply of inputs from related affiliates (Jedel and Kujawa, 1976). Opportunities for switching location are limited under these conditions. Intra-national shifts have not been widely detected, indeed the evidence suggests that job security in foreign-owned affiliates is comparable to that within indigenous firms (Ricks and Campagna, 1978). A number of cases of relocation within national boundaries have occurred where replacement plants have been constructed close to existing facilities, minimising the effects of dislocation (McKersie and Sengenberger, 1983, pp. 69-70).

A further constraint on mobility is an enterprise's degree of capital-intensity. Capital-intensity is likely to reduce the incentives for relocation. Heavily amortised capital costs and the relative bargaining advantage enjoyed by labour coupled with the limited wage cost savings offered by relocation mean that capital-intensive investments are likely to be amongst the most stable. These incentives are particularly pronounced in the case of MNE subsidiaries which tend to display higher than average capital-intensity (Dunning, 1976; Globerman, 1979; Stopford, 1979).

The limited credibility of the closure threat is reinforced with recognition of the alternative strategies available to MNEs. A more feasible longer-term bargaining strategy concerns the placing, elsewhere, of new investment. Over time the determinants of optimal location are likely to shift as corporate and host-nation advantages change. The threat of redirection of incremental investment may emerge as a bargaining tactic of considerable effect. A second strategy, highlighted in Chapter 4, relates to the development by MNEs of subcontracting relationships. Where cost pressures dictate the need for overseas production labour-intensive activities may be performed overseas by related or unrelated parties. This practice has been detected within both European (Bomers and Peterson, 1977) and US companies (US Tariff Commission, 1970). Where subcontracting is coupled with offshore assembly provisions in import tariffs, source and advanced host nation employment stability may be enhanced since these provisions encourage partial processing in source nation facilities. Repeal of OAPs might entail considerable job losses. One estimate for 1969 put the possible loss of US jobs at 37,000 (US Tariff Commission, 1970). The growth since 1969 of imports under US tariff provisions 807.00 and 806.30 (Helleiner, 1981) suggests that potential job losses would now be far greater. The magnitude of domestic job loss depends crucially on the extent to which processing activities are transferred overseas. The views of producers in labour-intensive sectors such as garment manufacture (Shearer, 1977) suggest that the displacement would be total.

Overall, the constraints on production location within MNEs suggest that this practice is not likely to present a major source of bargaining advantage. Indeed, within advanced nations the bunching of manufacturing job losses by both timing and sector (Ballance and Sinclair, 1983, ch. 5) suggests that this phenomenon may be traced to structural changes in the world economy bringing about a changing international division of labour. This view seems to be increasingly shared by union leaders (Bomers and Peterson, 1977). Our discussion does not preclude the possibility of MNEs adopting bargaining tactics utilising the threat of incremental investment being channelled elsewhere or subcontracting arrangements expanded.

The second source of MNE management bargaining power results from the supposed limited impact of strike action on affiliates. Kujawa (1979) argues that the multi-product nature of many MNEs means that production and revenue losses incurred on one product line in the event of a stoppage can be offset through cross-subsidisation. The effect of this is to reduce management disagreement costs of union demands. Clearly, this source of advantage does not depend on multinationality; rather it is characteristic of conglomerate organisation. A more specific advantage may result from the MNEs' ability to switch production across national boundaries.

The significance of production switching depends on two factors: the existence of duplicate facilities and the use of those facilities. A study of foreign-owned firms in the US revealed that over 70 per cent of respondents claimed to operate duplicate facilities outside the US. While only one firm admitted using overseas facilities to frustrate strike action in the US, 27 per cent of respondents reported that they would consider such action (Greer and Shearer, 1981). Cases of production switching appear few and far between (Bomers and Peterson, 1977; ILO, 1976a; Shearer, 1977). MNE management may be curtailed in strike circumvention by opposition in related plants. Evidence from a study of US MNEs revealed that 10 per cent of respondents had accepted union provisions at overseas plants refusing strike-breaking activities in the form of overtime or the handling of shipments with striking plants (Hershfield, 1975).

The opportunities for production switching are particularly limited for vertically-integrated MNEs. The costs of duplicating processes are likely to be exorbitant. Vertical integration by dramatically raising the repercussionary impact of a stoppage may endow organised labour with considerable bargaining power. The weakness of integrated MNEs is increasingly recognised (Bergsten *et al.*, 1978; Bomers and Peterson, 1977; Kujawa, 1979a). Although there has been no direct testing of this hypothesis there is some supportive evidence. Inter-industry regression analysis of strike activity and relative wages for a sample of foreign-owned firms in Britain revealed a negative sign on a related trade variable in strike equations which became positive in wage regressions (Enderwick and Buckley, 1983). The interpretation of these findings is that intra-enterprise trade tends to strengthen labour's bargaining power which in turn is reflected in a lower frequency of stoppages and higher wage share. Other research indicated that the foreign-owned/indigenous enterprise wage differential was greatest for direct workers in the larger-sized plants, those plants most likely to be closely integrated within global production systems (Buckley and Enderwick, 1983).

The third tenet of bargaining advantage refers to the expertise of management negotiators within MNEs. The arbitrage of experience across national boundaries may confer upon management a considerable advantage. The limited evidence which directly addresses this question is not supportive of any management advantage. Parent company influence over the composition of negotiating teams was found to be very much the exception in the case of foreign-owned firms in the US. Similarly, parent organisations offered no research support in the handling of collective bargaining issues (Jedel and Kujawa, 1977). Similar findings were reported from a study of European MNEs in the metal trades. This study revealed little evidence of participation in negotiation by management from related subsidiaries. This finding did not hold in the case of labour negotiators where outside union officials were often present (ILO, 1976b). One major exception to these findings may be provided by Japanese MNEs who display a high proclivity towards the exportation of source nation practices and personnel. For the majority of MNEs the considerable value of local knowledge in successful labour relations means that a great deal of discretion will be enjoyed by subsidiary management.

Our analysis suggests that greater validity attaches to the fourth element of the hypothesis: the insensitivity and obscurity of MNE negotiaton processes. The source of these difficulties appears to be not so much the failure to decentralise decision-making authority as the elaborate arrangements for higher level consultation within MNEs. There is little doubt that labour is disadvantaged in its dealings with MNEs by the inaccessibility of higher management and considerable delays introduced into the bargaining process by consultation requirements. We return to this question in the following chapter where possible remedies are examined.

Overall, our evaluation of the relative bargaining power of labour in its dealings with MNEs suggests that to date the hypothesis that labour is disadvantaged has been accepted too readily. We have sympathy with the view that MNE management negotiators have, on occasion, resorted to threat tactics with regard to the repositioning of new investment. The considerable constraints on relocation of facilities mean that this threat has little real credibility. Labour does appear to face difficulties in obtaining information for bargaining purposes. Similarly, bargaining procedures within MNEs present an obstacle for labour negotiators in their need for access to decision-making levels. However, the assertion that a multinational structure invariably places labour at a disadvantage is not compatible with a variety of evidence. The assertion appears particularly misplaced in the case of vertically-integrated MNEs where labour may enjoy considerable bargaining leverage. A more appropriate test of the hypothesis needs to be undertaken. One way forward which suggests itself would be multivariate analysis of the relative wage position of MNEs incorporating intra-enterprise trade as a proxy for vertical integration and dependency. A positive relationship would lend support to our view that unqualified generalisations regarding labour's relative bargaining power *vis-à-vis* MNEs, are misleading and unhelpful.

Conclusions

The analysis of this chapter reveals that MNEs do pursue industrial relations practices which often differ in type or degree from those normally observed in host nations. Their most distinctive features are a desire for decentralisation and independence in negotiation as well as an emphasis on the formalisation of procedures. The novel practices associated with MNEs fit in well with the intensive labour utilisation patterns noted in Chapter 4. Thus plant-based bargaining and disputes procedures as well as initiatives in union representation and the assertion of managerial prerogatives are all conducive to independence in the setting of effort-reward levels. A number of innovatory industrial relations practices pioneered in the UK by MNEs have become widely imitated. These UK initiatives are particularly significant given the inefficiency often associated with labour deployment in British industry (Pratten and Atkinson, 1976). Initiatives in productivity bargaining, for example, have not been widely observed outside the UK where union impediments to labour utilisation are less well established (Blanpain, 1977b).

Our findings lend support for union concerns in a number of areas. The most pressing difficulties are associated with the information disclosure practices of MNEs and their bargaining structures which may impede union access to key decision-makers.

We are sceptical of the overwhelming bargaining advantage supposedly enjoyed by MNE management. The comparable rates of industrial conflict suffered by MNEs and their extensive investments in bargaining protocols are inconsistent with a dominant bargaining position. The distinction between workplace and market bargaining power of MNE employees, introduced in Chapter 4, is illustrative in the present context. The vulnerability of many globally and regionally integrated MNEs to the threat of disruption provides employees with considerable workplace bargaining power. The significance for MNEs of short stoppages, often unofficial and unconstitutional, and their initiatives in containing conflict are consistent with the existence of high stoppage costs for MNEs. The eclectic model in highlighting the advantages of internalising transactions introduces the possibility of simultaneous internalisation of secondary stoppage costs through the device of common ownership (Enderwick, 1982c). The high level of disagreement costs faced by MNE management helps to explain their considerable efforts to ensure labour management accord. This conclusion questions the inevitability of multinational collective bargaining as a basis for labour action (Gennard, 1972) and raises the possibility that responses to the MNE may be effectively mounted at the enterprise or national level. This is one option examined in the final chapter.

Notes

1. For inclusion, stoppages must involve at least ten workers, last more than one day, or involve the loss of at least 100 working days.
2. The Badger Case (Blanpain, 1977) illustrates both the magnitude of compensation costs and the principle of parent company responsibility for meeting financial obligations.

6 LABOUR RESPONSES TO THE MNE

Introduction

The case for control of foreign investment arises from the likely divergence between objectives pursued by MNEs and those sought by source and host nations. Labour responses, as a more selective form of regulation, derive from the likelihood of MNEs generating both costs and benefits for labour. The view of organised labour that costs, to them, are likely to outweigh benefits, recognises the distributional impact of MNEs. In addition, counter action may be pursued in an attempt to redress the bargaining disadvantage supposedly imposed on labour by a multinational structure.

Economic theory provides little guidance in the design of policy responses to the MNE. The policy prescriptions of general equilibrium models of the international economy are inevitably limited.

Firstly, the underlying assumptions of perfectly competitive market structures and absence of externalities and knowledge imperfections in particular, question its usefulness as a framework for evaluating the impact of MNEs. For example, a significant externality may be generated where incremental investment by the individual firm lowers the return earned by all source nation foreign capital (Jasay, 1960; Kemp, 1962).

Secondly, such models are generally based on assumptions of global or national welfare maximisation despite the very real possibility of incompatibility between these objectives. A number of MNE practices may contribute to aggregate economic efficiency whilst imposing welfare costs on individual nations. The discriminatory pricing of technology may be a prerequisite for continuing innovation but is likely to be interpreted as a burden by nations with an inelastic demand for imported technologies. Furthermore, maximisation of national economic welfare might require source nation controls on capital outflows. Unrestricted foreign investment could lower welfare where post-tax foreign returns are less than those available on indigenous investments, where income flows and assets are lost through expropriation, or where source nation export prices are reduced through the competitive impact of overseas production with a concomitant worsening of the terms of trade (Bergsten *et al.*, 1978).

128

Thirdly, general equilibrium analysis ignores the distributional impact of welfare changes and incentives for selective opposition to DFI. Since capital outflows increase domestic capital returns at the expense of labour's share of national income, labour opposition to capital outflows is likely to be observed in major source nations.

Fourthly, the policy goals prompting MNE regulation may be incompatible with general equilibrium analysis. This is apparent, for example, in a desire to promote domestic employment. General equilibrium models do not address the possibilities of prolonged unemployment or significant adjustment costs.

Despite these deficiencies of neoclassical analysis little is available in the form of alternative paradigms. The essential incompatibility of neoclassical and eclectic perspectives on the MNE (Dunning, 1981, p. 81) is apparent despite the absence of any clear policy implications derived from eclectic models. At one extreme is the view of Rugman (1981, pp. 156-7), for whom 'regulation is always inefficient. Multinationals are always efficient.' This sort of gross simplification is based on the view that since MNEs bring greater exploitation of differences in comparative advantage they unreservedly increase global welfare. More considered analysis reveals that the MNE is likely to represent a second-best solution to the problem of maximising global wellbeing. In addition, a number of MNE practices, e.g. restrictive business practices, are likely to detract from efficient economic activity. However, abandonment of the general equilibrium framework leaves a vacuum which is likely to be filled by *ad hoc* evaluation based on particular conditions (Balogh and Streeten, 1960).

The limited contribution of theoretical perspectives of the MNE for the design of policy is reflected in labour responses. These responses have assumed disparate forms and varying degrees of direct labour involvement. For example, in the case of international codes of conduct direct labour involvement is apparent in the forums of the OECD and ILO but less so in the case of the US or International Chambers of Commerce. However, the development of non-government codes should be seen as a partial response to labour pressure, albeit pressure directed within other bodies. We may usefully classify the initiatives discussed in this chapter as labour responses to the MNE although they differ in the degree of direct labour initiation.

Following Bergsten *et al.* (1978) we may usefully classify these strategies in terms of their effect on relative power and their locus of enactment (see Table 6.1).

Table 6.1: Alternative Labour Responses to the MNE

Effect on bargaining power:	Reducing the power of MNEs	Increasing the power of labour
Level		
National	Host or source nation regulation of DFI	Co-determination and host councils
	Bilateral agreements	Source nation bargaining stipulations
International	Labour standards Multilateral forum on DFI Codes of conduct Information disclosure and collection	Transnational union co-operation

Source: Derived from Bergsten *et al.*, 1978, p. 54.

Reducing the Power of MNEs

National Initiatives

Attempts to control the activities of MNEs at the national level have focused on host and source nation regulation of DFI and the development of bilateral investment agreements. A number of host nations, e.g. Canada and Australia, systematically evaluate the expected contribution of foreign investments. The difficulty of action by one host nation is the danger that current and potential investments will be discouraged. The problem is particularly acute for nations forming part of a regional economic grouping where substitutability between hosts is high. As a means of lowering the relative power of MNEs *vis-à-vis* labour, evaluation of inward investment has little to offer. By its nature it invariably concentrates on readily quantifiable economic magnitudes such as direct employment creation, output and technology transference. Scant regard is likely to be given to employment displacement, income distribution and labour relations effects. The emphasis such policies place on the maximisation of net economic benefit within the host economy is well illustrated in the Canadian case. Indeed, recent proposals for an unfettered welcome to foreign investment with the host exercising a right to purchase, in the distant future, foreign-owned assets (Wonnacott, 1982) demonstrate the desire to maximise locally-retained benefits, regardless of their indigenous distribution.

Our discussion in the introductory section highlighted the probability that the distributional welfare impact of capital outflows would encourage labour opposition to outward investment. The analysis predicts that such opposition is most likely to be observed in major source nations. This follows from the fact that to be effective optimum capital controls require that the implementing nation be a sufficiently large source of DFI to affect overseas rates of return and prevent or limit retaliatory action. Consistent with this prediction are the efforts of the AFL-CIO to impose controls on US outward investment. The ill-fated Burke-Hartke bill sought, in a number of ways, to reduce the attractiveness of overseas production to US enterprises. The proposals focused on raising the incidence of domestic taxation on overseas earnings, controls on technology exports and the servicing of the US market from overseas bases, as well as increased information disclosure (Ruttenberg, 1971). The failure of this proposed legislation reflected its partisan nature.

Parent nation regulation of DFI, whilst eliminating the problem of host nation competition and substitution, is subject to a fundamental limitation. Where control is imposed in isolation regulated MNEs may suffer a competitive disadvantage if regulation raises costs or limits freedom of action. There are two probable corporate responses to source nation control. Some MNEs may formally incorporate themselves in unregulated third nations, creating a situation analogous to that found in shipping (Blake, 1976b). Alternatively, intense business lobbying may succeed in diluting the effectiveness of source nation imposed controls. A good example is provided by the partial regulation of outward investment pursued by the Swedish government. Here, controls have been highly selective focusing on the developmental impact of investments in a number of LDCs. This selectivity has probably ensured that Swedish MNEs have not been placed at a competitive disadvantage in comparison with unregulated MNEs.

An alternative to unilateral regulation of MNEs by host or source nation is the development of bilateral agreements between the two nations. A precedent for such a development may be found in the existence of double taxation treaties and insurance arrangements However, bilateral agreements are themselves subject to a number of shortcomings. If dual nation regulation raises MNE operating costs the possibility of a diversion of investment into non-participating economies arises. A fundamental criticism relates to any bilateral agreement in that preferential or detrimental treatment creates or maintains a distortion in global economic functioning (Grosse, 1982).

International Initiatives

The fundamental limitations of unilateral or bilateral action on MNE behaviour have prompted the search for international initiatives. The second important implication which may be derived from our introductory remarks is that efficient regulation of MNEs is likely to necessitate an international solution. In the absence of international co-ordination of national policies, diversity of regulation may induce sub-optimal MNE responses, or example, transfer pricing (Dunning, 1981, p. 393). International co-ordination of domestic policies would eliminate this problem of policy-derived imperfections. However, the feasibility of international solutions is limited by the implied subjugation of national sovereignty to supranational prescriptions. Reluctance to surrender domestic control over MNEs has resulted in a variety of third-best proposals varying in the severity of regulation and the means of ensuring compliance.

The least onerous international regulations encompassing labour relations are those imbedded in labour standards. The International Labour Organisation (ILO) has had a major direct and indirect impact on the labour practices of MNEs (and indigenous employers) through the setting of minimum standards of compliance. Between 1919 and 1968 the ILO introduced 128 binding Conventions and 132 Recommendations (ILO, 1969). These international instruments have had a tremendous direct impact. There were more than 3,400 ratifications by some 115 nations of 120 Conventions by 1968. Furthermore, national legislation and practices have been shaped to a considerable degree by the non-mandatory Recommendations adopted by the ILO Conference.

A number of proposals, more ambitious and selective in their aim of controlling MNEs, have focused on the establishment of a multilateral forum on DFI (Goldberg and Kindleberger, 1970; United Nations, 1974; Wallace, 1974). These proposals share a number of principles characteristic of liberal economic ideology. They advocate an open world economy subject to minimum social controls and the rule of international law. The proposal of Goldberg and Kindleberger is for a General Agreement for the International Corporation. The agreed principles would be administered by an international agency empowered to make non-binding recommendations. Whilst its remit, as originally conceived, paid little attention to labour issues there is no reason why minimum labour standards and guidelines could not be considered. The failure of these proposals to emerge in practical form highlights the problem of surrender of national sovereignty to supra-national bodies. Other proposals recognising this problem have suggested greater reliance on the rule of international law (Ball, 1967; Penrose, 1968) or confinement of international agencies to a consultative function (Rubin, 1971).

More progress has been achieved on limited regulation of MNEs, principally through the adoption of codes of conduct. The original stimulus to the development of codes came from the business lobby (Clee, 1966). Many MNE executives recognise the considerable benefits that codes may bring for them. Given the conflicting and, in their opinion, often unjustified criticisms levelled at MNEs international guidelines could moderate this discontent by highlighting the positive contribution of MNEs. Furthermore, if rules were consistent with principles of international law and in application did not distinguish between multinational and uninational enterprises, a greater uniformity of treatment would undoubtedly result.

Labour pressure for the development of guidelines has been prompted by the difficulties unions have faced in the economic sphere in their dealings with MNEs. The limited success of international union action has led to a search for political solutions to the problem of multinational business. The development of political regulation has undoubtedly been facilitated by increasing government intervention in economic affairs (Waldmann, 1980), the adverse publicity attracted by MNE involvement in the political affairs of host nations (Sampson, 1973) and revelations of illicit international payments (Jacoby, Eels and Nehemkis, 1977).

The earliest regulatory codes were non-governmental and were propagated by both business groups (International Chamber of Commerce, 1972; US Chamber of Commerce, 1975) and individual enterprises. The distinctive features of these codes are their generality and pliancy. A primary motive behind the development of non-governmental codes has been an attempt to preempt more onerous restrictions likely to be imposed by other bodies. The creators of multilateral codes have faced four major questions (Grosse, 1982).

The first relates to the problem of obtaining a consensus on proposals. The most widely accepted sets of guidelines (e.g. ILO, OECD) have developed through tripartite discussion involving government, business and labour representatives. The second consideration concerns the geographical coverage of guidelines. To some extent these two questions are related. It has proved easier to obtain agreement within multilateral forums such as the OECD than in truly international groupings like the United Nations. National governments, depending on whether they are major host or source nations of DFI, have displayed differences in the areas of regulation they emphasise. In general, the advanced Western economies as major MNE parent nations have sought to develop regulations which accommodate the growth of DFI within a competitive framework of minimal diversity of national policy. Amongst host nations the LDCs in particular have advocated mandatory controls on multinational business. These differences in orientation are a major explanatory factor in the long gestation period of the proposed UN code. The third and fourth questions are also interdependent to a considerable extent. They refer to the specificity and enforceability of rules. In general, the more specific guidelines are the easier it is to monitor and enforce compliance. Most codes of conduct currently in operation are of a voluntaristic nature. The major exception is provided by the Andean Common Market code which places mandatory controls, implemented through national legislation, on MNE subsidiaries. Unfortunately, from our perspective this code is of limited interest since it does not specifically address labour issues.

The two major sets of current guidelines which are very much concerned with labour issues are those of the ILO and OECD. Organised labour pressure for MNE regulation found early expression within the International Confederation of Free Trade Unions (ICFTU).[1] IN 1970 the ICFTU executive advocated the setting up of UN administration of a regulatory code on MNEs (ICFTU, 1970). By the mid-1970s the absence of an effective UN regulatory agency prompted proposals for an evolutionary code aiming towards enforceable rules. The form of enforcement was similar to that used by the ILO in its issuance of conventions. It is notable that other international trade union movements, for example the World Confederation of Labour (WCL), do not share this philosophy towards MNEs (WCL, 1973).

The results of labour pressure and the culmination of a number of sectoral studies of the impact of MNEs (ILO, 1975, 1976a, b, c) led in 1977[2] to the ILO Tripartite Declaration of Principles concerning Multinational Enterprises and Social Policy. The Declaration has four principal features (Gunter, 1981). Firstly, the principles are nonmandatory. Secondly, they are universal in the sense of applying to all enterprises, irrespective of ownership and multinationality. They have the same applicability for purely national private and public corporations as for MNEs. Thirdly, the principles are highly specific. They cover only the ILO's area of competence, employment and industrial relations matters. Fourthly, the Declaration recognises the evolutionary nature of the labour market effects of MNEs. They provide for review and amendment over the course of time.

The Declaration is of significance in four major areas. The first is a likely increasing integration of MNEs within the employment and labour relations framework of the host nation. This is apparent from the principles of non-discrimination and evolution. Furthermore, the voluntary nature of the principles and their compatibility with 15 Conventions and 19 Recommendations implies that they should be seen as a supplement to national custom and legislation. The second result is the apparent wish to propagate higher labour standards in the developing nations through the example of MNEs as model employers. The guidelines are likely to increase the spillover benefits of MNEs in the labour areas. As Chapter 3 noted there is considerable potential for increasing the contribution made by MNEs in a number of areas including training, the development of union representation and collective bargaining. Thirdly, the articles address a major labour concern, their access to corporate information. Paragraph 54 encourages the provision to worker representatives of information for bargaining purposes. In addition, the need for information on the overall operations of MNEs is recognised. Finally, the principles are non-committal on the issue of international collective bargaining. Whilst not creating any obstacles to the internationalisation of collective negotiation the emphasis on MNE integration within the host nation industrial relations system suggests the primacy of national bargaining structures.

Two important considerations arise over the question of the likely impact of the ILO Declaration. Firstly, the United States terminated its membership of the ILO just before the Declaration was adopted.[3] The effect of this is to limit coverage of the ILO articles and follow-up procedures. The second factor is the position of the ILO within the UN organisational umbrella. Because of the connections between the two institutions it is likely that the ILO principles will form part of the more comprehensive code currently under development within the UN (Baade, 1981). Depending on the acceptability of the UN code and its legal nature adoption is likely to increase significantly the impact of ILO principles.

The most significant code of conduct currently in operation is undoubtedly that of the Organisation for Economic Cooperation and Development (OECD). Its importance stems from two main features. Firstly, coverage of OECD members encompasses the main source and host nations of DFI.[4] Secondly, the guidelines have been in operation since June 1976[5] and have been amended in the light of changing conditions and incidents which have been referred to the Committee on International Investment and Multinational Enterprises (CIME) of the OECD. Review of the operation of the code occurred in 1979 and a further review is due in 1984.

The development and form of the OECD guidelines is similar to that of the ILO Declaration although the former enjoys a wider remit. The four major features of the OECD guidelines are its consultative development, voluntary nature, principle of non-discrimination and complementarity with national legislation. Acceptability of the guidelines is undoubtedly enhanced by their development within a consultative forum comprising government representatives and the Trade Union Advisory Committee (TUAC) and Business and Industry Advisory Committees (BIAC) of the OECD. To some extent the 1976 guidelines reflect consultative compromise since on a number of points the TUAC wished to see a strengthening of proposals. Furthermore, many unions interpret the present guidelines as merely the first step in a process culminating in binding controls (Blanpain, 1979). The voluntary nature of the guidelines reflects judicial necessity given the immense problems of ensuring legal enforceability. However, MNEs do not enjoy choice in acceptance since government adoption of the guidelines creates an expectation of MNE compliance. In addition, the guidelines could achieve legality if, in the course of time, they formed part of custom law. The principle of non-discrimination implies that the guidelines have the same applicability for domestic enterprises as they do for MNEs. Finally, the guidelines are designed as a supplement to national legislation. Where there is conflict between national laws and guideline recommendations, national law prevails ensuring state sovereignty. Although the OECD code covers more than employment and industrial relations issues it has had a significant impact on a number of areas of labour concern.

Firstly, the code encourages MNEs to adapt their employment practices, if necessary, in accord with local custom and legislation. Parent nation practices which are inconsistent with host nation methods are discouraged. This does not imply that all MNE innovations in the field of labour relations are prohibited; rather the question is one of impact on employees. If such practices are in the interest of host employees they may proceed. This is illustrated clearly in the Warner Lambert case (Blanpain, 1979, p. 217; Robinson, 1983, p. 131) where the CIME interpretation was that the guidelines did not prevent an MNE subsidiary from adapting wages and other conditions in the light of prevailing economic circumstances. Thus the guidelines do not prevent MNEs from engaging in concession bargaining, for example.

Secondly, compatible with local practices in all OECD nations is the encouragement of union recognition and development of collective bargaining. The guidelines reinforce the right of employees to collective representation and condone anti-union policies (Blanpain, 1979, p. 185; Robinson, 1983, p. 134).

Thirdly, the guidelines, and subsequent discussion, clarify the responsibilities of parent enterprises for the actions and liabilities of their subsidiaries (Blanpain, 1977b). The Badger case made clear the responsibility of the parent enterprise for the financial liabilities of its subsidiary, although this responsibility is not an unqualified one (Blanpain, 1979, p. 145). A responsibility also exists in the non-financial area where parent enterprises are obliged to provide such information and assistance as is necessary to enable subsidiaries to comply with local laws and practices. This principle is of significance in the disclosure of information on the economic performance of the MNE as a whole, the timing of disclosure and employee access to decision-making levels.

Fourthly, the OECD code specifically addresses the issue of access to key decision-makers (Blanpain, 1979, p. 145; Robinson, 1983, p. 137) and provides MNEs with a choice of meeting this requirement by delegating authority to subsidiary management or providing a duly authorised parent representative at subsidiary negoiations. In subsequent clarification of section 9 of the guidelines, which deal with the question of access, the CIME concluded that this right was a qualified one. Employee rights to information on the organisation's decision-making structure are confined to negotiating situations (Blanpain, 1983, p. 219). Furthermore, the CIME rejected the TUAC interpretation of section 9 as giving them a right of access to management based outside the nation concerned. The CIME view, supported by the BIAC, was that labour issues were primarily the concern of local management and should be dealt with at this level. Thus section 9 provides no right to by-pass local management (Blanpain, 1983, p. 28).

Fifthly, for union representatives a major section of the guidelines refers to the disclosure of information. A number of cases have been referred to the CIME over this question (Blanpain, 1979, pp. 199-217). Their view is that information disclosure is principally a national issue. Nevertheless, the guidelines provide assistance to union negotiators on a number of crucial issues. Section 3 foresees the need for disclosure on overall corporate performance where this is a requirement for meaningful bargaining and places the onus on parent enterprises to provide the necessary information to affiliates. Paragraph 6 lays down the requirement of reasonable notice in the case of changes likely to have a major impact on employee livelihood. 'Major change' is to be broadly interpreted and may cover lay-offs, closures, mergers and product line reorganisation.

These provisions have been the subject of considerable debate within the OECD. For the TUAC they do not go far enough. They desire not only prior notification but the right to negotiate over both the impact of, and grounds for, major decisions. While the wording of guideline 7 indicates prior notification the use of the word 'co-operation' implies consultation rather than meaningful negotiation. The BIAC position is that compliance with the disclosure provisions could create a number of problems. The major difficulties identified include the cost of compiling the required data, the need to preserve business confidentiality and the absence of agreed international standards of financial reporting (OECD, 1983b). Survey evidence from OECD MNEs highlights reluctance to disclose information on operating results and sales by geographical area and product line, principally because of the perceived threat to competitiveness (Blanpain, 1979, pp. 90-5; 1983, pp. 38-44). There is no doubt that from the trade union perspective these provisions do not go far enough. Indeed, the CIME's view that disclosure is primarily a national question allows MNEs to exploit national differences in reporting requirements and could result in large gaps in knowledge. This dissatisfaction has been a signficant influence on more ambitious proposals for increased information disclosure such as the so-called 'Vredeling Directive'.

The guidelines have been used to restrain MNE managements in cross-nation strikebreaking. The Hertz case illustrated a gap in the drafting of the 1976 Declaration. The relevant section, paragraph 8, dealt with threats of production switching or relocation as an unfair bargaining tactic. It did not specifically consider the cross-border transfer of strikebreaking labour. However, the CIME report made it clear that such tactics were incompatible both with the spirit of the guidelines and with the stipulations on *bona fide* negotiations. The 1979 Review provided the opportunity to include a passage condoning international transfer of employees as an unfair bargaining tactic. Whilst this undoubtedly provides some restraint on MNE bargaining power it does not preclude the possibility of intra-national transfer for MNEs with more than one establishment within a particular nation.

Finally, the guidelines do nothing to encourage the internationalisation of collective bargaining. Whilst increasing employee rights to information and access to key decision-makers the emphasis on national legislation and practices implies that international union groups must seek to achieve their aims both within this framework and in accord with the aspirations of nationally based union organisations.

Despite the undoubtable impact of the OECD code on both labour and non-labour questions a number of contentious issues remain. Firstly, the CIME has experienced difficulty in arriving at a meaningful definition of an MNE. While the guidelines side step the issue of definition the European Airlines Groupings case (Blanpain, 1983, pp. 119-35; Robinson, 1983, p. 135) and subsequent clarification highlight the primacy of decision-making structures as the defining characteristic. Such an intepretation is clearly sympathetic to union concerns but may prove difficult in operational terms. For example, the recent European Community proposal to create a new corporate structure, the European Economic Interest Group, designed to encourage cross-national support services, is indicative of the increasingly complex nature of business entities (Department of Trade and Industry, 1983). Developments of this type highlight the need for definition and clarification of the applicability of guideline provisions.

Secondly, the guidelines do not provide a remedy to the problem of divestment. Whilst stipulating the need for prior notification they cannot be used to prevent disinvestment, even in the case of profitable subsidiaries (Blanpain, 1979, pp. 150-73). Although governments are free to regulate plant closures within their framework of national law and practice, the guidelines make it clear that treatment of MNEs must not differ from that accorded indigenous enterprises. This area is likely to be one of acute concern in the immediate future, particularly within European nations. Again, labour dissatisfaction with progress in tackling this issue may lead to more radical proposals, perhaps centring on employee participation in decision-making.

Thirdly, codes of conduct have little to offer in the settlement of disputes. The CIME is concerned only with the discussion of issues; settlement is to be pursued within the nation raising the disputed matter. The ILO Declaration goes a little further in envisaging a disputes procedure passing from union-company discussion to the intervention of the relevant national government and finally the possibility of ILO investigation and recommendation. The truly tripartite structure of the ILO increases the probability of their recommendations being implemented.

Regulation of MNEs is also being pursued in other forums. Specialised codes on such matters as restrictive business practices (UNCTAD,

1980), the transfer of technology (UNCTAD, 1981) and prevention of illicit payments (UNESCO, 1978) are in force or in the process of development. More comprehensive regulation is being pursued within both the European Community (EC) and the United Nations (UN).

The approach of the European Community to the control of MNEs is somewhat out of step with that of other international organisations. The EC preference is for a series of legally binding measures covering specific issues. To date the major impact has been felt in the areas of information disclosure, taxation, anti-monopoly policy and employment protection. The uniqueness of this approach is primarily the result of the degree of economic and political integration desired by the Community and the effectiveness of labour pressure within Europe. Integration enables a transnational market to be regulated within a regional legislative framework. In addition, the European Community's approach to MNEs should be seen as one component of an industrial policy which places considerable emphasis on the strengthening of European capital *vis-à-vis* US MNEs (European Commission, 1976). At the same time this policy is concerned with restraining the economic power of MNEs where this might be used to the detriment of consumers, employees and less powerful competitors (Robinson, 1983, ch. 4). As well as the considerable progress made within the Community, particularly in the fields of information disclosure, employment protection and employee participation (Robinson, 1983, Part II), a broadening of Community action has seen the Lange-Gibbons proposals on closer co-operation between Europe and the US on anti-monopoly policy. Indeed, it is probably the export of EC experience with MNE control that represents the major potential impact of European initiatives in the regulation of international business.

The most ambitious attempt to develop a comprehensive code of conduct for MNEs is occurring within the UN. Work at the UN follows the setting up in 1972 of a Group of Eminent Persons whose subsequent report (UN, 1973) proposed the establishment of a Commission on Transnational Corporations. The considerable gestation period of the proposed UN code is primarily the result of the comprehensiveness of the controls envisaged and composition of the UN. The draft formulation which appeared in 1979 (Commission on Transnational Corporations, 1979) indicated that the code will comprise a set of voluntary rules which may be enforced by member nations if they so wish. The voluntary nature of the proposed code undoubtedly reflects considerable compromise in the course of discussion.

A number of areas of disagreement between LDCs and the advanced nations remain. One is the question of enforceability of the code. The LDCs display a preference for applying the code at the national level, heightening the role of host nation policy. Similarly, they oppose international adjudication of disputes. These attitudes raise something of a paradox. LDC acceptance of a voluntary code, given their preference for mandatory rules, implies that they will expect strict enforcement (Robinson, 1983, p. 15). Yet they are often the least well equipped to resolve disputes. In such a situation there is a strong case for an appropriately equipped international agency. Furthermore, reliance on domestic policy raises the probability of policy-induced imperfections with attendant sub-optimal MNE responses. Secondly, the balance of payments difficulties suffered by a large number of LDCs leads to them placing considerable emphasis on financial control of MNEs, particularly borrowing practices, profit repatriation and intra-company pricing. This aim may be at variance with the generally liberal financial regime desired by the Western nations. Thirdly, information disclosure represents an area that most major MNE source nations are anxious to protect, for both competitive and cost reasons. Continued secrecy is incompatible with the desire of most LDCs to open up and scrutinise the operations of MNEs (Grosse, 1982).

Despite the limited period in which codes of conduct have been in operation there has been some research on their impact (Grosse, 1980). Overall, this evidence indicates that codes are unlikely to generate any significant problems for participating nations. A survey of 28 US-based parent establishments revealed that the OECD code had no significant effect on location decisions. The majority of respondents indicated that location might be affected by mandatory rules, particularly financial and ownership restrictions. If regulation raised entry and control costs investment might be diverted to non-participating nations or retained in the source economy. Compatible with these views was some evidence of relocation, certainly in the initial period of operation, following the introduction of the restrictive mandatory Andean Code.

Interestingly, all respondents to this survey expressed the view that codes would have no impact on MNE labour relations. Such a view might reflect the high labour standards operated by respondents or the fact that labour relations provisions could be ignored or circumvented. If this latter conception is accurate it indicates that existing measures are either too weak or fail to tackle the critical issues. Clearly, more evidence is needed on the impact of codes. The case experience accumulated within the OECD since 1976 may have led to some modification of views held by MNE management.

On the basis of existing knowledge it does appear that codes of conduct offer a potentially effective and efficient method of regulating multinational business. The extent to which such regulation is efficient depends on the degree of uniformity imposed and centralisation of implementation. Where national policy differences are minimised the adverse effects of regulation (relocation, sub-optimal responses) appear minimal.

The problem of obtaining meaningful and current information on the operations of MNEs has led to the inclusion of information disclosure provisions in almost all codes of conduct. However, the significance of this problem, from the perspective of both union negotiators and host governments, has led to pressure for supplementary provisions. Two strategies are discernible. The first is a mandatory directive on employee information and consultation rights. The second is the establishment of an international agency charged with the collection, analysis and dissemination of information on the operations of MNEs.

It is within the European Community that the first strategy has been most actively pursued. In October 1980 the European Commission reached agreement on the content of a proposed directive on 'informing and consulting the employees of undertakings with complex structures, in particular transnational firms'. The purpose of the so-called 'Vredeling Directive' is to ensure that employees at local level within multi-plant enterprises are informed about decisions taken at higher levels which may have significant repercussions for them. Information rights are coupled with consultation procedures and include provisions enabling employee representatives to approach key decision-makers even when the latter are located in another country. Unlike the similar, though weaker, provisions of the ILO Declaration and OECD Guidelines, the Directive is a mandatory instrument.

The Directive requires that management of 'dominant undertakings' provide subsidiary management with information on the structure, economic and financial performance of the organisation, employment levels and probable trends, trends in production, sales and investment, including any plans for rationalisation or changes in working methods, and any plans likely to have a substantial impact on employee interests. The Directive, as originally conceived applied to enterprises with Community subsidiaries employing at least 100 people. Subsidiary management are required to disclose this information at least every six months. Failure to do so creates an obligation on the management of the dominant undertaking to respond to a request for such information from employee representatives (by-pass option).

The Directive contains far-reaching provisions for handling plant closures and restructuring. Where central management takes a decision on plant closure or transfer, changes in the activities of a plant, major organisational change or alters long-term co-operative relations with other undertakings, the reasons behind and effects of such decisions must be relayed to subsidiary management 40 days before implementation. The information must then be passed on to employee representatives within 30 days. Where management decisions are likely to have a direct impact on employees' terms of employment or working conditions employee representatives enjoy the right to consultations on measures planned to ameliorate adverse effects. Where subsidiary management fails to provide the necessary information or agree to consultation, employee representatives enjoy the right of access to management of the dominant undertaking.

This instrument, which greatly exceeds the information disclosure provisions of most national legislation (Bellace and Gospel, 1983), has been met by considerable business opposition. Lobbying by US- and Japanese-based MNEs has been particularly intense. Business concern has focused on the duplication of the Directive, covering areas addressed, albeit less stringently, by OECD and ILO codes and current and pending European Community legislation, as well as the administrative burden of regular reporting. In addition, the proposal raises the possibility that the authority of local management will be undermined by frequent resort to the by-pass mechanism, the danger to competitiveness of disclosure of highly sensitive information and the precedent mandatory provisions might create for other nations, particularly LDCs, seeking to regulate MNE operations. One defence put forward by a number of MNEs is the considerable progress they claim to have made in the voluntary development of consultative procedures. However, there is little doubt that the Vredeling Directive goes considerably beyond the scope and conditions of operation typical of joint consultative committees.

Business opposition, and the reluctance of some EC members towards the Vredeling Directive, resulted in considerable amendments in its passage through the European Parliament (Herman, 1983). These amendments lay down tighter procedures for the selection of employee representatives, introduce an overall enterprise size threshold of 1,000 employees for inclusion, reduce both the frequency and content of disclosure and provide greater management discretion over the disclosure of confidential business information (European Industrial Relations

Review, 1983). The most disabling amendments relate to the by-pass option and European representation of MNEs originating from outside the Community.

The European Parliament substantially weakened the right of employee representatives to consult with higher-level management. The right to consultation is replaced by an entitlement to write to management of the dominant undertaking requesting disclosure; the latter is then obliged to provide the necessary information to subsidiary management. Failure to comply with this request enables employee representatives to apply for a national court ruling requiring disclosure, reinforced, in necessary, by appropriate sanctions. This modification strikes at the very heart of the Directive in the opinion of its originator (Vredeling, 1983, p. 7).

The Commission's version of the Directive obliges MNEs with their headquarters outside the Community to ensure the presence of a duly delegated individual able to fulfil information and consultation requirements. In the absence of such a representative the obligation falls on the largest subsidiary within the European Community. This provision attracted a great deal of opposition, principally because of the danger of extra-territoriality. The Parliamentary text extends the responsibility to the management of individual subsidiaries. The effect of this is to create an anomalous situation where the employees of Community-based MNEs enjoy stronger safeguards than individuals employed by non-Community enterprises (Vredeling, 1983, p. 8). Submission to the European Council of Ministers of the final draft of this Directive is now awaited.

On a more general level recognition of the information deficiencies surrounding MNEs has resulted in the UN Commission on Transnational Corporations being charged with developing a comprehensive information system on MNEs. This data base is to be used to further research on the activities and impact of MNEs and in co-operative programmes with host governments seeking assistance in their dealings with MNEs. The CTC's computerised information system is now operational and comprises profiles of individual MNEs, industry and sectoral data, information on host nation and company agreements, and data on the international business environment. This experience has enabled a number of workshops to be held providing advice for negotiators from developing nations. Such a data bank is unlikely to provide an effective means of controlling MNEs in isolation and may be usefully allied with the introduction of regulatory codes (Grosse, 1982). Clearly, such information could be of considerable value to trades unions in dealing with

MNEs. We return to this possibility later in this chapter after considering international union activities.

Increasing the Power of Labour

A complementary strategy towards MNEs is one based on a strengthening of labour's relative power. Such an approach would have its major impact on the distribution of the economic product of MNEs. One advantage of this approach is that it would not necessarily imply a limitation on the size of the MNE-generated product since the efficacy of multinational business would not be impaired. It is a complementary strategy to the extent that MNE regulation would still be required to minimise the detrimental effects of international business. Again, we may distinguish between national and international initiatives.

National Initiatives

Labour responses to the MNE rooted at the national level raise a number of questions. Firstly, the question of whether responses should focus on source or host nations. A number of proposals have been offered for both cases. Secondly, controversy surrounds the issue of whether labour should pursue economic or political solutions to the MNE problem. The apparent weakness of labour in the economic sphere has led to considerable emphasis being placed on political remedies. The paradoxical nature of this has not gone undetected. In the US, for example, where labour has traditionally pursued its interests through collective bargaining, its support of the Burke-Hartke bill has been interpreted as a sign of economic impotency (Shearer, 1977). Thirdly, a number of writers have cast doubts on the likely effectiveness of national responses to the MNE. Popular allegations claim that MNEs enjoy the ability to evade, violate or influence national controls (Holland, 1975; Weinberg, 1975a).

Two major proposals have addressed host nation controls. Both are concerned with increasing labour's access to corporate decision-making processes. One widely held view is that the strongest hope for organised labour in combatting the MNE lies in power and influence at the level of the corporate board (Levinson, 1971). Sauvant (1981) has suggested the establishment of host country councils enjoying participation in the decision-making processes of particular MNEs. This form of regulation is seen as a supplement to external controls like codes of conduct. A variant of this approach, company councils, has made some progress within the international trade union movement but has faced problems of non-recognition and even opposition from MNEs. Sauvant recognises this obstacle and argues for the sanctioning of host councils by the UN in its forthcoming code.

Increased employee participation in enterprise decision-making has been a continuing concern in the European Community's industrial relations policy. The 'fifth' company law directive is designed to strengthen employee representation. While the ultimate objective remains the achievement of employee participation in company boards', in the shorter-term recognition of the diversity of national systems has led to acceptance of a variety of structures among member nations encompassing works councils, enterprise committees and shop steward combine committees. This flexiblity in acceptance of the inevitability of slow progress towards harmonisation of employee representation within the Community increases the likelihood of legislative proposals being adopted.

There are considerable advantages with a regionally-based initiative on employee participation. Introduction of such a scheme by a single government could have a detrimental effect on foreign investment flows. Home-based MNEs could be placed at a considerable competitive disadvantage in comparison with overseas MNEs if corporate flexibility and management discretion are constrained. Furthermore, union pressure for increased centralisation of decision-making, whilst enhancing labour's position, could adversely affect subsidiary management and performance. A similar increase in centralisation might be expected within foreign-based MNEs in an attempt to limit employee influence on decisions. There is some evidence from West Germany's experience of codetermination that such structures give greater control over home-based MNEs, but are far less effective in influencing overseas-based companies (Bomers and Peterson, 1977).

Source nation proposals, particularly within the US, have aimed at limiting the export of jobs to overseas affiliates. Kujawa (1978) proposes an amendment to national labour law obliging parent company executives and union officials to meet and discuss management decisions likely to have a significant impact on employee welfare. The proposal is not designed to curtail managerial prerogatives but primarily to offer employee representatives an opportunity to respond constructively to the economic pressures forcing the consideration of overseas production. Union officials would have the option of bargaining down to retain employment, if they so desired. Recent events have questioned the need for this type of legislative reform. Concession bargaining, which has been widespread within the US has focused in a number of cases on companies not considering initial or increased overseas involvement. Furthermore, the proposal is based on the implicit assumption that overseas production directly displaces source nation activity and is prompted primarily by cost, principally labour cost, considerations. Our discussion in Chapters 2 and 3 throws serious doubt on the empirical validity of such assumptions. This tendency to base analysis of the labour effects of MNEs on outmoded paradigms of international business (Kujawa, 1979a) is unhelpful (Enderwick, 1982b).

International Initiatives

A number of students of international business hold the view that the most effective long-term labour response to the MNE will involve some form of international union action (Gennard, 1972; Liebhaberg, 1980). However, there is no inevitability of international union action. Although many business enterprises now operate internationally it does not necessarily follow that labour groups will develop a similar structure (Olle and Schoeller, 1977). Indeed, there are several factors which suggest considerable impediments to international labour strategies.

Firstly, the structure of the international labour movement is not conducive to cohesive labour action. The international trade union movement is dominated by three global organisations responsible for the operations of international union groupings. The World Federation of Trade Unions (WFTU), with a claimed membership of 190 million, draws its support principally from the Communist Bloc. Its international arm comprises 11 Trade Unions' Internationals (TUIs). The democratic economies are served by the International Confederation of Free Trade Unions (ICFTU) with over 60 million members and 16 associated International Trade Secretariats (ITSs). The smallest grouping, with some 5 million members, is the World Confederation of Labour (WCL). Within this organisation are 12 industrial units described as International Trade Federations (ITFs), although the extent of their international involvement appears low (Rowan, Northrup and O'Brien, 1980). Superimposed upon the global and industrial organisations are a variety of regional, e.g. the European Trade Union Confederation (ETUC), and specialised international groupings, e.g. TUAC. Furthermore, major regional movements like the ETUC are now developing regional industry committees. There is inevitably some conflict between the ITSs and regionally-based industry committees (Windmuller, 1980). However, as a labour counter to the MNE it is the ITSs which have been most active.

Secondly, trade union action towards the MNE is always reactive. Labour responses and organisational changes are inevitably triggered by innovations in management policy. The result is likely to be hasty and *ad hoc* union reactions (Howarth, 1982). The analysis of Chapter 4 highlighted the need to consider management strategy as a significant influence on labour force cohesion both nationally and internationally. This question has been one largely ignored, certainly until recent times, in the industrial relations literature (Purcell and Sisson, 1983; Wood, 1982).

Thirdly, because of the impetus of managerial strategy in the internationalisation of business, labour responses have been largely defensive (Howarth, 1982). There has been little attempt by labour to use the dynamics of DFI to devise anticipatory responses (Enderwick, 1982b). This observation is clearly compatible with the frequent resort labour has made to government assistance and regulation in the absence of offensive strategies on its part. Organised labour has, to a considerable extent, misrepresented its unpreparedness in dealing with MNEs as economic impotence imposed upon it by a multinational structure (Weinberg, 1975b).

We can distinguish several forms of international union action (Levinson, 1975). The simplest form of international co-operation is the collection and exchange of information on the activities of MNEs. The next stage of co-operation is likely to be one of consultation. Demonstrations of solidarity, in the form of sympathy strikes, the banning of overtime, etc., comprise a third stage. A further form of international co-operation would involve the co-ordination of demands between subsidiaries. The final and most complete form would be true multinational collective bargaining based on a common claim and simultaneous termination of agreements.

To date, transnational union action has been limited in both its form and effectiveness (Northrup and Rowan, 1979). There has been a tendency for unions to concentrate on the first two stages of co-operation, the exchange of information and consultation. Blake (1973) has estimated that 60 per cent of international action takes these forms. The attraction of limited involvement is presumably the fact that it requires very little surrender of national union decision-making power to the international level. When co-operation occurs at a more advanced stage, unions have tended to focus on specific grievances and difficulties. This orientation has provided a stimulus to the development of ITSs. Their collection of data is extensive (Weinberg, 1978). The International Trade Secretariats also provide a forum for international consultation enabling, in one case, the United Automobile Workers of America (UAW) to provide evidence to an Australian arbitration involving employees of Holden (General Motors' Australian subsidiary).

ITSs have also achieved some success in the third stage of international co-operation, the demonstration of solidarity. Well publicised cases include the International Chemical and General Workers' Federation (ICF) support of unions in dispute with the Turkish subsidiary of Hoechst, the German chemical multinational. The tactics adopted by the ITSs, including the provision of financial assistance, the banning of overtime to maintain strike-bound plants, etc., tend to be most effective in pressing for the right of union recognition. There are tremendous problems involved in the co-ordination of international union action even to this limited extent. These difficulties perhaps explain why such action has tended to concentrate on single issues and has generally applied to subsidiaries of a single multinational. The major obstacles include differences in trade union ideologies, differences in national labour laws, such as the legality of sympathy strikes, and the problem of stimulating awareness of the mutual interests involved (Gennard, 1972). Evidence of the difficulties of organising international union action is provided by Blake (1972b). In an opinion survey of 94 UAW members in the Canadian subsidiary of Chrysler, Blake investigated willingness to undertake sympathy strikes in support of fellow Chrysler employees in the US, the UK and Mexico. Results indicated that the extent of solidarity in the form of sympathy strikes was 52, 13 and 12 per cent for the respective nations. The decline of support with geographical distance is significant. Whilst there was some evidence of increased support for less 'costly' forms of solidarity such as the restriction of overtime, the potential for international strike support appears very low.

The difficulties of organising for international union action provide a partial explanation of why the more advanced forms of international co-operation constitute no more than isolated incidents. There have been two significant attempts at the co-ordination of demands between subsidiaries. The first concerns the 1967 Chrysler wage parity agreement for Canada and the US (Blake, 1972). There appear to have been several factors conducive to this agreement. Apart from a high degree of union coverage within the same union between the two nations and no significant productivity differences, the path for such an agreement was laid two years previously when the two countries agreed to eliminate tariffs on trade in parts and vehicles (Treckel, 1972).

The second, and best-known, case is the St. Gobain agreement. In this case French, German, American and Italian affiliates of the French glass MNE agreed a co-ordinated wage strategy. After an early and generous settlement with the German and Italian unions a 26-day strike was initiated by the US union in pursuit of a wage claim based on global ability to pay. The co-operation of affiliates in refusing to work overtime was instrumental in ensuring a US settlement (Litvak and Maule, 1972). However, this case also displays features which dismiss the likelihood of a general tendency towards such co-ordination. The action concerned well organised unions in the developed nations, action was related to a clearly definable and short-term objective and the actual solidarity of the unions involved was never put to the test. The significance of these incidents should not be overstated (Northrup and Rowan, 1974).

Equally exceptional are cases of multinational collective bargaining (MCB) based on a common claim and simultaneous termination of agreements, although as a strategy it was discussed by the International Metalworkers' Federation (IMF) at their 1968 world conference (Trades Union Congress, 1970). The basic incentives to MCB are threefold. The erosion of union power associated with the growth of multinational business has triggered the idea of the need for international union structures as an effective counter. Secondly, if through MCB unions in the developed nations can successfuly alter the global wage structure, by raising wages in the low-wage nations, they may limit the job losses created by 'runaway' industries seeking lower cost sites (Ulman, 1975). Thirdly, an incentive to MCB is thought to be the precedent provided by the extension of domestic collective bargaining from the level of the plant or firm to an industry- or country-wide basis. Such an argument seriously understates the differences and additional difficulties involved in organising effective union strategies internationally. The extension of national bargaining on to the international plane involves qualitative differences which are not incurred in its domestic expansion. Such a precedent provides no real incentive to MCB.

The traditional impediments to multinational unionism have been outlined by a number of writers (Northrup, 1978; Ulman, 1975). Differences in labour legislation and practice obviously generate prob-. lems for the international co-ordination of union strategies. Whilst the exceptional cases of MCB indicate that such barriers are not insurmountable, they comprise a formidable constraint to such action (Smith, 1972). The diversity of law and practice has been a major source of stimulus to the view that multinational union co-operation is most likely to emerge initially within regional blocs such as the European Community, where harmonisation policies serve to create a fertile seedbed (Roberts, 1973; Smith, 1972). Recent analyses which highlight the increasing nationalisation and orientation towards the world economy of economic policies pursued by EC member states cast doubt on the likelihood of regional bargaining arrangements (Ziebura, 1982).

A second impediment exists in management opposition and union antipathy towards MCB. In certain cases management opposition may be prompted by a fear of countervailing power if unions can successfully organise globally; more generally concern focuses on the ability of unions to develop effective structures for decision-making and control at this level. One can envisage the imposition of a third tier to collective negotiation which, if effective, could restrain management flexibility, but if ineffective would simply serve to endanger existing arrangements. Conventional analyses of MCB which highlight the obstacles to such a development as being principally institutional, implicitly discount managerial strategy as an effective impediment to international bargaining. In contrast, the thrust of Chapter 4 was that the international operations of MNEs do create very considerable impediments in effectively segmenting labour groups by national boundaries and stratifying groups both within and between nations. The logical extension of this analysis is that bargaining structures are derived from management strategy and structure and MCB will be observed only when management permits its emergence (Gospel, 1983).

Management opposition may be mirrored at the level of the national union. International union co-operation presents two major problems for the national unions of particular nations. The first is the question of the appropriate vehicle for organising international action. One attraction of the ITSs is their lower susceptibility to the religious and ideological schisms which separate national unions. The bestowing of authority for international action on such bodies would involve a considerable loss of national sovereignty on the part of domestic union officials. Surrender of such power presupposes some recognition of the mutuality of interests between the various nations affected. There is little evidence of union awareness of communal interest and its development is likely to be seriously impaired by the increasingly significant domestic economic problems of major participants like the US and UK.

Thirdly, analysis of the prospects for MCB based on earlier theories of the MNE highlight the belief that overseas production is undertaken primarily for offensive motives (lower labour costs) and not for defensive reasons (market retention strategies), and that domestic and overseas production are directly substitutable. These beliefs have deflected union concern into the pursuit of national legislative or quasi-legislative responses. By emphasising the apparent lack of mutuality of labour concern between host and source nations such views may have worked to reinforce the divisions of union interest.

Fourthly, the changing patterns and forms of DFI discernible in recent years offer little incentive to MCB. Previous analyses of the prospects for MCB were based on the trend of direct investment in the postwar period up to the mid-1970s. Implicitly, the trend of this period was extrapolated into the indefinite future. Since the mid-1970s, important changes have occurred in the global pattern of direct foreign investment. Coupled with a slowing down in the growth rate of foreign investment the pattern of investment between the industrialised nations has become more balanced. European firms have achieved a considerable penetration of the US market. Divestment, particularly by US firms in Europe, has increased in significance (van den Bulcke *et al.*, 1979). Manufacturing investment in the LDCs is characterised by its export orientation and the servicing of regional or global markets. These changes have coincided with a diversity of forms of overseas involvement. Investments in the forms of joint ventures, turnkey operations and international subcontracting appear to be increasing in popularity (Oman, 1981).

A useful way of examining the impact of these developments on the probability of MCB is in terms of the necessary conditions for the emergence of stable bargaining cartels (McLean, 1977). Economic theory indicates that the likelihood of the development of a stable bargaining cartel depends upon:

    (i)   the common perception that co-operative action will yield mutual benefits;

    (ii) the extent to which cartel members are informed about the activities of non-members and substitution possibilities;

    (iii) the revelation and centralisation of information for policing agreements; and

    (iv) the existence of effective sanctions against transgressors.

In the context of this framework the more balanced pattern of cross-investment within the advanced nations is likely to increase awareness of the mutuality of labour interests. More nations are likely to experience simultaneously the costs and benefits of both inward and outward direct foreign investment. Offsetting this is the fact that there still remain enormous differences between countries in the relative importance of, and employment dependence upon, inward and outward investment (Gunter, 1981, p. 11). In addition, there are considerable differences in the sectoral distribution of cross-investment. This would tend to discourage multinational bargaining, particularly when involving ITSs organised principally along industry lines.

The rising importance of investment in the rapidly industrialising LDCs is also likely to retard the emergence of MCB. Not only are there likely to be substantially greater problems of cartel management in terms of points (ii) and (iii) — cost pressures may prompt the hiving-off of production facilities to low-cost centres and union differences are amplified — but there is evidence of government opposition to international union action which may be seen as a disguised form of protectionism pursued by unions in the advanced nations (Kassalow, 1978).

It is also likely that the changing forms of overseas involvement will discourage MCB. The diversity of forms represent attempts to adapt to changing conditions and host nation pressures. To the extent that such adaptation is successful the mutuality of union interest is probably reduced.

Finally, true multinational bargaining would necessitate the bridging of radically different national approaches to collective bargaining (Litvak and Maule, 1972). A global agreement would need to be related to the marginal subsidiary or nation and as such may not be acceptable to higher wage and productivity employees (Ruttenberg, 1974). Ulman (1975) argues that MCB is discouraged by the preference of national unions to pursue coercive wage claims based on the domestic inter-industrial wage structure rather than an international reference group within the global intra-industry wage structure. Concern has also focused on the possibility that MCB could lead to the emergence of a new 'labour aristocracy' weakening the labour solidarity required through a furtherance of particular interests at the expense of general welfare (Bomers and Peterson, 1977).

Despite these considerable obstacles exceptional cases of MCB have been documented and analysed (Miscimara, 1981; Northrup, Rowan and Laffer, 1977). Unions appear to have targeted the most promising MNEs. Survey evidence for the US found that companies approached tended to be the largest and most centralised in their labour relations (Hershfield, 1975). However, the most promising developments have occurred in the service industries of shipping and entertainment.

Both these cases appear exceptional in that they display traits highly conducive to MCB. Both involve an international demand for the industry's output and have been characterised by rapid technological change which has altered working conditions drastically. There is a low probability of factor and location substitution in both cases. These considerations have probably served to overcome national and ideological differences. This is particularly true in the entertainment industry where the threat of new technological opportunities has stimulated considerable concern. In the shipping industry pressure has stemmed from the poor working conditions offered by certain lines and facing employees of certain nationalities. In addition, both sectors are characterised by powerful and effective union organisation. It is also notable that both industries are likely to offer limited scope for the effectiveness of national action in terms of union leverage.

In conclusion, those cases of multinational union bargaining which have occurred appear to share certain characteristics which make them amenable to the development of stable bargaining coalitions. This conclusion is borne out by available empirical evidence. Only about 10 per cent of US (Hershfield, 1975) and British (Roberts and May, 1974) MNEs indicated that they had been approached on a transnational basis by unions. The frequency of 'looser' forms of union co-ordination is slightly higher. Analysis of trade union bodies confirms that incidence rates are higher for the less committal forms of co-operation such as exchange of information. Union responses appear to overstate considerably (Weinberg, 1978) the true extent and impact of their international activities (Northrup and Rowan, 1979).

Despite the exceptional cases, widespread transnational collective bargaining remains a remote development. Indeed in 1972 Blake (1972c) reported that the majority of US multinational managements did not anticipate significant union responses emerging for 9-12 years or more. With the hindsight of the last 12 years that time horizon appears unduly pessimistic from the point of view of management.

Conclusions

The analysis of this chapter has highlighted the underdevelopment of policy prescriptions derived from the eclectic model. However, given the role played by market imperfections in this approach there appears to be a formidable case for international regulation of MNEs. Controls introduced at this level may be useful in minimising the likelihood of policy-induced imperfections and suboptimal investment diversion effects. Controls which are designed to limit the power of MNEs may be usefully allied to labour strengthening proposals which have made only limited progress.

The evidence of this chapter and Chapter 4 enable us to hypothesise that the underdevelopment of labour responses to the MNE is due primarily to strategies being based on increasingly questionable assumptions about the nature of international business. Four assumptions appear critical. The first is the view that MNEs substantially enfeeble national unions as effective bargaining agents. The distinction between market bargaining power and workplace bargaining power is helpful in highlighting the superficial generality of this assumption. The second assumption follows directly from the first. It is that if nationally-based bargaining is rendered ineffective in the presence of MNEs then multinational union organisation is a logical inevitability. Not only is there nothing inevitable about the need for unions to adopt organisational structures similar to that of their employer counterparts, our analysis suggests that this may not necessrily be the most efficient form of response. A third crucial assumption is that the patterns and forms of overseas involvement characteristic of the 25 years immediately following the last world war will continue into the indefinite future. The changing forms and patterns of investment discernible since the mid-1970s appear likely to increase the obstacles to international union co-operation. Finally, previous analyses of MCB have highlighted the impediments to such a development as being principally institutional. Implicitly, managerial strategy as an effective constraint to international bargaining is discounted. In contrast, the thrust of this book is that the international operations of MNEs do create very formidable barriers.

While, overall, the above comments imply that the prospects for international union action are poorer than is generally assumed, this should not be a major source of concern to organised labour since our analysis implies that less ambitious strategies may, in certain cases, be a more effective counter to the MNE. The strategies implied centre on a strengthening of national union involvement in plant- and company-based bargaining, research on the vulnerability of selected MNEs, and consolidation of the activities of company- and industry-based international union movements.

The decentralisation of collective bargaining which MNEs have pursued in a variety of host nations may create problems for union officials. The trend in Britain, for example, where MNEs have pioneered the formalistion of workplace bargaining and disengagement from multi-employer agreements has tended to erode the effective bargaining position of national union officials. Given the multi-plant status of many larger MNEs within host nations, the position of union representatives in establishment and corporate bargaining is of considerable significance. Effective union responses to the MNE imply a far greater role for union officials in both the monitoring and determination of establishment agreements within MNEs. An appropriate vehicle for achieving this might be combine committees which appear highly valued by MNE employees (Buckley and Enderwick, 1984).

A second strategy implication is the need to examine the 'geneology of production' in an attempt to identify those MNEs vulnerable to national bargaining overtures. Effective national bargaining may be limited to those MNEs characterised by regional or global vertical or horizontal integration. Here we would disagree with the view of Kujawa (1979a) who argues that an MNE must possess a fully transnationally integrated production system to be in the same position as a national firm in the event of production disruption. Rather our view is that even partial integration could generate considerable strike costs for MNEs, costs which would be considered an 'externality' by uni-plant national companies. While total income flows might not be halted for partially integrated MNEs, the same applies for conglomerate uni-national firms. Furthermore, stock holding costs, incurred to defray sales losses in the event of work stoppages, are likely to be substantially higher for MNEs. The need for substantial stock holding within MNEs might result from their desire to retain customer loyalty resulting from entry to intermediate markets as an independent seller in an attempt to achieve scale economies where internal demand alone implies output at suboptimal levels (Lall, 1980b). Although some progress has been made in explaining differences by nationality and industry in the incidence of internal trade (Buckley and Pearce, 1981) a considerable amount of work remains to be done.

The role of existing international union arrangements is a third important implication. Clearly, nationally-based action is likely to be enhanced by the collection and exchange of information on the activities of MNEs. This role is one which might be usefully undertaken within ITSs and company councils. Important stimulants to this work lie in the information disclosure provisions of existing and pending codes, and within the European Community, the Vredeling Directive. Furthermore, unions would benefit from greater contact and exchange with the information compilation activities of the UN through its CTC. Information acquisition and analysis, particularly as an input to pro-active labour strategies, is an area where union resources should be increased and directed with more effectiveness.

Notes

1. The structure and operations of this and other world trade union movements are discussed later in this chapter.

2. The declaration was formally adopted by the Governing Body of the ILO on 16 November 1977 and is reprinted in Appendix 1.

3. The United States withdrawal was not the result of the Tripartite Declaration; indeed the US played a significant role in its drafting.

4. One exception is Turkey which did participate in the Declaration.

5. The 1976 Declaration and Guidelines are reproduced in Appendix 2.

7 POLICY IMPLICATIONS AND CONCLUSIONS

Introduction

Preceding chapters have highlighted a number of important policy implications of the operations of MNEs. The findings are of particular interest to DFI source nations, host, particularly LDC, economies, and the labour movement. In this chapter we outline the major implications for these three groups in their attempts to regulate MNEs. In addition, we attempt an assessment of the research questions set out in Chapter 1. Finally, concluding comments pinpoint some unsettled issues and areas requiring further research.

Source Nation Policy

The analysis of Chapters 3 and 6 indicated the likelihood of interest group pressures to restrict outward DFI. The sources of such pressure include a widely-held belief that overseas production represents a substitute for exporting from the source nation. This view has been propagated by outmoded conceptions of the MNE such as the Product Cycle Model and classical position general equilibrium models of international trade. The results of such views include AFL-CIO sponsorship of the ill-fated Burke-Hartke bill in the US and Japanese union opposition to the proposed Nissan investment in Britain.

Our analysis suggests that there is no sound economic case for restriction of outward investment. Apart from the very distinct possibility that restrictions on MNEs could adversely affect source nation welfare, it is unclear that impediments to DFI would be effective. The increasingly difficult investment conditions existing since the late 1970s have revealed the adaptability of MNEs and the range of alternative forms international involvement may assume. It is quite possible that controls on subsidiary production would simply increase the volume of technology licensed internationally (Harberger, 1978). The opportunities for substitution of alternative forms of international market servicing are highlighted by the eclectic approach (Dunning, 1981, Part 1). Support for this approach is provided by recent research indicating that the licensing option is often considered simultaneously with DFI (Contractor, 1981; Telesio, 1979) rather than sequentially (Rugman, 1980). The likely effects of an enforced rise in international licensing include a fall in recipient and source nation welfare. For the licensor the lower comparative private return on licensing as opposed to subsidiary production means a fall in the profitability of technological advantages and a lower incentive to R&D investment. Furthermore, even a temporary restriction on DFI could lead to a permanently increased flow of technology licensing. This possibility arises from the finding that there are significant learning curve effects in the efficiency of technology transfer (Davidson, 1980; Teece, 1977). Even if previously imposed restrictions on DFI are lifted, and DFI continues to offer a more profitable mode of overseas market servicing, there may not occur a mass swich towards DFI. If learning effects accruing from the licensing experience lead to a lowering of the average costs of licensing the profit differential offered by DFI may be partially, or totally, eliminated. Finally, the possibility that unilaterally imposed regulation of MNEs will exacerbate market imperfections, prompting welfare-reducing corporate responses, suggests the limited value of source nation controls.

A second, and more positive, policy implication for source nations concerns the need for adjustment. The analysis of Chapter 3 highlighted the role trade adjustment might play in the event of international capital flows. Internal adjustment, involving the inter-industry movement of labour and capital resources, may be impaired by a variety of market imperfections. Obvious imperfections exist where factor prices are inflexible and geographical or skill mismatches exist between expanding and contracting sectors. Similarly, restructuring will be impeded where there is a divergence between the private and social costs of adjustment. Whether adjustment arising from the internationalisation of production is more or less difficult than changes stemming from technological progress, demand shifts or increased import penetration is not clear. The heterogeneity of MNE activity is likely to exacerbate the problem of factor mismatch. Similarly, the widespread development of ILMs within MNEs increases labour immobility where the loss of specific training and seniority rights implies the possibility of private adjustment costs exceeding social costs. Offsetting these factors are the opportunities for intra-industry adjustment achievable within MNEs. A number of source nation enterprises have responded to the competitive pressures of recent years by upgrading the capital and skill content of their activities, often within the same industry. Where adjustment takes this form the likelihood of factor mismatch is lowered.

The targets of adjustment policy explicitly address three major objectives (Wolf, 1979). The first is an attempt to lower the social costs of adjustment and facilitate change. The second refers to the equity issue of encouraging a sharing of adjustment costs through redistribution from the affected minority to the population in general. Thirdly, adjustment may be facilitated where the 'transparency' of policy costs and benefits is heightened. In the design of policy to achieve these targets a number of questions arise. The first is the source of adjustment pressure. In the present case it would be necessary to quantify the contribution made by international trade and investment to the need for adjustment. A second consideration, clearly related to the first, is the question of whether trade- and investment-impacted labour and capital should be treated as a special case. Finally, policy variation in the extent of reliance on market forces is likely to be observed. The degree of government involvement and its role in facilitating or displacing market forces is a crucial policy variable.

There has been some research on the employment implications of trade expansion. Most studies focus on LDC exports, particularly manufactures. As Chapter 2 indicated, MNEs play a major role in such trade for a number of rapidly industrialising LDCs. Thus these studies may be indicative of the employment adjustment burden imposed by export platform investments. Unfortunately, as Chapter 3 revealed there has been very little analytical study of source nation employment effects of outward investment and certainly no estimates of the adjustment problems this might have created.

There is considerable agreement, for a number of nations, that the employment adjustment of a balanced trade expansion with LDCs is low in aggregate terms (Cable, 1982; Frank, 1977; Kierzkowski, 1980; Wolter, 1976). For the US, the work of Frank suggests that the potential employment losses associated with productivity growth and domestic demand shifts are some six to nine times greater than those generated by net expansions of foreign trade. A similar estimate was reported for West Germany (Wolter, 1976). Aggregative results of this type do tend to understate the probable adjustment burden. Evidence from countries such as Belgium (De Grauwe *et al.*, 1979) and the UK (Cable, 1982) suggests that imports from LDCs are characterised by a high unskilled labour content whereas advanced nation exports embody large amounts of physical and human capital. This implies that even a balanced trade expansion (i.e. simultaneous increase in imports and exports) will involve a net displacement of workers as labour shifts to the capital-intensive export sector. De Grauwe *et al.* suggest that the total number of workers required to shift would be nearly three times higher for a balanced trade expansion with LDCs as compared with advanced nations. This finding reinforces the important point that job gains and losses resulting from an increasing global division of labour do not occur on a one-for-one basis. In the poorest LDCs the displacement of one European Community worker is likely to create between 9 and 23 jobs while the replacement of a US worker might be expected to create between 13 and 33 positions (Lydall, 1975).

Further understatement of the restructuring costs of trade expansion with LDCs occurs when the sectoral specificity of adjustment is ignored. The work of Cable (1982) suggests that for the UK the most significant effects would be experienced in the sectors of textiles and clothing, footwear, leather goods and wood and furniture. World Bank projections of LDCs manufactured trade suggests that increased penetration will occur, in the next few years, in non-traditional areas, particularly engineering. Incremental employment growth will be lowest for unskilled and semi-skilled production workers (Balassa, 1981).

The above paragraph suggests that there may be a case for treating trade- and investment-impacted workers as a special case. Evidence from both Britain (Cable, 1982) and the US (Mitchell, 1976) indicates that such workers are likely to be predominantly manual, unskilled, and engaged in relatively low-wage occupations overrepresented among women. These characteristics are likely to be correlated with below average mobility. Furthermore, the industry-wide impact of trade and investment adjustment raises human capital investment losses and job search costs. Where employment declines are experienced by the majority of employers within an industry displaced workers face the loss of industry-specific training investments and the prospect of job search in a different industry (Hight, 1978).

Despite these considerations the US experience with selective assistance to trade-impacted workers throws doubts on any claim to special treatment. Trade adjustment assistance (TAA) was first authorised in the US by the 1962 Trade Expansion Act. For eligibility workers were required to demonstrate that the principal cause of their unemployment was the reduction of trade barriers. Some 48,000 workers were assisted between 1963 and 1975 (Mitchell, 1976). Workers assisted in this period appeared to display traits likely to be associated with adjustment difficulties (Bale, 1973; McCarthy, 1974). Considerable liberalisation of eligibility criteria occurred with the passing of the 1974 Trade

Act under which displaced workers had to show that increasing imports (not necessarily the result of a lowering of trade barriers) were a major (not necessarily the principal) cause of their unemployment. The effect of this was to increase considerably the number receiving assistance. In the fiscal year 1980, $1.6 billion was paid to 536,000 claimants (Rosenberg, 1983). Econometric research has indicated that the relaxation of eligibility criteria in 1974 led to a substantial change in the type of employee assisted. Increasingly, those receiving TAA were to be found in heavy durable manufacturing industries such as steel and automobiles which were badly affected by the recessionary conditions of the late 1970s and early 1980s. While TAA under the 1962 Act had the effect of increasing average employment duration this appeared to be spent in productive job search (Neumann, 1978). Those assisted after 1974 fell into two distinct groups. The first, and largest, comprising some 72 per cent of recipients, were found to be on temporary lay-off and resumed the same employment at the end of lay-off. These individuals suffered little in the way of earnings losses as a result of employment. Their losses were very similar to those incurred by recipients of unemployment insurance. The second group, those permanently displaced, suffered substantial earnings losses, and obtained little benefit from the employment services offered within TAA (Corson and Nicholson, 1981).

These studies raise three important points. Firstly, it is apparent that cost-effective assistance for trade- or investment-impacted workers requires a strict definition of the proposed target group. Liberalisation of criteria appears to lead to the inclusion of a large number of recession-impacted individuals, in the US case, those on temporary lay-off. Job search and mobility allowances are wasted on such individuals. Secondly, the employment service aspect of TAA appears inadequate for those individuals most severely affected, the permanently displaced. This suggests that assistance should pay greater attention to fostering positive adjustment. Thirdly, the US experience, certainly after 1974, suggests that there is no case for special treatment of trade-impacted displaced workers. Their problems and adjustment costs, certainly for the majority, do not differ significantly from those of the generally unemployed. This point would be reinforced by a firm commitment to positive restructuring creating an environment receptive to adjustment.

The views that trade-impacted workers do not justify special treatment (Magee, 1979) and the dangers of programme proliferation (National Association of Manufacturers', 1962) appear to have been accepted by current US policy makers. The gradual elimination of the TAA programme has seen an initial increase in qualification for eligibility, a tying of assistance to those already enrolled on an approved training course and finally a reallocation of expenditures towards all unemployed with an emphasis on training, relocation and job search assistance (Rosenberg, 1983).

The changing US position towards market-reliance and market-freeing assistance policies is duplicated in the British case with legislation limiting the power of trade unions (Taylor, 1983) and abolishing wages councils (Pond, 1983). Both policies are expected to facilitate restructuring through increased wage and labour flexibility. Reforms of this nature have received some support from recent OECD pronouncements on the need for positive adjustment policies (OECD, 1983). Such policies should ensure that assistance to structurally declining areas contributes to restructuring and is not considered as a source of rents by entrepreneurs or employees (Burton, 1979). Action, which should ideally be of a temporary nature, could be reduced progressively according to a predetermined timetable. Adoption of more positive adjustment policies could be encouraged by reform of Article XIX of GATT which provides for emergency controls on imports where serious injury is experienced by domestic producers. The present form of this Article encourages purely defensive action. Suggestions for reform (Tumlir, 1974) have concentrated on linking emergency action to a commitment to positive adjustment.

More ambitious suggestions for reform, particularly those implying that trade- and investment-induced adjustment presents distinct problems, are unlikely to be received sympathetically at the present time. the ICFTU has proposed the development of an International Reconversion Fund designed to cover rationalisation and restructuring costs of trade-affected industries in the advanced nations. The contribution of particular nations to the Fund would be positively related to total and *per capita* national income and negatively to share of LDC manufactures in total imports. Such a Fund would encourage positive adjustment in two main ways. Firstly, restrictive import controls would be made less attractive where adjustment costs are partially funded externally. Secondly, since individual contributions are inversely related to LDC import penetration, encouragement is given to import absorption. Such a scheme could be extended to encompass DFI-induced adjustment but is unlikely to be given serious consideration at the present time.

This section has necessarily been restricted to a consideration of trade-impacted adjustment. Even if one accepts the role played by MNEs in the increased export of manufactures from LDCs the adjustment burden created by export platform investments appears extremely insignificant. Unfortunately, there has been little useful research on the extent to which outward investment displaces domestic employment. However, the discussion of Chapter 3 implied that the degree of substitutability between domestic and overseas production was limited in the general case. This would suggest that the employment dislocation effects of DFI are limited. Clearly, this conclusion may be invalidated by systematic investigation of this question and by the possibility that the skill mismatch in source nations resulting from MNE operations may exacerbate labour market bottlenecks (Frank and Freeman, 1978b).

Host Nation Policy

Three major policy implications arise in the case of host nations. For advanced host economies a major problem in recent years has been the high divestment rates of MNEs. For LDC hosts a recurring question has been the feasibility of alternatives to the MNE or, at least, the extraction of increased development stimulus from the operations of MNEs.

It is unclear whether the high divestment rates exhibited by MNEs in recent years are likely to be a transitory or permanent feature of multinational business. High and rising rates of corporate failure and labour shedding have been symptomatic of the economic difficulties of the last few years. Despite the very diverse motives for disinvestment there is some evidence that the recession has forced a reconsideration of market servicing postures within Europe, particularly for US MNEs (Hood and Young, 1982). The selectivity of rationalisation is also suggestive of powerful underlying structural pressures.

For policy purposes a useful distinction may be drawn between short-term and long-term investment instability. The principal source of short-term instability is commercial non-viability. A variety of factors have been associated with voluntary disinvestment in the longer term. Poor performance, as reflected by an inadequate return on investment, or excessive demands on management time and capital inputs are the most frequently cited factors. Environmental factors, including host-government pressures, poor market prospects and small size, are also important.

Host nation policy towards divestment is likely to focus on both anticipation and management of the divestment process. Empirical analysis indicates several factors that appear crucial in both the deter- mination and timing of disinvestment decisions. Interesting evidence emerges on the role of government grants and financial inducements to DFI. The withdrawal of such inducements does not appear to prompt disinvestment (Sachdev, 1975). This finding could be explained if it is accepted that commercially viable projects should not be jeopardised by the withdrawal of such aid, particularly if the grants accurately reflect break-even subsidies (Ashcroft and Ingham, 1979; Yannopoulos and Dunning, 1976).

A number of studies have highlighted the importance of source country influences in the timing of action. There is some evidence that recent unsatisfactory corporate financial performance in the source nation may be an important trigger to the disinvestment process (Hood and Young, 1980; Torneden, 1975). It is not clear whether the motive for this is to release resources to allow for increased attention to be paid to source nation difficulties, or because unprofitable affiliates cannot be maintained under such conditions. The latter is intuitively more appealing.Thus disinvestment is unlikely to provide a panacea for parent company problems in most situations. It may occur, however, in cases where subsidiary operations are a drain on corporate resources. The disinvestment decision may be based on the unprofitability of overseas operations but the timing of that decision may be prompted by domestic difficulties. This implies that the likelihood of disinvest- ment is probably greatest when domestic and subsidiary operations experience difficulties simultaneously. This view that loss-making over- seas operations may be carried is reinforced by Toreden's findings that disinvestments are often preceded by key management changes in the parent corporation. An individual not involved in the initial acquisition or establishment decision may see the need for divestment or be polit- ically able to take such a decision.

The difficulties of predicting disinvestment are indicated by findings that such decisions are invariably taken by top management in the source nation. Few firms appear to consider pre-disinvestment discussion with host government representatives (Torneden, 1975). This is reported of US firms in particular, who discount the usefulness of government assistance proposals or see such suggestions as likely to restrict their manoeuvrability (Boddewyn, 1979). Despite the apparent remoteness of decision-making some indications of impending disin- vestment may be detected. The disinvestment decision is one charac- terised by a comparatively long gestation period. There is, on average, a time lapse of some six months between the suggestion of disinvestment and commitment to it. Implementation may take a further 24 months (Torneden, 1975). This period is likely to witness visits to the subsidiary by parent company experts, the granting of 'recovery' periods, or the use of intermediaries such as bankers and consultants. Whilst US firms appear most impatient in their financial performance expectations they may be more willing to utilise expert intermediaries (Boddewyn, 1979). These findings offer a number of suggestions for the design of policy towards inward investment.

Firstly, there is a need for commercial viability to be explicitly incorporated into the investment evaluation process. Whilst this should form an initial stage of evaluation for any agency there are two important factors which need stressing. One is that when financial assistance is offered there is likely to be a divergence between private and total cost. Where this divergence is substantial the appraisal of risk by the private investor may be heavily discounted. Government assistance provides a form of risk underwriting. This reinforces the need for commercial assessment by the sponsoring agency. This does not necessarily imply that projects which would not be commercially viable in the absence of state aid should be rejected. There may be a case for assisting projects to become commercially viable, particularly if there are substantial benefits likely to accrue to the host economy. The other factor is the rising concern with employment creation objectives. This, in the context of the economic decline of peripheral regions in a number of host economies, may influence the evaluation process and lead to giving undue weight to the employment effects of an investment project. This could result in a superficial evaluation of the full costs and benefits of the project.

Secondly, attention should focus on the form and method of administration of incentives. Thus generous export profit tax allowances discriminate in favour of export-oriented branch plants and may discourage local linkages. Although stability may be encouraged by the development of domestic linkages the way this is achieved appears critical. More success is likely to be achieved by a policy of attracting compatible industries than by, for example, imposition of minority ownership requirements. There is evidence that if firms are denied their preferred location choices the alternative may be no investment at all (Buckley, Hartley and Sparkes, 1980). Similarly, difficulties with joint-venture partners constitute a source of disinvestment pressure (Hood and Young, 1980; Sachdev, 1975).

Thirdly, the above analysis has highlighted the stability advantages which follow from a selective approach to DFI. Selection should focus on attracting industries with growth potential and not those entering the maturity stage of their life-cycle where cost pressures may necessitate relocation to Third World sites. Selection should also be based on an evaluation of the comparative advantages of a host region.

Finally, the centralisation of divestment decisions within MNEs indicates the considerable benefits which might accrue to host government representatives in the management of divestment disruptions where prior notification is a mandatory requirement. Clearly, the provisions envisaged within the original formulation of the Vredeling Directive could offer substantial advantages for both labour and government representatives.

For less developed host economies there is a general preoccupation with increasing the benefits obtainable from DFI. The discussion of Chapter 3 suggests that DFI might bring shallow development where local linkages are poor, training benefits are not widely diffused or inappropriate technologies are employed. The importance of the competitive pressure faced by MNE subsidiaries as a stimulus to development was also stressed. Two main courses of action suggest themselves. The first concerns the attraction of alternatives to DFI or the 'unbundling' of the package of assets (management, capital, technology, etc.) transferred within the MNE. The second focuses on raising the relative bargaining power of LDC governments in their dealings with MNE investors.

Breaking up of the bundle of assets transferred within the MNE investment package may assume a variety of forms including joint ventures, technical collaboration in the form of licensing, and management contracts. These alternative arrangements are most fully developed in the resource field. The possibilities of unbundling are revealed by DFI where capital is raised locally, implying the profitable separation of at least this element (Casson, 1979). Untying the MNE package offers two principal benefits to LDC hosts. Firstly, by encouraging more effective competition among suppliers, and even increasing the number of potential suppliers, the cost of externally provided development packages may be substantially reduced. Furthermore, the supply of alternative modes may constitute a competitive stimulus to incumbent MNEs. Secondly, reconstitution of the elements of the package by the host nation offers benefits of learning by doing and the opportunity to increase positive development externalities.

Studies of MNEs producing in the LDCs suggest that the more technologically sophisticated enterprises are often unwilling to disassemble their asset packages (Frank, 1980). The major reasons cited for this reluctance include the likelihood of insufficient revenue (appropriability problem), the difficulty of maintaining quality where branded technology is transferred, the danger that new competition will be established and the belief that certain elements are inseparable. The widespread existence of subcontracting arrangements suggests that at least technology and marketing skills may be in joint supply (Casson, 1979). The appropriation problem and danger of licensee competition imply that suppliers will impose conditions protective of their monopoly assets. The most widespread restrictive terms relate to limitations on the production and marketing locations open to licensees as well as the licensors' right to incremental improvements on imported technologies (UNCTAD, 1974). Other devices, particularly prevalent in the case of 'core' technologies (Casson, 1979), include the engineering of technological indivisibility and over-specification (Hoogvelt, 1982). The reluctance of many MNEs to license technology, and the unattractive terms often attached to licensing agreements, suggests the value of investigating alternative sources of supply. Non-multinational firms represent one alternative. Analysis of the Indian case suggests that such firms are often more willing to supply technology and may provide it at lower cost (Alam and Langrish, 1981). Cost savings may be possible where non-branded technologies are provided. Offsetting this potential saving are the higher search costs incurred in identifying the less prestigious enterprises able to supply non-proprietary technologies.

It is not clear that unbundling represents a cost effective alternative to DFI (Bardhan, 1982). The financing of projects may be easier to achieve where foreign investors have an equity share. Many LDCs lack the requisite skills effectively to co-ordinate all the elements of the investment package and any short-term cost gains may be eclipsed by the discouragement of long-term relationships between MNEs and LDCs. Furthermore, it is debatable whether LDCs are 'overcharged' for technology within the typical DFI package. Because LDCs display a relatively elastic demand for imported technologies discriminating MNE monopolists will charge them a lower than average price (Johnson, 1970). The higher transfer resource costs entailed in technology licensing impose welfare losses on both licensee and licensor nations (Caves, Crookell and Killing, 1983). There is also evidence that licensed technologies tend to be older than those transferred to LDCs through subsidiary production (Mansfield and Romeo, 1980).

International licensing could be encouraged by reform of the patent system (Casson, 1979). Magee (1977b) has suggested the introduction of legal guarantees granting international temporal monopolies over product and process technologies. Simple patents of limited duration, obtainable at low cost, would encourage the development and transfer of less complex technologies by MNEs, partially overcoming the appropriability problem which encourages firms to concentrate on the most sophisticated technologies. A significant labour market benefit of such reform would be the increased likelihood of appropriate (labour-intensive) technologies becoming available to those LDCs unable profitably to absorb more advanced processes. Indeed, the ability of recipient LDCs to benefit from control over the reconstitution of components of the DFI package is a critical constraint on the use of licensing. Where LDCs lack the capability to derive learning advantages from the restructuring of imported technologies there may be a case for allowing DFI. Over time, the opportunities for converting DFI packages to contractual licensing or subcontracting modes increase as operating procedures become standardised and skills more widely diffused (Casson, 1979).

The limitations to attempts to break up the DFI package, particularly the considerable imperfection within the market for technology, suggest the utility of less ambitious proposals focusing on increasing the relative bargaining strength of LDCs and the degree of effective competition faced by MNE subsidiaries.

A major problem facing host governments is the fact that their relative bargaining power *vis-à-vis* MNEs is likely to be lowest at the entry negotiation stage. As the MNE commits resources, as operations become increasingly standardised and host government familiarity with the activities of MNEs rises, the balance of power shifts in favour of the host nation. Vernon (1971) has characterised this problem in terms of the 'obsolescing bargain'. As negotiating advantage changes over the project life cycle renegotiation becomes increasingly attractive to the host state (Stoever, 1979). The problems of a weak host bargaining position and MNE protection from vigorous competition are related. Where governments hold a poor bargaining position they may be forced to concede to MNE demands for market protection. Empirical studies of relative bargaining strength suggest that the MNE's position will be stronger where it is in possession of complex technologies characterised by extensive product diversity and differentiation and where it retains control over market access (Fagre and Wells, 1981). Where there are alternative sources of investment funds or potential suppliers of technology the MNE's position is substantially weakened. This weakening of position is likely to be reflected in a lower return on investment. Support for this hypothesis is to be found in historical data for UK overseas investment indicating that a higher return was obtained on capital invested in colonised LDCs than on investments outside the British Empire (Svedberg, 1982). The rise of alternative DFI sources, particularly Japan and a number of rapidly developing LDCs, suggests that in recent years host governments may have experienced a strengthening of their bargaining power. Unfortunately, the significant decline in overseas investment rates during the present recession has increased the degree of competition between potential hosts with some inflation of incentives proferred to MNEs (OECD, 1983). This is an area whether further investigation, particularly on the sensitivity of DFI to incentives, is urgently required. The limited evidence available for LDCs suggests that the effectiveness of fiscal incentives is slight (Shah and Toye, 1978) or non-existent (Lim, 1983). If this is true fiscal provisions provide only a source of rent to inward investors. Research in this area may be usefully complemented by the work of the UN Centre on Transnational Corporations in advising and training LDC host governments in business-government neogtiations.

Implications for the Labour Movement

Our analysis has raised a number of important implications for labour. In summary, we have argued that effective labour responses to the MNE are unlikely to develop in the near future, at the international level. The obstacles to multinational collective bargaining are formidable and are reinforced by consideration of managerial strategies with regard to labour force cohesion. However, as Ulman (1975) argues it is not sufficient to explain the general absence of multinational bargaining simply in terms of the impediments it faces. Rather, we have argued that multinationalisation of business has severly weakened the bargaining power of a number of integrated MNEs. These enterprises appear vulnerable to plant- and company-based bargaining overtures.

For organised labour strategies need to be reformulated in a number of ways. Firstly, a more professional approach is required. In particular, responses to the MNE should be underpinned by conceptual understanding of the dynamics of international business. We have argued, in a number of places, that the eclectic approach offers a useful vehicle for such analysis. Secondly, one advantage of conceptualisation of the issues raised by MNEs would be the opportunity for developing anticipatory labour strategies. It is important that labour organisations increasingly assume the initiative in negotiating with the MNE. Analysis of the changing global distribution of comparative advantage would enable identification of those sectors sensitive to multinationalisation and import competition. The work of institutions like the World Bank suggests the significant changes that are likely to occur in the world economy over the next few years. Increasingly, labour difficulties will be experienced in the non-traditional manufacturing industries and even in service sectors where producers are increasingly turning to international subcontracting arrangements, e.g. publishing and retail clothing multiples. Thirdly, there is a need for considerable re-orientation of the focus of union action towards the MNE. Our analysis suggests a two-tier approach with a continuing role for ITSs, particularly enterprise-specific world councils. Their principal contribution would be one of information assimilation and analysis and as a bargaining agent for those sectors facing a weak negotiating position at the national level. Complementing the role of ITSs would be a strengthening of national union representation of MNE employees. As MNEs have pursued decentralisation of bargaining structures within particular host and source nations the need for labour combine committees, encompassing employee representatives within individual plants of specific MNEs, has increased. There is a need for consolidation of these developments and increased professionalism in their dealings with MNEs.

Unfortunately, recent trends in strategies and priorities discernible within the international labour movement do not suggest that the areas we have stressed are likely to receive favourable consideration in the near future. In recent years recessionary pressures have reduced the power of individal unions and impeded the development of international union co-operation. The result has been a consolidation of action within national union centres (e.g. TUC, AFL-CIO, DGB, etc.) at the expense of ITSs. This development helps to explain the increasing resort labour has made to national and regional political solutions (Busch, 1983). Adoption of the strategies suggested in this book would thus necessitate a substantial and positive reorientation of union thinking. Given the pressures facing the labour movements of most economies in the present recession the issues raised by MNEs are unlikely to be accorded great priority. However, as recessionary conditions ease these questions will assume increasing significance. Hopefully, reconsideration of labour responses might occur at that time.

In our evaluation of the labour problems generated by multinational business, information deficiencies and remoteness of decision-making consistently emerge as major issues facing the labour movement. As Chapter 6 indicated the principal initiatives in this area have occurred within the umbrella of voluntary codes of conduct for MNEs. The most significant impending developments are contained within proposals being pursued by the European Community. Unfortunately, from the point of view of labour, little reliance should be placed on these initiatives. Despite their systematic weakening in progress through the Community's legislative structure considerable opposition remains. At the time of writing (November 1983) British resistance suggests the likelihood of considerable delay and opposition to both the draft Vredeling Directive and Fifth Directive on harmonisation of company law. The British position (*British Business*, 1983) emphasises the voluntary promotion of employee involvement in consultation and decision-making and stresses the cumbersome nature of European Community legislation in this area. This suggests that labour will continue to experience information difficulties in bargaining with MNEs. Empirical evidence on information disclosure indicates that where national legislation is ineffectual disclosure remains underdeveloped. Even where employees enjoy rights to specific information problems may persist. In Germany, a nation where employees enjoy considerable access to information and decision-makers, survey evidence revealed that only 4 per cent of respondents felt sufficiently well informed about plant closures and relocations (Hartmann and Marsh, 1983). This suggests that national legislation is unlikely to provide the type of information that employees need in dealing with MNEs, reinforcing the role for union initiatives in this area.

Conclusions and Further Research

In conclusion we may reconsider the major research questions set out in Chapter 1. Firstly, our analysis, and particularly the data examined in Chapter 2, confirms that MNEs have played a major role in the changing international division of labour. This role has been a direct one where enterprises have invested in overseas production facilities. A number of MNEs now service demand in advanced economies from LDC based export platforms. An indirect role is also discernible. Here the competitive pressures provided by MNEs have forced restructuring within uninational enterprises. This reorganisation has assumed a variety of forms including labour displacing capital investment, the introduction of more flexible working practices and international subcontracting. These pressures have been accentuated by the growth of European and Japanese overseas investment. However, it is important to recognise that internationalisation of the world economy comprises more than just the operations of MNEs. Technological dependency and the truncation of national industries like computers, which rely on vital inputs from overseas, are likely to exist even in the absence of MNEs (Cox, 1982).

Secondly, the concentration of DFI by industry and area, particularly in respect of export-oriented Third World investments, creates the need for adjustment in the advanced nations. This adjustment has been achieved most easily within those sectors dominated by MNEs. Restructuring has exhibited a number of forms including further internationalisation, increased automation and concessionary bargaining. Those sectors badly affected by rising import penetration, including textiles, clothing and footwear, have pursued political solutions to their problems, solutions which have too often discouraged positive adjustment.

Thirdly, the potential instability of overseas investment was examined. Divestment has been an issue of pressing concern in a number of advanced host economies. It is unclear whether this development is solely the result of the present recession or whether divestment forms a conscious element of corporate strategy for MNEs. This is an area where further research is needed.

Fourthly, our analysis of the labour market effects of DFI within LDCs was subject to a number of limitations. Opportunities for increasing the development impact were apparent in a number of areas. More controversy surrounds the question of what constitutes appropriate technologies for LDCs. Further investigation of the short- and long-term employment effects of different technologies would be useful. A similar controversy surrounds the longer-term developmental effects of DFI. The implication of neoclassical models, that the accumulation of overseas capital creates opportunities for self-sustaining development through technological progress and productivity growth (Frankel, 1965), has been disputed by dependency theorists (Bornschier, 1980). Again, this vital question has received insufficient attention.

Fifthly, our reconsideration of the effects of MNEs on labour's relative bargaining power cautions against the dangers of generalisation. It is possible that in a number of cases labour enjoys a strong position in its dealings with MNEs. At this stage we have only been able to offer a variety of indirect evidence in support of this hypothesis and clearly it requires direct testing.

Sixthly, our discussion of the spillover effects of DFI suggests that these have been significant. In the LDCs training investments and management education have been increased by the presence of MNEs. However, there appear to be a number of areas where these positive externalities might be enhanced. Within the advanced host nations many of the innovative labour practices pioneered by MNEs have been readily absorbed despite some suspicion on the part of organised labour.

An obvious limitation to our analysis is the underdevelopment of the theoretical labour market and policy implications of the emerging eclectic model of international business. In a number of places we have been forced to rely on the theoretical guidance offered by general equilibrium models of international trade. Not only are such models based on unhelpful assumptions about the operations of MNEs, it is impossible to reconcile this approach with the eclectic model. Hopefully, further work within the eclectic paradigm will allow progress in analysing the labour market effects of MNEs. A fruitful area for further work is suggested by the compatibility between the internalisation concept and the development of internal labour markets. In addition, more research is urgently required on the twin problems of investment- and export-substitution which represent fundamental questions facing systematic research in this area.

Overall, our analysis lends considerable support to the view that multinational labour relations represent an extension in scope and complexity rather than a departure in terms of character (Weinberg, 1975b). The labour issues generated by MNEs primarily represent quantitative rather than qualitative differences.

APPENDIX 1: INTERNATIONAL LABOUR ORGANISA-TION — TRIPARTITE DECLARATION OF PRINCIPLES CONCERNING MULTINATIONAL ENTERPRISES AND SOCIAL POLICY (adopted by the Governing Body of the International Labour Office, November 1977)

The Governing Body of the International Labour Office;

Recalling that the International Labour Organisation for many years has been involved with certain social issues related to the activities of multinational enterprises;

Noting in particular that various Industrial Committees, Regional Conferences, and the International Labour Conference since the mid-1960s have requested appropriate action by the Governing Body in the field of multinational enterprises and social policy;

Having been informed of the activities of other international bodies, in particular the UN Commission on Transnational Corporations and the Organisation for Economic Co-operation and Development (OECD);

Considering that the ILO, with its unique tripartite structure, its competence, and its longstanding experience in the social field, has an essential role to play in evolving principles for the guidance of governments, workers' and employers' organisations, and multinational enterprises themselves;

Recalling that it convened a Tripartite Meeting of Experts on the Relationship between Multinational Enterprises and Social Policy in 1972, which recommended an ILO programme of research and study, and a Tripartite Advisory Meeting on the Relationship of Multinational Enterprises and Social Policy in 1976 for the purpose of reviewing the ILO programme of research and suggesting appropriate ILO action in the social and labour field;

Bearing in mind the deliberations of the World Employment Conference;

Having thereafter decided to establish a tripartite group to prepare a Draft Tripartite Declaration of Principles covering all of the areas of ILO concern which relate to the social aspects of the activities of multinational enterprises, including employment creation in the developing countries, all the while bearing in mind the recommendations made by the Tripartite Advisory Meeting held in 1976;

175

Having also decided to reconvene the Tripartite Advisory Meeting to consider the Draft Declaration of Principles as prepared by the tripartite group;

Having considered the Report and the Draft Declaration of Principles submitted to it by the reconvened Tripartite Advisory Meeting;

Hereby approves the following Declaration which may be cited as the Tripartite Declaration of Principles concerning Multinational Enterprises and Social Policy, adopted by the Governing Body of the International Labour Office, and invites governments of States Members of the ILO, the employers' and workers' organisations concerned and the multinational enterprises operating in their territories to observe the principles embodied therein.

1   Multinational enterprises play an important part in the economies of most countries and in international economic relations. This is of increasing interest to governments as well as to employers and workers and their respective organisations. Through international direct investment and other means such enterprises can bring substantial benefits to home and host countries by contributing to the more efficient utilisation of capital, technology and labour. Within the framework of development policies established by governments, they can also make an important contribution to the promotion of economic and social welfare; to the improvement of living standards and the satisfaction of basic needs; to the creation of employment opportunities, both directly and indirectly; and to the enjoyment of basic human rights, including freedom of association, throughout the world. On the other hand, the advances made by multinational enterprises in organising their operations beyond the national framework may lead to abuse of concentrations of economic power and to conflicts with national policy objectives and with the interest of the workers. In addition, the complexity of multinational enterprises and the difficulty of clearly perceiving their diverse structures, operations and policies sometimes give rise to concern either in the home or in the host countries, or in both.

2   The aim of this Tripartite Declaration of Principles is to encourage the positive contribution which multinational enterprises can make to economic and social progress and to minimise and resolve the difficulties to which their various operations may give rise, taking into account the United Nations resolutions advocating the Establishment of a New International Economic Order.

3   This aim will be furthered by appropriate laws and policies, measures and actions adopted by the governments and by co-operation among the governments and the employers' and workers' organisations of all countries.

4   The principles set out in this Declaration are commended to the governments, the employers' and workers' organisations of home and host countries and to the multinational enterprises themselves.

5   These principles are intended to guide the governments, the employers' and workers' organisations and the multinational enterprises in taking such measures andd actions and adopting such social policies, including those based on the principles laid down in the Constitution and the relevant Conventions and Recommendations of the ILO, as would further social progress.

6   To serve its purpose this Declaration does not require a precise legal definition of multinational enterprises; this paragraph is designed to facilitate the understanding of the Declaration and not to provide such a definition. Multinational enterprises include enterprises, whether they are of public, mixed or private ownership, which own or control production, distribution, services or other facilities outside the country in which they are based. The degree of autonomy of entities within multinational enterprises in relation to each other varies widely from one such enterprise to another, depending on the nature of the links between such entities and their fields of activity and having regard to the great diversity in the form of ownership, in the size, in the nature and location of the operations of the enterprises concerned. Unless otherwise specified, the term 'multinational enterprise' is used in this Declaration to designate the various entities (parent companies or local entities or both or the organisation as a whole) according to the distribution of responsibilities among them, in the expectation that they will co-operate and provide assistance to one another as necessary to facilitate observance of the principles laid down in the Declaration.

7   This Declaration sets out principles in the fields of employment, training, conditions of work and life and industrial relations which governments, employers' and workers' organisations and multinational enterprises are recommended to observe on a voluntary basis; its provisions shall not limit or otherwise affect obligations arising out of ratification of any ILO Convention.

General policies

8   All the parties concerned by this Declaration should respect the sovereign rights of States, obey the national laws and regulations, give due consideration to local practices and respect relevant international standards. They should respect the Universal Declaration of Human Rights and the corresponding International Covenants adopted by the General Assembly of the United Nations as well as the Constitution of the International Labour Organisation and its principles according to which freedom of expression and association are essential to sustained progress. They should also honour commitments which they have freely entered into, in conformity with the national law and accepted international obligations.

9   Governments which have not yet ratified Conventions Nos. 87, 98, 111 and 122 are urged to do so and in any event to apply, to the greatest extent possible, through their national policies, the principles embodied therein and in Recommendations Nos. 111, 119 and 122.[1] Without prejudice to the obligation of governments to ensure compliance with Conventions they have ratified, in countries in which the Conventions and Recommendations cited in this paragraph are not complied with, all parties should refer to them for guidance in their social policy.

10   Multinational enterprises should take fully into account established general policy objectives of the countries in which they operate. Their activities should be in harmony with the development priorities and social aims and structure of the country in which they operate. To this effect, consultations should be held between multinational enterprises, the government and, wherever appropriate, the national employers' and workers' organisations concerned.

11   The principles laid down in this Declaration do not aim at introducing or maintaining inequalities of treatment between multinational and national enterprises. They reflect good practice for all. Multinational and national enterprises, wherever the principles of this Declaration are relevant to both, should be subject to the same expectations in respect of their conduct in general and their social practices in particular.

12   Governments of home countries should promote good social practice in accordance with this Declaration of Principles, having regard to the social and labour law, regulations and practices in host countries

as well as to relevant international standards. Both host and home country governments should be prepared to have consultations with each other, whenever the need arises, on the initiative of either.

Employment

Employment promotion

13   With a view to stimulating economic growth and development, raising living standards, meeting manpower requirements and over-coming unemployment and underemployment, governments should declare and pursue, as a major goal, an active policy designed to promote full, productive and freely-chosen employment.[2]

14   This is particularly important in the case of host country governments in developing areas of the world where the problems of unemployment and underemployment are at their most serious. In this connection, the general conclusions adopted by the Tripartite World Conference on Employment, Income Distribution and Social Progress and the International Division of Labour (Geneva, June 1976) should be kept in mind.[3]

15   Paragraphs 13 and 14 above establish the framework within which due attention should be paid, in both home and host countries, to the employment impact of multinational enterprises.

16   Multinational enterprises, particularly when operating in developing countries, should endeavour to increase employment opportunities and standares, taking into account the employment policies and objectives of the governments, as well as security of employment and the long-term development of the enterprise.

17   Before starting operations, multinational enterprises should wherever appropriate, consult the competent authorities and the national employers' and workers' organisations in order to keep their manpower plans, as far as practicable, in harmony with national social development policies. Such consultation, as in the case of national enterprises, should continue between the multinational enterprises and all parties concerned, including the workers' organisations.

18   Multinational enterprises should give priority to the employment, occupational development, promotion and advancement of nationals of the host country at all levels in co-operation, as appropriate, with representatives of the workers employed by them or of the organisa-

tions of these workers and governmental authorities.

19   Multinational enterprises, when investing in developing countries, should have regard to the importance of using technologies which generate employment, both directly and indirectly. To the extent permitted by the nature of the process and the conditions prevailing in the economic sector concerned, they should adapt technologies to the needs and characteristics of the host countries. They should also, where possible, take part in the development of appropriate technology in host countries.

20   To promote employment in developing countries, in the context of an expanding world economy, multinational enterprises, wherever practicable, should give consideration to the conclusion of contracts with national enterprises for the manufacture of parts and equipment, to the use of local raw materials and to the progressive promotion of the local processing of raw materials. Such arrangements should not be used by multinational enterprises to avoid the responsibilities embodied in the principles of this Declaration.

Equality of opportunity and treatment

21   All governments should pursue policies designed to promote equality of opportunity and treatment in employment, with a view to eliminating any discrimination based on race, colour, sex, religion, political opinion, national extraction or social origin.[4]

22   Multinational enterprises should be guided by this general principle throughout their operations without prejudice to the measures envisaged in paragraph 18 or to government policies designed to correct historical patterns of discrimination and thereby to extend equality of opportunity and treatment in employment. Multinational enterprises should accordingly make qualifications, skill and experience the basis for the recruitment, placement, training and advancement of their staff at all levels.

23   Governments should never require or encourage multinational enterprises to discriminate on any of the grounds mentioned in paragraph 21, and continuing guidance from governments, where appropriate, on the avoidance of such discrimination in employment is encouraged.

Security of employment

24   Governments should carefully study the impact of multinational

enterprises on employment in different industrial sectors. Governments as well as multinational enterprises themselves, in all countries should take suitable measures to deal with the employment and labour market impacts of the operations of multinational enterprises.

25   Multinational enterprises equally with national enterprises, through active manpower planning, should endeavour to provide stable employment for their employees and should observe freely-negotiated obligations concerning employment stability and social security. In view of the flexibility which multinational enterprises may have, they should strive to assume a leading role in promoting security of employment, particularly in countries where the discontinuation of operations is likely to accentuate long-term unemployment.

26   In considering changes in operations (including those resulting from mergers, take-overs or transfers of production) which would have major employment effects, multinational enterprises should provide reasonable notice of such changes to the appropriate government authorities and representatives of the workers in their employment and their organisations so that the implications may be examined jointly in order to mitigate adverse effects to the greatest possible extent. This is particularly important in the case of the closure of an entity involving collective lay-offs or dismissals.

27   Arbitrary dismissal procedures should be avoided.[5]

28   Governments, in co-operation with multinational as well as national enterprises, should provide some form of income protection for workers whose employment has been terminated.[6]

Training

29   Governments, in co-operation with all the parties concerned, should develop national policies for vocational training and guidance, closely linked with employment.[2] This is the framework within which multinational enterprises should pursue their training policies.

30   In their operations, multinational enterprises should ensure that relevant training is provided for all levels of their employees in the host country, as appropriate, to meet the needs of the enterprise as well as the development policies of the country. Such training should, to the extent possible, develop generally useful skills and promote career

opportunities. This responsibility should be carried out, where appropriate, in co-operation with the authorities of the country, employers' and workers' organisations and the competent local, national or international institutions.

31   Multinational enterprises operating in developing countries should participate, along with national enterprises, in programmes, including special funds, encouraged by host governments and supported by employers' and workers' organisations. These programmes should have the aim of encouraging skill forrmation and development as well as providing vocational guidance, and should be jointly administered by the parties which support them. Wherever practicable, multinational enterprises should make the services of skilled resource personnel available to help in training programmes organised by governments as part of a contribution to national development.

32   Multinational enterprises, with the co-operation of governments and to the extent consistent with the efficient operation of the enterprise, should afford opportunities within the enterprise as a whole to broaden the experience of local management in suitable fields such as industrial relations.

Conditions of work and life

Wages, benefits and conditions of work

33   Wages, benefits and conditions of work offered by multinational enterprises should be not less favourable to the workers than those offered by comparable employers in the country concerned.

34   When multinational enterprises operate in developing countries, where comparable employers may not exist, they should provide the best possible wages, benefits and conditions of work, within the framework of government policies.[7] These should be related to the economic position of the enterprise, but should be at least adequate to satisfy basic needs of the workers and their families. Where they provide workers with basic amenities such as housing, medical care or food, these amenities should be of a good standard.[8]

35   Governments, especially in developing countries, should endeavour to adopt suitable measures to ensure that lower income groups and less developed areas benefit as much as possible from the activities of multinational enterprises.

Safety and health

36   Governments should ensure that both multinational and national enterprises provide adequate safety and health standards for their employees. Those governments which have not yet ratified the ILO Conventions on Guarding of Machinery (No. 119), Ionising Radiation (No. 115), Benzene (No. 136) and Occupational Cancer (No. 139) are urged nevertheless to apply to the greatest extent possible the principles embodied in these Conventions and in their related Recommendations (Nos. 118, 114, 144 and 147). The Codes of Practice and Guides in the current list of ILO publications on Occupational Safety and Health should also be taken into account.[9]

37   Multinational enterprises should maintain the highest standards of safety and health, in conformity with national requirements, bearing in mind their relevant experience within the enterprise as a whole, including any knowledge of special hazards. They should also make available to the representatives of the workers in the enterprise, and upon request, to the competent authorities and the workers' and employers' organisations in all countries in which they operate, information on the safety and health standards relevant to their local operations, which they observe in other countries. In particular, they should make known to those concerned any special hazards and related protective measures associated with new products and processes. They, like comparable domestic enterprises, should be expected to play a leading role in the examination of causes of industrial safety and health hazards and in the application of resulting improvements within the enterprise as a whole.

38   Multinational enterprises should co-operate in the work of international organisations concerned with the preparation and adoption of international safety and health standards.

39   In accordance with national practice, multinational enterprises should co-operate fully with the competent safety and health authorities, the representatives of the workers and their organisations, and established safety and health organisations. Where appropriate, matters relating to safety and health should be incorporated in agreements with the representatives of the workers and their organisations.

Industrial relations

40   Multinational enterprises should observe standards of industrial relations not less favourable than those observed by comparable employers in the country concerned.

Freedom of association and the right to organise

41   Workers employed by multinational enterprises as well as those employed by national enterprises should, without distinction whatsoever, have the right to establish and, subject only to the rules of the organisation concerned, to join organisations of their own choosing without previous authorisation.[10] They should also enjoy adequate protection against acts of anti-union discrimination in respect of their employment.[11]

42   Organisations representing multinational enterprises or the workers in their employment should enjoy adequate protection against any acts of interference by each other or each other's agents or members in their establishment, functioning or administration.[12]

43   Where appropriate, in the local circumstances, multinational enterprises should support representative employers' organisations.

44   Governments, where they do not already do so, are urged to apply the principles of Convention No. 87, Article 5, in view of the importance, in relation to multinational enterprises, of permitting organisations representing such enterprises or the workers in their employment to affiliate with international organisations of employers and workers of their own choosing.

45   Where governments of host countries offer special incentives to attract foreign investment, these incentives should not include any limitation of the workers' freedom of association or the right to organise and bargain collectively.

46   Representatives of the workers in multinational enterprises should not be hindered from meeting for consultation and exchange of view among themselves, provided that the functioning of the operations of the enterprise and the normal procedures which govern relationships with representatives of the workers and their organisations are not thereby prejudiced.

47   Governments should not restrict the entry of representatives of employers' and workers' organisations who come from other countries

at the invitation of the local or national organisations concerned for the purpose of consultation on matters of mutual concern, solely on the grounds that they seek entry in that capacity.

Collective bargaining

48   Workers employed by multinational enterprises should have the right, in accordance with national law and practice, to have representative organisations of their own choosing recognised for the purpose of collective bargaining.

49   Measures appropriate to national conditions should be taken, where necessary, to encourage and promote the full development and utilisation of machinery for voluntary negotiation between employers or employers' organisations and workers' organisations, with a view to the regulation of terms and conditions of employment by means of collective agreements.[13]

50   Multinational enterprises, as well as national enterprises, should provide workers' representatives with such facilities as may be necessary to assist in the development of effective collective agreements.[14]

51   Multinational enterprises should enable duly authorised representatives of the workers in their employment in each of the countries in which they operate to conduct negotiations with representatives of management who are authorised to take decisions on the matters under negotiation.

52   Multinational enterprises, in the context of bona fide negotiations with the workers' representatives on conditions of employment, or while workers are exercising the right to organise, should not threaten to utilise a capacity to transfer the whole or part of an operating unit from the country concerned in order to influence unfairly those negotiations or to hinder the exercise of the right to organise; nor should they transfer workers from affiliates in foreign countries with a view to undermining bona fide negotiations with the workers' representatives or the workers' exercise of their right to organise.

53   Collective agreements should include provisions for the settlement of disputes arising over their interpretation and application and for ensuring mutually respected rights and responsibilities.

54   Multinational enterprises should provide workers' representatives with information required for meaningful negotiations with the entity involved and, where this accords with local law and practices, should

also provide information to enable them to obtain a true and fair view of the performance of the entity or, where appropriate, of the enterprise as a whole.[15]

55   Governments should supply to the representatives of workers' organisations on request, where law and practice so permit, information on the industries in which the enterprise operates, which would help in laying down objective criteria in the collective bargaining process. In this context, multinational as well as national enterprises should respond constructively to requests by governments for relevant information on their operations.

Consultation

56   In multinational as well as in national enterprises, systems devised by mutual agreement between employers and workers and their representatives should provide, in accordance with national law and practice, for regular consultation on matters of mutual concern. Such consultation should not be a substitute for collective bargaining.[16]

Examination of grievances ·

57   Multinational as well as national enterprises should respect the right of the workers whom they employ to have all their grievances processed in a manner consistent with the following provision: any worker who, acting individually or jointly with other workers, considers that he has grounds for a grievance should have the right to submit such grievance without suffering any prejudice whatsoever as a result, and to have such grievance examined pursuant to an appropriate procedure.[17] This is particularly important whenever the multinational enterprises operate in countries which do not abide by the principles of ILO Conventions pertaining to freedom of association, to the right to organise and bargain collectively and to forced labour.[18]

Settlement of industrial disputes

58   Multinational as well as national enterprises jointly with the representatives and organisations of the workers whom they employ should seek to establish voluntary conciliation machinery, appropriate to national conditions, which may include provisions for voluntary arbitration, to assist in the prevention and settlement of industrial disputes between employers and workers. The voluntary conciliation machinery should include equal representation of employers and workers.[19]

Geneva, 16 November 1977.

Notes

1. Convention (No. 87) concerning Freedom of Association and Protection of the Right to Organise; Convention (No. 98) concerning the Application of the Principles of the Right to Organise and to Bargain Collectively; Convention (No. 111) concerning Discrimination in Respect of Employment and Occupation; Convention (No. 122) concerning Employment Policy. Recommendation (No. 111) concerning Discrimination in Respect of Employment and Occupation; Recommendation (No. 119) concerning Termination of Employment at the Initiative of the Employer; Recommendation (No. 122) concerning Employment Policy.

2. Convention (No. 122) and Recommendation (No. 122) concerning Employment Policy.

3. ILO, World Employment Conference, Geneva, 4-17 June 1976.

4. Convention (No. 111) and Recommendation (No. 111) concerning Discrimination in Respect of Employment and Occupation; Convention (No. 100) and Recommendation (No. 90) concerning Equal Remuneration for Men and Women Workers for Work of Equal Value.

5. Recommendation (No. 119) concerning Termination of Employment at the Initiative of the Employer.

6. Convention (No. 142) and Recommendation (No. 150) concerning Vocational Guidance and Vocational Training in the Development of Human Resources.

7. Recommendation (No. 116) concerning Reduction of Hours of Work.

8. Convention (No. 110) and Recommendation (No. 110) concerning Conditions of Employment of Plantation Workers; Recommendation (No. 115) concerning Workers' Housing; Recommendation (No. 69) concerning Medical Care; Convention (No. 130) and Recommendation (No. 134) concerning Medical Care and Sickness.

9. The ILO Conventions and Recommendations referred to are listed in 'Publications on Occupational Safety and Health', ILO, Geneva 1976, pp. 1-3.

10. Convention No. 87, Article 2.

11. Convention No. 98, Article 1 (1).

12. Convention No. 98, Article 2 (1).

13. Convention No. 98, Article 4.

14. Convention (No. 135) concerning protection and facilities to be afforded to workers' representatives in the undertaking.

15. Recommendation (No. 129) concerning Communication between Management and Workers within Undertakings.

16. Recommendation (No. 94) concerning Consultation and Co-operation between Employers and Workers at the Level of the Undertaking; Recommendation (No. 129) concerning Communications within the Undertaking.

17. Recommendation (No. 130) concerning the Examination of Grievances within the Undertaking with a View to their Settlement.

18. Convention (No. 29) concerning Forced or Compulsory Labour; Convention (No. 105) concerning the Abolition of Forced Labour; Recommendation (No. 35) concerning Indirect Compulsion to Labour.

19. Recommendation (No. 92) concerning Voluntary Conciliation and Arbitration.

List of international labour Conventions and Recommendations referred to in the Tripartite Declaration of Principles concerning Multinational Enterprises and Social Policy

Conventions

Convention (No. 29) concerning Forced or Compulsory Labour, 1930.

Convention (No. 87) concerning Freedom of Association and Protection of the Right to Organise, 1948.

Convention (No. 98) concerning the Application of the Principles of the Right to Organise and to Bargain Collectively, 1949.

Convention (No. 100) concerning Equal Remuneration for Men and Women Workers for Work of Equal Value, 1951.

Convention (No. 105) concerning the Abolition of Forced Labour, 1957.

Convention (No. 110) concerning Conditions of Employment of Plantation Workers, 1958.

Convention (No. 111) concerning Discrimination in Respect of Employment and Occupation, 1958.

Convention (No. 115) concerning the Protection of Workers against Ionising Radiations, 1960.

Convention (No. 119) concerning the Guarding of Machinery, 1963.

Convention (No. 122) concerning Employment Policy, 1964.

Convention (No. 130) concerning Medical Care and Sickness Benefits, 1969.

Convention (No. 135) concerning Protection and Facilities to be Afforded to Workers' Representatives in the Undertaking, 1971.

Convention (No. 136) concerning Protection against Hazards of Poisoning arising from Benzene, 1971.

Convention (No. 139) concerning Prevention and Control of Occupational Hazards caused by Carcinogenic Substances and Agents, 1974.

Convention (No. 142) concerning Vocational Guidance and Vocational Training in the Development of Human Resources, 1975.

Recommendations

Recommendation (No. 35) concerning Indirect Compulsion to Labour, 1930.

Recommendation (No. 69) concerning Medical Care, 1944.

Recommendation (No. 90) concerning Equal Remuneration for Men and Women Workers for Work of Equal Value, 1951.

Recommendation (No. 92) concerning Voluntary Conciliation and

Arbitration, 1951.

Recommendation (No. 94) concerning Consultation and Co-operation between Employers and Workers at the Level of the Undertaking, 1952.

Recommendation (No. 110) concerning Conditions of Employment of Plantation Workers, 1958.

Recommendation (No. 111) concerning Discrimination in Respect of Employment and Occupation, 1958.

Recommendation (No. 114) concerning the Protection of Workers against Ionising Radiations, 1960.

Recommendation (No. 115) concerning Workers' Housing, 1961.

Recommendation (No. 116) concerning Reduction of Hours of Work, 1962.

Recommendation (No. 118) concerning the Guarding of Machinery, 1963.

Recommendation (No. 119) concerning Termination of Employment at the Initiative of the Employer, 1963.

Recommendation (No. 122) concerning Employment Policy, 1964.

Recommendation (No. 129) concerning Communications between Management and Workers within the Undertaking, 1967.

Recommendation (No. 130) concerning the Examination of Grievances Within the Undertaking with a View to their Settlement, 1967.

Recommendation (No. 134) concerning Medical Care and Sickness Benefits, 1969.

Recommendation (No. 144) concerning Protection against Hazards of Poisoning arising from Benzene, 1971.

Recommendation (No. 147) concerning Prevention and Control of Occupational Hazards caused by Carcinogenic Substances and Agents, 1974.

Recommendation (No. 150) concerning Vocational Guidance and Vocational Training in the Development of Human Resources, 1975.

APPENDIX 2: ORGANISATION FOR ECONOMIC CO-OPERATION AND DEVELOPMENT — DECLARATION ON INTERNATIONAL INVESTMENT AND MULTINATIONAL ENTERPRISES (21 June 1976)

The governments of OECD member countries

Considering

- that international investment has assumed increased importance in the world economy and has considerably contributed to the development of their countries;
- that multinational enterprises play an important role in this investment process;
- that co-operation by Member countries can improve the foreign investment climate, encourage the positive contribution which multinational enterprises can make to economic and social progress, and minimise and resolve difficulties which may arise from their various operations;
- that, while continuing endeavours within the OECD may lead to further international arrangements and agreements in this field, it seems appropriate at this stage to intensify their co-operation and consultation on issues relating to international investment and multinational enterprises through inter-related instruments each of which deals with a different aspect of the matter and together constitute a framework within which the OECD will consider these issues:

Declare:

Guidelines for multinational enterprises

I   that they jointly recommend to multinational enterprises operating in their territories the observance of the Guidelines as set forth in the Annex hereto having regard to the considerations and understandings which introduce the Guidelines and are an integral part of them;

National treatment

II   (1) that Member countries should, consistent with their needs to maintain public order, to protect their essential security interests and to fulfil commitments relating to international peace and security,

190

accord to enterprises operating in their territories and owned or controlled directly or indirectly by nationals of another Member country
(hereinafter referred to as 'Foreign-Controlled Enterprises') treatment
under their laws, regulations and administrative practices, consistent
with international law and no less favourable than that accorded in
like situations to domestic enterprises (hereinafter referred to as
'National Treatment');

(2) that Member countries will consider applying 'National
Treatment' in respect of countries other than Member countries;

(3) that Member countries will endeavour to ensure that their
territorial subdivisions apply 'National Treatment';

(4) that this Declaration does not deal with the right of Member
countries to regulate the entry of foreign investment or the conditions
of establishment of foreign enterprises;

International investment incentives and disincentives

III (1) that they recognise the need to strengthen their co-operation
in the field of international direct investment;

(2) that they thus recognise the need to give due weight to the
interests of Member countries affected by specific laws, regulations
and administrative practices in this field (hereinafter called 'measures')
providing official incentives and disincentives to international direct
investment;

(3) that Member countries will endeavour to make such measures
as transparent as possible, so that their importance and purpose can be
ascertained and that information on them can be readily available;

Consultation procedures

IV that they are prepared to consult one another on the above
matters in conformity with the Decisions of the Council relating to
Inter-Governmental Consultation Procedures on the Guidelines for
Multinational Enterprises, on National Treatment and on International
Investment Incentives and Disincentives;

Review

V that they will review the above matters within three years with
a view to improving the effectiveness of international economic co-
operation among Member countries on issues relating to international
investment and multinational enterprises;

II(b) ANNEX TO THE DECLARATION OF 21 JUNE 1976 BY GOVERNMENTS OF OECD MEMBER COUNTRIES ON INTERNATIONAL INVESTMENT AND MULTINATIONAL ENTERPRISES

Guidelines for multinational enterprises

1   Multinational enterprises now play an important part in the economies of Member countries and in international economic relations, which is of increasing interest to governments.Through international direct investment, such enterprises can bring substantial benefits to home and host countries by contributing to the efficient utilisation of capital, technology and human resources between countries and can thus fulfil an important role in the promotion of economic and social welfare. But the advances made by multinational enterprises in organising their operations beyond the national framework may lead to abuse of concentrations of economic power and to conflicts with national policy objectives. In addition, the complexity of these multinational enterprises and the difficulty of clearly perceiving their diverse structures, operations and policies sometimes give rise to concern.

2   The common aim of the Member countries is to encourage the positive contributions which multinational enterprises can make to economic and social progress and to minimise and resolve the difficulties to which their various operations may give rise. In view of the transnational structure of such enterprises, this aim will be furthered by co-operation among the OECD countries where the headquarters of most of the multinational enterprises are established and which are the location of a substantial part of their operations. The guidelines set out hereafter are designed to assist in the achievement of this common aim and to contribute to improving the foreign investment climate.

3   Since the operations of multinational enterprises extend throughout the world, including countries that are not Members of the Organisation, international co-operation in this field should extend to all States. Member countries will give their full support to efforts undertaken in co-operation with non-member countries, and in particular with developing countries, with a view to improving the welfare and living standards of all people both by encouraging the positive contributions which multinational enterprises can make and by minimising

and resolving the problems which may arise in connection with their activities.

4   Within the Organisation, the programme of co-operation to attain these ends will be a continuing, pragmatic and balanced one. It comes within the general aims of the Convention on the Organisation for Economic Co-operation and Development (OECD) and makes full use of the various specialised bodies of the Organisation, whose terms of reference already cover many aspects of the role of multinational enterprises, notably in matters of international trade and payments, competition, taxation, manpower, industrial development, science and technology. In these bodies, work is being carried out on the identification of issues, the improvement of relevant qualitative and statistical information and the elaboration of proposals for action designed to strengthen inter-governmental co-operation. In some of these areas procedures already exist through which issues related to the operations of multinational enterprises can be taken up. This work could result in the conclusion of further and complementary agreements and arrangements between governments.

5   The initial phase of the co-operation programme is composed of a Declaration and three Decisions promulgated simultaneously as they are complementary and inter-connected in respect of guidelines for multinational enterprises, national treatment for foreign-controlled enterprises and international investment incentives and disincentives.

6   The guidelines set out below are recommendations jointly addressed by Member countries to multinational enterprises operating in their territories. These guidelines, which take into account the problems which can arise because of the international structure of these enterprises, lay down standards for the activities of these enterprises in the different Member countries. Observance of the guidelines is voluntary and not legally enforceable. However, they should help to ensure that the operations of these enterprises are in harmony with national policies of the countries where they operate and to strengthen the basis of mutual confidence between enterprises and States.

7   Every State has the right to prescribe the conditions under which multinational enterprises operate within its national jurisdiction, subject to international law and to the international agreements to which it has subscribed. The entities of a multinational enterprise located in various countries are subject to the laws of these countries.

8   A precise legal definition of multinational enterprises is not

required for the purposes of the guidelines. These usually comprise companies or other entities whose ownership is private, state or mixed, established in different countries and so linked that one or more of them may be able to exercise a significant influence over the activities of others and, in particular, to share knowledge and resources with the others. The degree of autonomy of each entity in relation to the others varies widely from one multinational enterprise to another, depending on the nature of the links between such entities and the fields of activity concerned. For these reasons, the guidelines are addressed to the various entities within the multinational enterprise (parent companies and/or local entities) according to the actual distribution of responsibilities among them on the understanding that they will co-operate and provide assistance to one another as necessary to facilitate observance of the guidelines. The word 'enterprise' as used in these guidelines refers to these various entities in accordance with their responsibilities.

9   The guidelines are not aimed at introducing differences of treatment between multinational and domestic enterprises; wherever relevant they reflect good practice for all. Accordingly, multinational and domestic enterprises are subject to the same expectations in respect of their conduct wherever the guidelines are relevant to both.

10   The use of appropriate international dispute settlement mechanisms, including arbitration, should be encouraged as a means of facilitating the resolution of problems arising between enterprises and Member countries.

11   Member countries have agreed to establish appropriate review and consultation procedures concerning issues arising in respect of the guidelines. When multinational enterprises are made subject to conflicting requirements by Member countries, the governments concerned will co-operate in good faith with a view to resolving such problems either within the Committee on International Investment and Multinational Enterprises established by the OECD Council on 21st January 1975 or through other mutually acceptable arrangements.

Having regard to the foregoing considerations, the Member countries set forth the following guidelines for multinational enterprises with the understanding that Member countries will fulfil their responsibilities to treat enterprises equitably and in accordance with international law and international agreements, as well as contractual obligations to which they have subscribed:

General policies

Enterprises should

1 take fully into account established general policy objectives of the Member countries in which they operate;

2 in particular, give due consideration to those countries' aims and priorities with regard to economic and social progress, including industrial and regional development, the protection of the environment, the creation of employment opportunities, the promotion of innovation and the transfer of technology;

3 while observing their legal obligations concerning information, supply their entities with supplementary information the latter may need in order to meet requests by the authorities of the countries in which those entities are located for information relevant to the activities of those entities, taking into account legitimate requirements of business confidentiality;

4 favour close co-operation with the local community and business interests;

5 allow their component entities freedom to develop their activities and to exploit their competitive advantage in domestic and foreign markets, consistent with the need for specialisation and sound commercial practice;

6 when filling responsible posts in each country of operation, take due account of individual qualifications without discrimination as to nationality, subject to particular national requirements in this respect;

7 not render — and they should not be solicited or expected to render — any bribe or other improper benefit, direct or indirect, to any public servant or holder of public office;

8 unless legally permissible, not make contributions to candidates for public office or to political parties or other political organisations;

9 abstain from any improper involvement in local political activities.

Disclosure of information

Enterprises should, having due regard to their nature and relative size in the economic context of their operations and to requirements of business confidentiality and to cost, publish in a form suited to improve public understanding a sufficient body of factual information on the structure, activities and policies of the enterprise as a whole, as a supplement, in so far as necessary for this purpose, to information to be disclosed under the national law of the individual countries in which they operate. To this end, they should publish within reasonable time limits, on a regular basis, but at least annually, financial statements and other pertinent information relating to the enterprise as a whole, comprising in particular:

Employment and industrial relations

Enterprises should, within the framework of law, regulations and prevailing labour relations and employment practices, in each of the countries in which they operate,

1   respect the right of their employees, to be represented by trade unions and other bona fide organisations of employees, and engage in constructive negotiations, either individually or through employers' associations, with such employee organisations with a view to reaching agreements on employment conditions, which should include provisions for dealing with disputes arising over the interpretation of such agreements, and for ensuring mutually respected rights and responsibilities;

2   (a) provide such facilities to representatives of the employees as may be necessary to assist in the development of effective collective agreements,

       (b) provide to representatives of employees information which is needed for meaningful negotiations on conditions of employment;

3   provide to representatives of employees where this accords with local law and practice, information which enables them to obtain a true and fair view of the performance of the entity or, where appropriate, the enterprise as a whole;

4   observe standards of employment and industrial relations not less favourable than those observed by comparable employers in the host country;

5   in their operations, to the greatest extent practicable, utilise,

train and prepare for upgrading members of the local labour force in co-operation with representatives of their employees and, where appropriate, the relevant governmental authorities;

6   in considering changes in their operations which would have major effects upon the livelihood of their employees, in particular in the case of the closure of an entity involving collective lay-offs or dismissals, provide reasonable notice of such changes to representatives of their employees, and where appropriate to the relevant governmental authorities, and co-operate with the employee representatives and appropriate governmental authorities so as to mitigate to the maximum extent practicable adverse effects;

7   implement their employment policies including hiring, discharge, pay, promotion and training without discrimination unless selectivity in respect of employee characteristics is in furtherance of established governmental policies which specifically promote greater equality of employment opportunity;

8   in the context of bona fide negotiations[1] with representatives of employees on conditions of employment, or while employees are exercising a right to organise, not threaten to utilise a capacity to transfer the whole or part of an operating unit from the country concerned in order to influence unfairly those negotiations or to hinder the exercise of a right to organise;[2]

9   enable authorised representatives of their employees to conduct negotiations on collective bargaining or labour management relations issues with representatives of management who are authorised to take decisions on the matters under negotiation.

Science and technology

Enterprises should

1   endeavour to ensure that their activities fit satisfactorily into the scientific and technological policies and plans of the countries in which they operate, and contribute to the development of national scientific and technological capacities, including as far as appropriate the establishment and improvement in host countries of their capacity to innovate;

2   to the fullest extent practicable, adopt in the course of their business activities practices which permit the rapid diffusion of tech-

nologies with due regard to the protection of industrial and intellectual property rights;

3   when granting licences for the use of industrial property rights or when otherwise transferring technology do so on reasonable terms and conditions.

(i)   the structure of the enterprise, showing the name and location of the parent company, its main affiliates, its percentage ownership, direct and indirect, in these affiliates, including shareholdings between them;

(ii)   the geographical areas[3] where operations are carried out and the principal activities carried on therein by the parent company and the main affiliates;

(iii)   the operating results and sales by geographical area and the sales in the major lines of business for the enterprise as a whole;

(iv)   significant new capital investment by geographical area and, as far as practicable, by major lines of business for the enterprise as a whole;

(v)   a statement of the sources and uses of funds by the enterprise as a whole;

(vi)   the average number of employees in each geographical area;

(vii)   research and development expenditure for the enterprise as a whole;

(viii)   the policies followed in respect of intra-group pricing;

(ix)   the accounting policies, including those on consolidation, observed in compiling the published information.

Competition

Enterprises should, while conforming to official competition rules and established policies of the countries in which they operate,

1   refrain from actions which would adversely affect competition in the relevant market by abusing a dominant position of market power, by means of, for example,

    (a)   anti-competitive acquisitions,

    (b)   predatory behaviour toward competitors,

    (c)   unreasonable refusal to deal,

    (d)   anti-competitive abuse of industrial property rights,

    (e)   discriminatory (i.e. unreasonably differentiated) pricing and using such pricing transactions between affiliated enterprises as a means of affecting adversely competition outside these enterprises;

2   allow purchasers, distributors and licensees freedom to resell, export, purchase and develop their operations consistent with law, trade conditions, the need for specialisation and sound commercial practice;

3   refrain from participating in or otherwise purposely strengthening the restrictive effects of international or domestic cartels or restrictive agreements which adversely affect or eliminate competition and which are not generally or specifically accepted under applicable national or international legislation;

4   be ready to consult and co-operate, including the provision of information, with competent authorities of countries whose interests are directly affected in regard to competition issues or investigations. Provision of information should be in accordance with safeguards normally applicable in this field.

Financing

Enterprises should, in managing the financial and commercial operations of their activities, and especially their liquid foreign assets and liabilities, take into consideration the established objectives of the countries in which they operate regarding balance of payments and credit policies.

Taxation

Enterprises should

1   upon request of the taxation authorities of the countries in which they operate, provide, in accordance with the safeguards and relevant procedures of the national laws of these countries, the information necessary to determine correctly the taxes to be assessed in connection with their operations, including relevant information concerning their operations in other countries;

2   refrain from making use of the particular facilities available to them, such as transfer pricing which does not conform to an arm's length standard, for modifying in ways contrary to national laws the tax base on which members of the group are assessed.

Notes

1. Bona fide negotiations may include labour disputes as part of the process of negotiation. Whether or not labour disputes are so included will be determined by the law and prevailing employment practices of particular countries.

2. Subsequently amended in the 1979 Review (amended language in italics): In the context of bona fide negotiations with representatives of employees on conditions of employment, or while employees are exercising a right to organise, not threaten to utilise a capacity to transfer the whole or part of an operating unit from the country concerned *nor transfer employees from the enterprises' component entities in other countries* in order to influence unfairly those negotiations or to hinder the exercise of a right to organise.

3. For the purposes of the guideline on disclosure of information the term 'geographical area' means groups of countries or individual countries as each enterprise determines is appropriate in its partiuclar circumstances. While no single method of grouping is appropriate for all enterprises or for all purposes, the factors to be considered by an enterprise would include the significance of operations carried out in individual countries or areas as well as the effects on its competitiveness, geographic proximity, economic affinity, similarities in business environments and the nature, scale and degree of interrelationship of the enterprises' operations in the various countries.

BIBLIOGRAPHY

Addison, J.T. (1982) 'Are Unions Good for Productivity?', *Journal of Labor Research*, 3, 125-38
—— and A.H. Barnett (1982) 'The Impact of Unions on Productivity', *British Journal of Industrial Relations*, 20, 145-62
—— and W.S. Siebert (1979) *The Market for Labor: An Analytical Treatment*, Goodyear, Santa Monica
Adler, M. and G.V.G. Stevens (1974) 'The Trade Effects of Direct Investment', *Journal of Finance*, 29, 665-76
AFL-CIO (1979) *Needed: A Constructive Foreign Trade Policy*, AFL-CIO Industrial Union Department, Washington
Agarwal, J. (1976) 'Factor Proportions in Foreign and Domestic Firms in Indian Manufacturing', *Economic Journal*, 86, 589-94
Aharoni, Y. (1971) 'On the Definition of a Multinational Corporation', *Quarterly Review of Economics and Business*, 11, 27-38
Ahluwalia, M. (1974) 'Income Inequality', in H. Chenery *et al.*, *Redistribution with Growth*, Oxford University Press, Oxford
Aho, M.C. and D.J. Rousslang (1979) *The Impact of LDC Trade on US Workers: Demographic and Occupational Characteristics of Workers in Trade-Sensitive Industries*, US Department of Labor, Washington, DC
Alam, G. and J. Langrish (1981) 'Non-Multinational Firms and Transfer of Technology to Less Developed Countries', *World Development*, 9, 383-7
Aliber, R.Z. (1970) 'A Theory of Direct Investment', in C.P. Kindleberger (ed.), *The International Corporation*, MIT Press, Cambridge, Mass., 17-34
Allen, T.W. (1973) *Direct Investment of European Enterprises in South East Asia*, Economic Cooperation Centre for the Asian and Pacific Region, No. 3, Bangkok
Alsegg, R.G. (1971) *Control Relationships Between American Corporations and their European Subsidiaries*, AMA Research Study 107, American Management Association Inc., New York
Anell, L. (1981) *Recession, The Western Economies and the Changing World Order*, Frances Pinter, London
Armstrong, R.B. (1979) 'National Trends in Office Construction, Employment and Headquarter Location in US Metropolitan Areas', in P.W. Daniels (ed.), *Spatial Patterns of Office Growth and Location*, John Wiley, London
Arnison, J. (1971) *The Million Pound Strike*, Lawrence and Wishart, London
Arrighi, G. (1970) 'International Corporations, Labour Aristocracies and Economic Development in Tropical Africa', *Journal of Modern African Studies*, 6, 141-69
—— (1982) 'A Crisis of Hegemony', in S. Amin *et al.* (eds.), *Dynamics of Global Crisis*, Macmillan, London
Arrow, K. (1970) 'The Organisation of Economic Activity: Issues Pertinent to the Choice of Market Versus Non Market Allocation', in R.H. Haveman and J. Margolis (eds.), *Public Expenditures and Policy Analysis*, Markham Publish-

ing, Chicago

Ashcroft, B. and K.P.D. Ingham (1979) 'Company Adaptation and the Responses to Regional Policy: A Comparative Analysis of MNC Subsidiaries and Indigenous Companies', *Regional Studies*, 13, 25-37

Baade, H.W. (1981) 'Codes of Conduct for Multinational Enterprises: An Introductory Survey', in N. Horn (ed.), *Legal Problems of Codes of Conduct for Multinational Enterprises*, Studies in Transnational Economic Law, Vol. 1, Kluwer, Deventer

Bacon, R.W. and W.A. Eltis (1974) *The Age of US and UK Machinery*, NEDO Monograph 3, National Economic Development Office, London

Baerresen, D.W. (1971) *The Border Industrialisation Programme of Mexico*, D.C. Heath, Lexington

Baily, P.J. (1979) *Employment Effects of Multinational Enterprises: A Survey of Relevant Studies Relating to the Federal Republic of Germany*, International Labour Office, Geneva, Multinational Enterprises Programme, Working Paper 2

Balassa, B. (1981) *The Newly Industrialising Countries in the World Economy*, Pergamon Press, New York

Bale, M. (1973) *Adjustment to Freer Trade: An Analysis of the Adjustment Assistance Provisions of the Trade Expansion Act of 1962*, Ph.D. Dissertation submitted to University of Wisconsin, Madison

Ball, G. (1967) 'Cosmocorp: The Importance of Being Stateless', *Columbia Journal of World Business*, 2, 25-30

Ballance, R.H., J.A. Ansari and H.W. Singer (1982) *The International Economy and Industrial Development: The Impact of Trade and Investment on the Third World*, Wheatsheaf Books, Brighton

—— and S. Sinclair (1983) *Collapse and Survival: Industry Strategies in a Changing World*, World Industry Studies 1, Allen and Unwin, London

Balmer-Cao, T-H. (1979) 'Système Politique, Répartition des Revenues et Pénétration des Entreprises Multinationales', *Annuaire Suisse de Science Politique*

Balogh, T. and P. Streeten (1960) 'Domestic versus Foreign Investment', *Bulletin of Oxford University Institute of Statistics*, 22, 213-24

Baranson, J. (1967) *Manufacturing Problems in India: The Cummins Diesel Experience*, Syracuse University Press, New York

Bardhan, P.K. (1982) 'Imports, Domestic Production, and Transnational Vertical Integration: A Theoretical Note', *Journal of Political Economy*, 90, 1020-34

Barrera, M. (1979) 'Colonial Labor and Theories of Inequality: The Case of International Harvester', in R. Cohen *et al.* (eds.), *Peasants and Proletarians: The Struggles of Third World Workers*, Hutchinson, London

Behrman, J.N. and W.A. Fischer (1980) *Overseas R&D Activities of Transnational Companies*, Oelgeschlager, Gunn and Hain, Cambridge, Mass

Bellace, J. R. and H.F. Gospel (1983) 'Disclosure of Information to Trade Unions: A Comparative Perspective', *International Labour Review*, 122, 57-74

Belli, R.D. and L.C. Maley (1974) 'Sales by Majority-Owned Foreign Affiliates of US Companies, 1966-1972,' *Survey of Current Business*, 54, 25-40

Benson, I. and J. Lloyd (1983) *New Technology and Industrial Change*, Kogan Page, London

Bergsten, C.F. (1976) *An Analysis of US Foreign Direct Investment Policy and Economic Development*, AID Discussion Paper 36, Washington, DC

—— T. Horst and T.H. Moran (1978) *American Multinationals and American Interests*, Brookings Institution, Washington

Berthomieu, C. and A. Hanaut (1980) 'Can International Subcontracting Promote Industrialisation?', *International Labour Review*, 119, 335-49

Biersteker, T.J. (1978) *Distortion or Development: Contending Perspectives on the Multinational Corporation*, MIT Press, Cambridge, Mass

Blake, D.H. (1972) 'Corporate Structure and International Unionism', *Columbia Journal of World Business*, 7, 19-26

—— (1972b) 'Multinational Corporation, International Union and International Collective Bargaining: A Case Study of the Political, Social and Economic Implications of the 1967 UAW-Chrysler Agreement', in H. Gunter (ed.), *Transnational Industrial Relations*, Macmillan, London

—— (1972c) 'The Internationalisation of Industrial Relations', *Journal of International Business Studies*, 3, 17-32

—— (1973) 'Cross-National, Cooperative Strategies: Union Responses to the MNCs', in K.P. Tudyka (ed.), *Multinational Corporations and Labour Unions*, SUN, Werkuitgave

—— (1973b) 'International Labor and Regulation of Multinational Corporations: Proposals and Prospects', *San Diego Law Review*, 11, 179-205

Blam, Y. and R.G. Hawkins, (1975) *Forms of Foreign Investment and the External Trade of Developing Countries*: University of Reading Discussion Papers in International Investment and Business Studies

Blanpain, R. (1970) 'American Involvement in Belgium', in A. Kamin (ed.), *Western European Labor and the American Corporation*, Bureau of National Affairs, Washington

—— (1977) *The Badger Case and the OECD Guidelines for Multinational Enterprises*, Kluwer, Deventer

—— (1977b) 'Multinationals Impact on Host Country Industrial Relations', in R.F. Banks and J. Stieber (eds.), *Multinationals, Unions and Labor Relations in Industrialised Countries*, Cornell University Press, New York

—— (1979) *The OECD Guidelines for Multinational Enterprises and Labour Relations 1976-1979: Experience and Review*, Kluwer, Deventer

—— (1983) *The OECD Guidelines for Multinational Enterprises and Labour Relations 1979-1982: Experience and Mid-Term Report*, Kluwer, Deventer

Boddwyn, J.J. (1979) 'Divestment: Local vs Foreign and US vs European Approaches', *Management International Review*, 18, 21-8

—— (1983) 'Foreign Direct Divestment Theory Is It the Reverse of FDI Theory?', *Weltwirlschaftliches Archiv*, 119, 345-55

Bomers, G.B.J. and R.B. Peterson (1977) 'Multinational Corporations and Industrial Relations: The Case of West Germany and the Netherlands', *British Journal of Industrial Relations*, 15, 45-62

Booz, Allen and Hamilton (1979) *The Electronics Industry in Scotland: A Proposed Strategy*, Scottish Development Agency, Glasgow

Bornschier, V. (1978) 'Cross-National Evidence of the Effects of Foreign Investment and Aid on Economic Growth and Inequality: A Survey of Findings and a Reanalysis', *American Journal of Sociology*, 84, 651-83

—— (1980) 'Multinational Corporations and Economic Growth: A Cross-National Test of the Decapitisation Thesis', *Journal of Development Economics*, 7, 191-210

—— (1982) 'World Economic Integration and Policy Responses: Some Developmental Impacts', in H. Makler, A. Martinelli and N. Smelser (eds.), *The New International Economy*, Sage, London

Bos, H.C., M. Sanders and C. Secchi (1974) *Private Foreign Investment in Developing Countries: A Quantitative Study on the Evaluation of the Macroeconomic Effects*, D. Riedel, Dordrecht

Breidenstein, G. (1976) 'International Division of Labour and Structural Unemployment', *Intereconomics*, 4, 115-19

Brewer, A. (1980) *Marxist Theories of Imperialism: A Critical Survey*, Routledge and Kegan Paul, London

British Business (1983) 'Government Seeks Views on EC Employee and Company Law Proposals', November, 18, 587

Brown, W. (1981) *The Changing Contours of British Industrial Relations*, Basil Blackwell, Oxford

Buckley, P.J. (1983) 'New Theories of International Business: Some Unresolved Issues', in M. Casson (ed.), *The Growth of International Business*, Allen and Unwin, London

—— Z. Berkova and G.D. Newbould (1983) *Direct Investments in the United Kingdom by Smaller European Firms*, Macmillan, London

—— and Casson, M. (1976) *The Future of the Multinational Enterprise*, Macmillan, London

—— and M. Casson (1981) 'The Optimal Timing of a Foreign Direct Investment', *Economic Journal*, 91, 75-87

—— and H. Davies (1981) 'Foreign Licensing in Overseas Operations', in R.G. Hawkins (ed.), *Research in International Business and Finance*, JAI Greenwich, Conn

—— and J.H. Dunning (1976) 'The Industrial Structure of US Direct Investment in the UK', *Journal of International Business Studies*, 7, 5-17

—— and P. Enderwick (1983) 'Comparative Pay Levels in Domestically-Owned and Foreign-Owned Plants in UK Manufacturing – Evidence from the 1980 Workplace Industrial Relations Survey', *British Journal of Industrial Relations*, 21, 395-400

—— and P. Enderwick (1984) *The Industrial Relations Practices of Foreign-Owned Firms in Britain*, Macmillan, London

—— A.G. Hartley and J.R. Sparkes (1980) *The Employment Effects of Intra-EEC Foreign Direct Investment*, EEC Programme of Research and Actions on the Development of the Labour Market, study 78/1 Brussels

—— and R.D. Pearce (1981) 'Market Servicing by Multinational Manufacturing Firms: Exporting versus Foreign Production', *Managerial and Decision Economics*, 2, 229-46

Burton, J. (1979) *The Job Support Machine: A Critique of the Subsidy Morass*, Centre for Policy Studies, London

Busch, G.K. (1983) 'The Shifting Balance of Power in the International Labour Movement', *Multinational Business*, 3, 18-25

Business International Corporation (1980) *The Effects of US Corporate Foreign Investment 1970-1978*, Business International Special Research Study, New York

Cable, V. (1977) 'British Protectionism and LDC Imports', *Overseas Development Institute Review*, 11, 29-48

—— (1982) 'Cheap Imports and Jobs: the Impact of Competing Manufactured Imports from Low Labour Cost Countries on UK Employment', in W.P. Maunder (ed.), *Case Studies in Development Economics*, Heinemann, London

Calvert, A.L. (1981) 'A Synthesis of Foreign Direct Investment Theories and Theories of the Multinational Firm', *Journal of International Business Studies*, 12, 43-59

Caporaso, J.A. (1982) 'Industrialisation in the Periphery: The Evolving Global Division of Labor', *International Studies Quarterly*, 25, 347-84

Casson, M. (1979) *Alternatives to the Multinational Enterprise*, Macmillan, London

—— (1982) 'Transaction Costs and the Theory of the Multinational Enterprise', in A.M. Rugman (ed.), *New Theories of the Multinational Enterprise*, Croom Helm, London

Castles, S. (1979) 'Review of F. Frobel *et al*. The New International Division of Labour', *Capital and Class*, 7, 122-30

Caves, R.E. (1971) 'International Corporations: The Industrial Economics of Foreign Investment', *Economica*, 38, 1-27

—— (1980) 'Productivity Differences Among Industries', in R.E. Caves and L.B. Krause (eds.), *Britain's Economic Performance*, Brookings Institution, Washington, DC

—— (1982) *Multinational Enterprise and Economic Analysis*, Cambridge University Press, Cambridge

—— H. Crookell and J.P. Killing (1983) 'The Imperfect Market for Technology Licenses', *Oxford Bulletin of Economics and Statistics*, 45, 249-67

Central Policy Review Staff (1975) *The Future of the British Car Industry*, HMSO, London

Chase-Dunn, C. (1975) 'The Effects of International Economic Dependence on Development and Inequality: a Cross-National Study', *American Sociological Review*, 40, 720-38

Chen, E.K. (1983) 'Factor Proportions of Foreign and Local Firms in Developing Countries: A Theoretical and Empirical Note', *Journal of Development Economics*, 12, 267-74

Child, S. (1982) 'Multinationals and the Transfer of Technology to LDCs', *Multinational Business*, 18-20

Chopra, J., J.J. Boddwyn, R.L. Torneden (1978) 'US Foreign Divestment: A 1972-1975 Updating', *Columbia Journal of World Business*, 13, 14-18

Chruden, J.H. and A.W. Sherman (1972) *Personnel Practices of American Companies in Europe*, American Management Association, New York

Chudnovsky, D. (1982) 'The Changing Remittance Behaviour of United States Manufacturing Firms in Latin America', *World Development*, 10, 513-21

Chudson, W.A. (1971) *The International Transfer of Commercial Technology to Developing Countries*, United Nations Institute for Training and Research Report No. 13, New York

Chung, B.S. and C.H. Lee (1980) 'The Choice of Production Techniques by Foreign and Local Firms in Korea', *Economic Development and Cultural Change*, 29, 135-40

Chung, W.K. (1978) 'Sales by Majority-Owned Foreign Affiliates of US Companies, 1976', *Survey of Current Business*, 58, 31-40

Clee, G.H. (1966) 'Guidelines for Global Business', *Columbia Journal of World Business*, 1, 97-104

Coase, R.H. (1937) 'The Nature of the Firm', *Economica*, 4, 386-405

Cohen, B.I. (1973) 'Comparative Behaviour of Foreign and Domestic Export Firms in a Developing Economy', *Review of Economics and Statistics*, 55, 190-7

Commission on Transnational Corporations (1979) *Transnational Corporations: A Code of Conduct; A Composite Text of Formulations by the Chairman and Elements Prepared by the Centre on Transnational Corporations*, Working paper No 10, UN, CTC, New York

Constas, K.J. and R.P. Vichas (1981) 'Patterns and Performance of Multinational and Domestic Food Wholesale Firms', *Managerial and Decision Economics*, 2, 25-31

Contractor, F. (1981) *International Technology Licensing: Compensation, Costs and Negotiation*, Lexington Books, Lexington, Mass

Corson, W. and W. Nicholson (1981) 'Trade Adjustment Assistance For Workers: Results of a Survey of Recipients Under the Trade Act of 1974', in R.G. Ehrenberg (ed.), *Research in Labor Economics*, Vol. 4, JAI Press, Greenwich, Conn

Courtney, W.H. and D.M. Leipziger (1975) 'Multinational Corporations in LDCs: The Choice of Technology', *Oxford Bulletin of Economics and Statistics*, 37, 297-304

Cox, R.W. (1976) 'Labor and the Multinationals', *Foreign Affairs*, 54, 354-65

—— (1982) 'Production and Hegemony: Toward a Political Economy of World Order', in H.K. Jacobson and D. Sidjanski (eds.), *The Emerging International Economic Order*, Sage Publications, London

Crum, R. and G. Gudgin (1978) *Non-Production Activities in UK Manufacturing Industry*, European Economic Commission, Brussels

Curhan, J.P., W.H. Davidson and R. Suri (1977) *Tracing the Multinationals: A Sourcebook on US-based Enterprises*, Ballinger, Cambridge, Mass

Currie, J. (1979) *Investment: the Growing Role of Export Processing Zones*, Economist Intelligence Unit, Special Report 64, London

Daniel, W.W. and N. Millward (1983) *Workplace Industrial Relations in Britain: the DE/PSI/SSRC Survey*, Heinemann Educational Books, London

Daniels, J.D. and F. Robles (1982) 'The Choice of Technology and Export Commitment: the Peruvian Textile Industry', *Journal of International Business Studies*, 13, 67-89

Davidson, W.H. (1980) *Experience Effects in International Investment and Technology Transfer*, UMI Research Press, Ann Arbor

Davies, G. and I. Thomas (1976) *Overseas Investment in Wales*, Christopher Davies, Cardiff

Deane, R.S. (1970) *Foreign Investment in New Zealand Manufacturing*, Sweet and Maxwell, Wellington, NZ

Deaton, D.R. and P.B. Beaumont (1980) 'The Determinants of Bargaining Structure; Some Large-Scale Evidence for Britain', *British Journal of Industrial Relations*, 18, 202-16

De Grauwe, P., W. Kennes, T. Petters and R. Van Straelen (1979) 'Trade Expansion with Less Developed Countries and Employment: A Case Study of Belgium', *Weltwirlschaftliches Archiv*, 65, 99-115

de la Torre, J. (1974) 'Foreign Investment and Export Dependency', *Economic*

Development and Cultural Change, 23, 133-50

—— R.B. Stobaugh and P. Telesio (1973) 'US Multinational Enterprises and Changes in the Skill Composition of US Employment', in D. Kujawa (ed.), *American Labor and the Multinational Corporation*, Praeger, New York

Department of Trade and Industry (1983) *Draft EC Regulation on the European Economic Interest Grouping (EEIG): A Consultative Document*, London

Desatrick, R.L. and M.L. Bennett (1977) *Human Resource Management in the Multinational Company*, Gower, Aldershot

De Vos, T. (1981) *US Multinationals and Worker Participation in Management: The American Experience in the European Community*, Aldwych Press, London

Dixon, M., S. Jonas and E. McGaughan (1983) 'Changes in the International Division of Labor and Low-Wage Labor in the United States', in A. Bergesen (ed.), *Crisis in the World-System*, Sage Publications, Beverly Hills

Doeringer, P. and M. Piore (1971) *Internal Labor Markets and Manpower Analysis*, D.C. Heath, Lexington

Dunning, J.H. (1966) 'US Subsidiaries in Britain and their UK Competitors: A Case Study in Business Ratios', *Business Ratios*, 5-18

—— (1969) *The Role Of American Investment in the British Economy*, PEP Broadsheet 507, Political and Economic Planning, London

—— (1970) *Studies in International Investment*, Allen and Unwin, London

—— (1976) *US Industry in Britain*, EAG Business Research Study, Wilton House, London

—— (1977) 'Trade, Location of Economic Activity and the MNE: A Search for an Eclectic Approach', in B. Ohlin, P.O. Hesselbom and P.M. Wijkman (eds.), *The International Allocation of Economic Activity*, Macmillan, London

—— (1979) 'Explaining Changing Patterns of International Production: In Defence of the Eclectic Theory', *Oxford Bulletin of Economics and Statistics*, 41, 269-96

—— (1981) *International Production and the Multinational Enterprise*, Allen and Unwin, London

—— (1983) 'Changes in the Level and Structure of International Production: The Last One Hundred Years', in M. Casson (ed.), *The Growth of International Business*, Allen and Unwin, London, 84-139

—— and R.D. Pearce (1981) *The World's Largest Industrial Enterprises*, Gower, Farnborough

The Economist (1982) 'As American as Raw Fish', 284, 56-8

Edwards, B. (1977) *Multinational Business and the Trade Unions*, Spokesman, London

Edwards, P.K. (1980) 'Size of Plant and Strike-Proneness', *Oxford Bulletin of Economics and Statistics*, 42, 145-56

Edwards, R. (1979) *Contested Terrain: The Transformation of the Workplace in the Twentieth Century*, Heinemann Educational Books, London

Emmanuel, A. (1972) *Unequal Exchange, A Study of the Imperialism of Trade*, New Left Books, London

—— (1982) *Appropriate or Underdeveloped Technology?*, John Wiley, Chichester

Enderwick, P. (1979) 'Multinationals and Labour: A Review of Issues and Responses', *Management Bibliographies and Reviews*, 5, 219-42

—— (1982) 'How Stable is Direct Foreign Investment?', *Journal of Irish Business and Administrative Research*, 4, 87-97

—— (1982b) 'Labour and the Theory of the Multinational Corporation', *Industrial Relations Journal*, 13, 32-43

—— (1982c) 'Strike Costs and Public Policy', *Journal of Public Policy*, 2, 347-64

—— (1983) 'Productivity and Labour Utilisation: The Experience of Foreign-Owned Firms', *Journal of General Management*, 9, 38-50

—— (1984) *Ownership Nationality and Industrial Relations Practices in British Non-Manufacturing Industries*, mimeographed

—— and P.J. Buckley (1982) 'Strike Activity and Foreign Ownership: An Analysis of British Manufacturing 1971-1973', *British Journal of Industrial Relations*, 20, 308-21

—— and P.J. Buckley (1983) 'The Determinants of Strike Activity in Foreign-Owned Plants: Inter-industry Evidence from British Manufacturing Industry 1971-1973', *Managerial and Decision Economics*, 4, 83-8

Erdilek, A. (1976) 'Can the Multinational Corporation be Incorporated into the General Equilibrium Theory of International Trade and Investment?', *Social and Economic Studies*, 25, 280-90

European Commission (1976) *Survey of Multinational Enterprises*, European Commission, Vol. 1, 6

European Industrial Relations Review (1983) 'Transnationals: Shaping EEC Law', *European Industrial Relations Review*, 109, 21-5

Evans, P. (1979) *Dependent Development: The Alliance of Multinational, State and Local Capital in Brazil*, Princeton University Press, Princeton, NJ

Fagre, N. and L.T. Wells (1982) 'Bargaining Power of Multinationals and Host Governments', *Journal of International Business Studies*, 13, 9-23

Fairchild, L.G. (1977) 'Performance and Technology of US and National Firms in Mexico', *Journal of Development Studies*, 14, 14-34

Finger, J.M. (1976) 'Trade and Domestic Effects of the Offshore Assembly Provision in the US Tariff', *American Economic Review*, 66, 598-611

—— (1977) 'Offshore Assembly Provisions in the West German and Netherlands Tariffs: Trade and Domestic Effects', *Weltwirlschaftliches Archiv*, 113, 237-49

Fishwick, F. (1982) *Multinational Companies and Economic Concentration in Europe*, Gower, Aldershot

Flanders, A. (1964) *The Fawley Productivity Agreement*, Faber and Faber, London

—— (1970) 'Labor-Management Relations and the Democratic Challenge', in A. Kamin (ed.), *Western European Labor and the American Corporation*, Bureau of National Affairs, Washington

Forsyth, D.J.C. (1972) *US Investment in Scotland*, Praeger Special Studies, London

—— (1973) 'Foreign-Owned Firms and Labour Relations: A Regional Perspective', *British Journal of Industrial Relations*, 11, 20-28

—— and R.F. Solomon (1977) 'Choice of Technology and Nationality of Ownership in Manufacturing in a Developing Country', *Oxford Economic Papers*, 29, 258-82

Frank, A.G. (1981) *Reflections on the World Economic Crisis*, Hutchinson, London

—— (1981a) *Crisis in the Third World*, Heinemann Educational Books, London

Frank, C. (1977) *Foreign Trade and Domestic Aid*, Brookings Institution, Washington, DC

Frank, I. (1980) *Foreign Enterprise in Developing Countries*, Johns Hopkins University Press, Baltimore

Frank, R.H. and R.T. Freeman (1978) *Distributional Consequences of Direct Foreign Investment*, Academic Press, London

—— (1978b) 'The Distributional Consequences of Direct Foreign Investment', in W. Dewald (ed.), *The Impact of International Trade and Investment on Employment*, US Department of Labor, Washington, DC

Frankel, M. (1965) 'Home Versus Foreign Investment: A Case Against Capital Export,' *Kyklos*, 18, 411-433

Franko, L.G. (1975) *Multinational Enterprise, The International Division of Labour in Manufactures and the Developing Countries*, International Labour Office, Geneva, World Employment Programme Research Working Paper 4

—— (1976) *The European Multinationals: A Renewed Challenge to American and British Big Business*, Harper and Row, London

—— and S. Stephenson (1982) 'The Micro Picture: Corporate and Sectoral Developments', in L. Turner and N. McMullen (eds.), *The Newly Industrialising Countries: Trade and Adjustment*, Allen and Unwin, London

Freedman, A.L. (1977) *Industry and Labour: Class Struggle at Work and Monopoly Capitalism*, Macmillan, London

Freeman, O.L. and W. Persen (1980) 'Multinational Corporations: Some Facts and Figures', *Economic Impact*, 34, 47-53

Freeman, R.B. (1980) 'The Effect of Unionism on Worker Attachment to Firms', *Journal of Labor Research*, 1, 29-63

—— and J. Medoff (1979) 'The Two Faces of Unionism', *The Public Interest*, 69-93

Frobel, F., J. Heinrichs, and O. Kreye (1980) *The New International Divison of Labour: Structural Unemployment in Industrialised Countries and Industrialisation in Developing Countries*, Cambridge University Press, Cambridge

Gartman, D. (1979) 'Origins of the Assembly Line and Capitalist Control of Work at Ford', in A. Zimbalist (ed.), *Case Studies on the Labor Process*, Monthly Review Press, New York

Gennard, J. (1972) *Multinational Corporations and British Labour: A Review of Attitudes and Responses*, British North American Committee, London

—— and M.D. Steuer (1971) 'The Industrial Relations of Foreign-Owned Subsidiaries in the United Kingdom', *British Journal of Industrial Relations*, 9, 143-59

George, K.D., R. McNabb and J. Shorey (1977) 'The Size of the Work Unit and Labour Market Behaviour', *British Journal of Industrial Relations*, 15, 265-78

Giddy, I.H. (1978) 'The Demise of the Product Cycle Model in International Business Theory', *Columbia Journal of World Business*, 13, 90-7

Girvan, N. (1972) *Multinational Corporations and Dependent Underdevelopment in Mineral Export Economies*, Yale University Press, New Haven

—— (1976) *Corporate Imperialism: Conflict and Expropriation*, M.E. Sharpe, New York

Globerman, S. (1979) 'Foreign Direct Investment and Spillover Efficiency Benefits in Canadian Manufacturing Industries', *Canadian Journal of Economics*,

12, 42-56

Goldberg, P.M. and C.P. Kindleberger (1970) 'Toward a GATT For Investment: a Proposal for Supervision of the International Corporation', *Law and Policy in International Business*, 2, 295-323

Gospel, H.F. (1983) 'New Managerial Approaches to Industrial Relations: Major Paradigms and Historical Perspective', *Journal of Industrial Relations*, 25, 162-76

Graham, E.M. (1978) 'Transatlantic Investment by Multinational Firms: A Rivalistic Phenomenon?', *Journal of Post-Keynesian Economics*, 1, 82-99

Gray Report (1972) Government of Canada, *Foreign Direct Investment in Canada* (The Gray Report), Government Printing Office, Ottawa

Greer, C.R. and J.C. Shearer (1981) 'Do Foreign-Owned Firms Practice Unconventional Labor Relations?', *Monthly Labor Review*, 104, 44-8

Grosse, R. (1980) *Foreign Investment Codes and Location of Direct Investment*, Praeger, New York

—— (1982) 'Codes of Conduct for Multinational Enterprises', *Journal of World Trade Law*, 16, 414-34

Gudgin, G., R. Crum and S. Bailey (1979) 'White Collar Employment in UK Manufacturing Industry', in P.W. Daniels (ed.), *Spatial Patterns of Office Growth and Location*, John Wiley, London

Gunter, H. (1975) *Multinational Corporations and Labour: A World-Wide Theme with Variations*, paper presented to the 1975 Asia Regional Conference on Industrial Relations, Tokyo

—— (1981) *ILO Research on Multinational Enterprises and Social Policy: An Overview*, International Labour Office, Geneva, Multinational Enterprises Programme, Working Paper 15

—— (1981a) 'The Tripartite Declaration of Principles (ILO): Standards and Follow-Up', in N. Horn (ed.), *Legal Problems of Codes of Conduct for Multinational Enterprises*, Studies in Transnational Economic Law, Vol. 1, Kluwer, Deventer

Hamill, J. (1982) *Labour Relations in Foreign-Owned Firms in the UK*, Ph.D. Thesis submitted to Paisley College, Scotland

—— (1983) 'The Labour Relations Practices of Foreign-Owned and Indigenous Firms', *Employee Relations*, 5, 14-16

Hamilton, F.E.I. (1976) 'Multi-National Enterprise and the European Economic Community', *Tijdschrift Voor Economische en Sociale Geographie*, 67, 258-78

Hancock, M. (1983) 'Transnational Production and Women Workers', in A. Phizacklea (ed.), *One Way Ticket: Migration and Female Labour*, Routledge and Kegan Paul, London

Harberger, A.C. (1978) 'Comment', in W.G. Dewald (ed.), *The Impact of International Trade and Investment on Employment*, US Department of Labor, Washington, DC

Harrison, R. (1982) 'Assisted Industry, Employment Stability and Industrial Decline: Some Evidence from Northern Ireland', *Regional Studies*, 16, 267-85

Hartmann, H. and A.I. Marsh (1983) 'Information as a Trade Union Strategy: Research on a Systematic Approach to Comparative Data', *Labour and Society*, 8, 209-24

Hawkins, R.G. (1972) *Job Displacement and the Multinational Firm: A Methodological Review*, New York University Center for Multinational Studies, Occasional Paper No 3

—— and M.J. Jedel (1975) 'US Jobs and Foreign Investment', in D. Kujawa (ed.), *International Labor and the Multinational Enterprise* Praeger, New York

Hedlund, G. (1981) 'Autonomy of Subsidiaries and Formalisation of Headquarters – Subsidiary Relationships in Swedish MNEs', in L. Otterbeck (ed.), *The Management of Headquarters – Subsidiary Relationships in Multinational Corporations*, Gower, Farnborough

Heise, P.A. (1973) 'The Multinational Corporation and Industrial Relations: Discussion', *Labor Law Journal* 24, 480-3

Helleiner, G.K. (1976) 'Transnational Enterprise, Manufactured Exports, and Employment in Less Developed Countries', *Economic and Political Weekly*, 11, 247-76

—— (1981) *Intra-Firm Trade and the Developing Countries*, Macmillan, London

—— (1981b) 'Intra-Firm Trade and the Developing Countries: An Assessment of the Data', in R. Murray (ed.), *Multinationals Beyond the Market*, Harvester Press, Brighton

—— and R. Lavergne (1979) 'Intra-Firm Trade and Industrial Exports to the United States', *Oxford Bulletin of Economics and Statistics*, 41, 297-312

Hellinger, S.H. and D.A. Hellinger (1976) *Unemployment and the Multinationals*, Kennikat, New York

Helliwell, J.F. (ed.) (1976) *Aggregate Investment*, Penguin Modern Economics Readings, Penguin, Harmondsworth

Hendricks, W.E. and L.M. Kahn (1982) 'The Determinants of Bargaining Structure in US Manufacturing Industries', *Industrial and Labor Relations Review*, 35, 181-95

Herman, F. (1983) 'The European Parliament and the Vredeling Proposal', in R. Blanpain *et al.*, *The Vredeling Proposal: Information and Consultation of Employees in Multinational Enterprises*, Kluwer, Deventer

Hershfield, D.C. (1975) *The Multinational Union Faces the Multinational Company*, Conference Board Report No 658, Conference Board, New York

Hewitt, G. (1980) 'Research and Development Performed Abroad by US Manufacturing Multinationals', *Kyklos*, 33, 308-26

Hight, J. (1978) 'Comment', in W.G. Dewaid (ed.), *The Impact of International Trade and Investment on Employment*, US Department of Labor, Washington, DC

Hill, H. (1982) 'Vertical Inter-Firm Linkages in LDCs: A Note on the Philippines', *Oxford Bulletin of Economics and Statistics*, 44, 261-71

Hirsbrunner, J.E. (1974) 'Manpower Training and Development in Multinational Companies', *Public Personnel Management*, 3, 378-84

Hirschey, R.C. and R.E. Caves (1981) 'Internationalisation of Research and Transfer of Technology by Multinational Enterprises', *Oxford Bulletin of Economics and Statistics*, 42, 115-30

Holland, S. (1975) *The Socialist Challenge*, Quartet, London

Hone, A. (1974) 'Multinational Corporations and Multinational Buying Groups', *World Development*, 2, 145-9

Hood, N. (1977) 'The Long-term Impact of Multinational Enterprise on Industrial Geography: The Scottish Case', *Scottish Geographical Magazine*, 93
—— (1979) *The Economics of Multinational Enterprise*, Longmans, London
—— (1980) *European Development Strategies of US Owned Manufacturing Companies Located in Scotland*, Report prepared for the Scottish Economic Planning Department, HMSO, Edinburgh
—— (1982) *Multinationals in Retreat. The Scottish Experience*, Edinburgh University Press, Edinburgh
—— and S. Young (1976) 'US Investment in Scotland – Aspects of the Branch Factory Syndrome', *Scottish Journal of Political Economy*, 23, 279-94
Hoogvelt, A.M.M. (1982) *The Third World in Global Development*, Macmillan, London
Horst, T. (1972) 'Firm and Industry Determinants of the Decision to Invest Abroad: An Empirical Study', *Review of Economics and Statistics*, 54, 258-66
—— (1974) *American Exports and Foreign Direct Investments*, Harvard Institute of Economic Research, Discussion Paper No 362
Howard, C.G. (1971) 'The Extent of "Nativisation" of Management in Overseas Affiliates of Multinational Firms: a World-Wide Study', *Indian Management*, 10, 11-20
Howarth, N. (1982) 'The Trade Union Response to Multinationals', in S. Maxwell (ed.), *Scotland, Multinationals and the Third World*, Mainstream Publishing, Edinburgh
Howenstine, N.G. (1982) 'Growth of US Multinational Companies', *Survey of Current Business*, 62, 34-46
Hufbauer, G.C. and F.M. Adler (1968) *Overseas Manufacturing Investment and the Balance of Payments*, US Treasury Department, Tax Policy Research Study No. 1, Washington
Hughes, H. and P.S. You (eds.) (1969) *Foreign Investment and Industrialisation*, Australian National University Press, Canberra
Hymer, S. (1972) 'The Multinational Corporation and the Law of Uneven Development', in J. Bhagwati (ed.), *Economics and the World Order*, Macmillan, London
—— (1976) *The International Operations of National Firms: a Study of Direct Investment*, MIT Press, Cambridge, Mass. (previously unpublished doctoral dissertation, 1960)
ICTFU (1971) *Economic and Social Bulletin*, 19, 22-3
—— (1983) *Trade Unions and the Transnationals, Export Processing Zones*, Special Issue No. 3, March
Industrial Relations Review and Reports (1981) 'Staff Status – Issues and Trends', *Industrial Relations Review and Reports*, 248, 2-8
Inohara, H. (1982) *Japanese Subsidiaries in Europe: Promotion of Local Personnel*, Sophia University, Institute of Comparative Culture, Business Series, Bulletin No 89, Tokyo
International Labour Organisation (1969) *The ILO: In Service of Social Progress*, International Labour Office, Geneva
—— (1976) *Wages and Working Conditions in Multinational Enterprises*, International Labour Office, Geneva
—— (1976a) *Multinationals in Western Europe: The Industrial Relations Experience*, International Labour Office, Geneva

—— (1976b) *Social and Labour Practices of some European-Based Multinationals in the Metal Trades*, International Labour Office, Geneva

—— (1976c) *The Impact of Multinational Enterprises on Employment and Training*, International Labour Office, Geneva

—— (1981a) *Employment Effects of Multinational Enterprises in Industrialised Countries*, International Labour Office, Geneva

—— (1981b) *Employment Effects of Multinational Enterprises in Developing Countries*, International Labour Office, Geneva

—— (1981c) *Multinationals' Training Practices and Development*, International Labour Office, Geneva

Iyanda, O. and J.A. Bells (1979) *Employment Effects of Multinational Enterprises in Nigeria*, International Labour Office, Geneva, Multinational Enterprises Programme, Working Paper 10

Jackson, P.M. (1982) *The Political Economy of Bureaucracy*, Philip Allan, Oxford

Jacoby, N.H., P. Mehemkis and R. Eells (1977) *Bribery and Extortion in World Business*, Macmillan, London

Jasay, A.E. (1960) 'The Social Choice Between Home and Overseas Investment', *Economic Journal*, 70, 105-13

Jedel, M.J. and D. Kujawa (1976) *Management and Employment Practices of Foreign Direct Investors in the United States*, in U.S. Department of Commerce, Foreign Direct Investment in the United States: Report to the Congress, Vol. 5, Appendix 1, Government Printing House, Washington, DC

—— (1977) 'Industrial Relations Profiles of Foreign-owned Manufactures in the United States', in R.F. Banks and J. Stieber (eds.), *Multinationals, Unions and Labor Relations in Industrialised Countries*, Cornell University Press, New York

Jenkins, R. (1979) 'The Export Performance of Multinational Corporations in Mexican Industry', *Journal of Development Studies*, 15, 89-107

—— (1982) 'Dependent Industrialisation in the Third World', in S. Maxwell (ed.) , *Scotland, Multinationals and the Third World*, Mainstream, Edinburgh

Jo, S.H. (1976) *The Impact of Multinational Firms on Employment and Income: The Case of South Korea*, International Labour Office, Geneva, Multinational Enterprises Programme, Working Paper 7

Johnson, H.G. (1970) 'The Efficiency and Welfare Implications of the Multinational Corporation' in C.P. Kindleberger (ed.), *The International Corporation: A Symposium*, MIT Press, Cambridge, Mass

Jones, D.T. and S.J. Prais (1978) 'Plant Size and Productivity in the Motor Industry: Some International Comparisons', *Oxford Bulletin of Economics and Statistics*, 40, 131-51

Jordan, G.L. and J.E. Valhne (1981) *Domestic Employment Effects of Direct Investment Abroad by Two Swedish Multinationals*, International Labour Office, Geneva, Multinational Enterprises Programme, Working Paper 13

Juhl, P. (1979) 'On the Sectoral Patterns of West German Manufacturing Investment in Less Developed Countries: The Impact of Firm Size, Factor Intensities and Protection', *Weltwirlschaftliches Archiv*, 115, 508-19

Kamata, S. (1983) *Japan in the Passing Lane: An Insider's Account of Life in a Japanese Auto Factory*, Allen and Unwin, London

Kassalow, E.M. (1978) 'Aspects of Labour Relations in Multinational Companies:

An Overview of Three Asian Countries', *International Labour Review*, 117, 273-87

Kelly, J.E. (1982) *Scientific Management, Job Redesign, and Work Performance*, Academic Press, London

Kemp, M.C. (1962) 'Foreign Investment and the National Advantage', *Economic Record*, 38, 56-62

Kierzkowski, H. (1980) 'Displacement of Labour by Imports of Manufactures', *World Development*, 8, 753-62

Killick, T. (1982) 'Employment in Foreign-Owned Manufacturing Plants', *British Business*, 11, 536-7

Kindleberger, C.P. (1969) *American Business Abroad*, Yale University Press, New Haven

King, J. and P. Regan (1976) *Relative Income Shares*, Macmillan, London

Knickerbocker, F.T. (1973) *Oligopolistic Reaction and Multinational Enterprise*, Graduate School of Business Administration, Harvard University, Boston

Kojimi, K. (1977) 'Transfer of Technology to Developing Countries –Japanese Type Versus American Type', *Hitotsubashi Journal of Economics*, 18

—— (1978) *Direct Foreign Investment*, Croom Helm, London

Kravis, I.B. and R.E.Lipsey (1982) 'The Location of Overseas Production and Production for Export by U.S. Multinational Firms', *Journal of International Economics*, 12, 201-23

Kreye, O., V. Frobel and J. Heiricks (1980) 'Western Europe's Economic Development and the N.I.E.O.', in E. Lazlo and J. Kurtzman (eds.), *Western Europe and the New International Economic Order*, Pergamon, Oxford

Kroner, M.L. (1980) 'U.S. International Transactions in Royalties and Fees 1967-1978', *Survey of Current Business*, 60, 29-35

Kujawa, D. (1971) *International Labour Relations Management in the Automotive Industry: A Comparative Study of Chrysler, Ford and General Motors*, Praeger, New York

—— (1978) 'U.S. Labor, Multinational Enterprise and the National Interest: A Proposal for Labor Law Reform', *Law and Policy in International Business*, 10, 941-68

—— (1979a) 'Collective Bargaining and Labor Relations in Multinational Enterprise: A U.S. Public Policy Perspective', in R. Hawkins (ed.), *Economic Effects of Multinational Enterprises*, J.A.I. Press, Greenwich, Conn

—— (1979b) 'The Labour Relations of U.S. Multinational Corporations Abroad: Comparative and Prospective Views', *Labour and Society*, 4, 3-25

—— (1980) 'Labor Relations of U.S. Multinationals Abroad', in B. Martin and E.M. Kassalow (eds.), *Labor Relations in Advanced Industrial Societies: Issues and Problems*, Carnegie Endowment, New York

Kumar, K. (1982) 'Third World Multinationals: A Growing Force in International Relations', *International Studies Quarterly*, 26, 397-424

—— and M.G. McLeod (1981) *Multinationals from Developing Countries*, D.C. Heath, Lexington

Labour Research (1980) 'U.K. Multinationals', *Labour Research*, 69, 2-4

Lall, S. (1973) 'Transfer-Pricing by Multinational Manufacturing Firms', *Oxford Bulletin of Economics and Statistics*, 35, 173-93

—— (1979) 'Multinationals and Market Structure in an Open Developing Economy: The Case of Malaysia', *Weltwirlschaftliches Archiv*, 115, 325-50

—— (1979b) *The Indirect Employment Effects of Multinational Enterprises in Developing Countries*, International Labour Office, Geneva, Multinational Enterprises Programme, Working Paper 3

—— (1980) 'Offshore Assembly in Developing Countries', *National Westminster Bank Review*, 14-23

—— (1980b) 'Vertical Inter-Firm Linkages in LDCs: An Empirical Study', *Oxford Bulletin of Eonomics and Statistics*, 42, 203-25

—— (1982) *Developing Countries as Exporters of Technology*, Macmillan, London

—— and P. Streeten (1977) *Foreign Investment, Transnationals and Developing Countries*, Macmillan, London

Lamont, D.F. (1970) 'American Business: Success or Failure in the Messogiorno', *Italian-American Business*, 21, 38-46

Landsberg, M. (1979) 'Export-Led Industrialisation in the Third-World: Manufacturing Imperialism', *Review of Radical Political Economics*, 11, 50-63

Langdon, S. (1981) *Multinational Corporations in the Political Economy of Kenya*, Macmillan, London

Lecaillon, J.F. Paukert, C. Morrisson and D. Germidis (1983) *Income Distribution and Economic Development: An Analytical Survey*, International Labour Office, Geneva

Lecraw, D. (1977) 'Direct Investment by Firms from Less Developed Countries', *Oxford Economic Papers*, 29, 442-57

Leibenstein, H. (1976) *Beyond Economic Man*, Harvard University Press, Cambridge, Mass

Leigh, R. and D.J. North (1978) 'Acquisitions in British Industry: Implications for Regional Development', in F.E.I. Hamilton (ed.), *Contemporary Industrialisation: Spatial Analysis and Regional Development*, Longmans, London

Levinson, C. (1971) 'The Multinational Corporation', *ICF Bulletin*

Levinson, K. (1975) *Multinational Corporations and Trade Unions*, University of Uppsala Project Report, mimeographed

Liebhaberg, B. (1980) *Industrial Relations and Multinational Corporations in Europe*, Gower, Aldershot

Lim, D. (1977) 'Do Foreign Companies Pay Higher Wages than Their Local Counterparts in Malaysian Manufacturing?', *Journal of Development Economics*, 4, 55-6

—— (1982) 'Fiscal Incentives and Direct Foreign Investment in Less Developed Countries', *Journal of Development Studies*, 19, 207-12

Lim, L. and P.E. Fong (1977) *The Electronics Industry in Singapore*, University of Singapore, Economic Research Centre

—— (1982) 'Vertical Linkages and Multinational Enterprises in Developing Countries', *World Development*, 10, 585-95

Lincoln, R.A. (1975) *US Direct Investment in the UK*, Economist Intelligence Unit, QER Special No. 23, London

Lipsey, R.E. (1982) 'Studies of Multinational Firms', *NBER Reporter*, 7-10

—— I.B. Kravis and R.A. Roldan (1982) 'Do Multinational Firms Adapt Factor Proportions to Relative Factor Prices?', in A.O. Krueger (ed.), *Trade and Employment in Developing Countries*, Vol. 2, University of Chicago Press, Chicago

—— and M.Y. Weiss (1981) 'Foreign Production and Exports in Manufacturing

Industries', *Review of Economics and Statistics*, 63, 488-94

Little, J.S. (1978) 'Locational Decisions of Foreign Direct Investors in the United States', *New England Economic Review*, 43-63

Litvak, I.A. and C.J. Maule (1972) 'The Unions Response to International Corporations', *Industrial Relations*, 12, 62-71

Lloyd, P.A. (1982) *A Third World Proletariat?*, Allen and Unwin, London

Long, F. (1981) 'Multinational Corporations and the Non-Primary Sector Trade of Developing Countries. A Survey of Available Data', *Economia Internazionale*, 34, 376-99

Lydall, H.F. (1975) *Trade and Employment: A Study of the Effects of Trade Expansion on Employment in Developing and Developed Countries*, International Labour Office, Geneva

Magee, S.P. (1977) 'Information and Multinational Corporations. An Appropriability Theory of Direct Foreign Investment', in J. Bhagwati (ed.), *The New International Economic Order*, MIT Press, Cambridge, Mass

—— (1977b) 'Multinational Corporations, Industry Technology Cycle and Development', *Journal of World Trade Law*, 11, 297-321

—— (1979) 'Jobs and the Multinational Corporation: The Home-Country Perspective', in R.G. Hawkins (ed.), *The Economic Effects of Multinational Corporations, Research in International Business and Finance*, Vol. 1, JAI Press, Greenwich, Conn

—— (1981) 'The Appropriability Theory of the Multinational Corporation', *Annals of the American Academy of Political and Social Science*, 458, 123-35

Mahler, V.A. (1981) 'Mining, Agriculture and Manufacturing. The Impact of Foreign Investment on Social Distribution in Third World Countries', *Comparative Political Studies*, 14, 267-97

Mansfield, E. and A. Romeo (1980) 'Technology Transfer to Overseas Subsidiaries by US-Based Firms', *Quarterly Journal of Economics*, 95, 737-50

Mason, R.H. (1973) 'Some Observations on the Choice of Technology by Multinational Firms in Developing Countries', *Review of Economics and Statistics*, 55, 349-55

Massey, D. and R. Meegan (1982) *The Anatomy of Job Loss*, Methuen, London

McAleese, D. and M. Counahan (1979) 'Stickers or Snatchers? Employment in Multinational Corporations during the Recession', *Oxford Bulletin of Economics and Statistics*, 41, 345-58

—— and D. McDonald (1978) 'Employment Growth and the Development of Linkages in Foreign-Owned and Domestic Manufacturing Enterprises', *Oxford Bulletin of Economics and Statistics*, 40, 321-39

McCarthy, J.E. (1974) *Trade Adjustment Assistance: A Case Study of the Shoe Industry in Massachusetts*, Ph.D. Dissertation submitted to Tufts University

McKersie R.B. and P. Cappelli (1982) *Concession Bargaining*, Alfred P. Sloan School of Management, MIT Working Paper 1322-82

—— and L.C. Hunter (1972) *Pay, Productivity and Collective Bargaining*, Macmillan, London

—— and W. Sengernberger (1983) *Job Losses in Major Industries: Manpower Strategy Responses*, OECD, Paris

McLean, R.A. (1977) 'Bargaining Cartels and Multinational Industrial Relations', *Columbia Journal of World Business*, 12, 107-12

McMullan, N. (1982) *The Newly Industrialising Countries: Adjusting to Success*, British North American Committee, Washington

Medoff, J. (1979) 'Layoffs and Alternatives Under Trade Unions in the United States', *American Economic Review*, 69, 380-95

Meller, P. and A. Mizala (1982) 'US Multinationals and Latin American Manufacturing Employment Absorption', *World Development*, 10, 115-26

Michalet, C.A. (1976) *The Multinational Companies and the New International Division of Labour*, International Labour Office, Geneva, World Employment Programme, Research Working Paper 5

Michel, A. (1983) 'The Internationalisation of the Economy and Inequalities of Class and Sex', *Current Sociology*, 31, 209-11

Miller, R.U. and M.A. Zaidi (1982) 'Human Capital and Multinationals: Evidence from Brazil and Mexico', *Monthly Labor Review*, 105, 45-7

Millward, N. (1979) 'Research Note: The Strike Record of Foreign-Owned Manufacturing Plants in Great Britain', *British Journal of Industrial Relations*, 17, 99-104

Miscimara, P.A. (1981) 'The Entertainment Industry: Inroads in Multinational Collective Bargaining', *British Journal of Industrial Relations*, 19, 49-65

Mitchell, D.J.B. (1976) *Labor Issues of American International Trade and Investment*, Johns Hopkins University Press, Baltimore

Moll, E. (1967) 'Technical Assistance and Private Enterprise', *OECD Observer*, 31, 35-7

Morley, S.A. and G.W. Smith (1977a) 'The Choice of Technology: Multinational Firms in Brazil', *Economic Development and Cultural Change*, 25, 239-64
—— (1977b) 'Limited Search and the Technology Choices of Multinational Firms in Brazil', *Quarterly Journal of Economics*, 91, 263-88

Moxon, R.W. (1975) 'The Motivation for Investment in Offshore Plants: The Case of the US Electronics Industry', *Journal of International Business Studies*, 6, 51-65

Mundell, R.A. (1957) 'International Trade and Factor Mobility', *American Economic Review*, 47, 321-35

Murray, P. and J. Wickham (1982) 'Technocratic Ideology and the Reproduction of Inequality: The Case of the Electronics Industry in the Republic of Ireland', in G. Day (ed.), *Diversity and Decomposition in the Labour Market*, Gower, Aldershot

Musgrave, P.B. (1975) *Direct Investments Abroad and the Multinationals: Effects on the United States Economy*, Report to the Subcommittee on Multinational Corporations of the Committee on Foreign Relations, United States Senate, Washington

National Association of Manufacturers (1962) in *Trade Expansion Act of 1962*, US Congress, Senate Committee on Finance, Washington, DC, pp. 1630-1

Nayyar, D. (1978) 'Transnational Corporations and Manufactured Exports from Poor Countries', *Economic Journal*, 88, 59-84

Negandhi, A.R. (1983) 'External and Internal Functioning of American, German and Japanese Multinational Corporations: Decisionmaking and Policy Issues', in W.H. Goldberg (ed.), *Governments and Multinationals*, Oelgeschlager, Gunn and Hain, Cambridge, Mass
—— and B.R. Baliga (1979) *Quest for Survival and Growth: a Comparative Study of American, European and Japanese Multinationals*, Praeger, New

York

—— (1981) *Tables are Turning: German and Japanese Multinational Companies in the United States*, Oelgeschlager, Gunn and Hain, Cambridge, Mass

Nelson, R.R. (1981) 'Research on Productivity Growth and Productivity Differences: Dead Ends and New Departures', *Journal of Economic Literature*, 14, 1029-64

Neumann, G.R. (1978) 'The Direct Labor Market Effects of the Trade Adjustment Assistance Program: The Evidence From the TAA Survey', in W. Dewald (ed.), *The Impact of International Trade and Investment on Employment*, US Department of Labor, Washington, DC

Newbould, G.D., P.J. Buckley and J. Thurwell (1978) *Going International – the Experience of Smaller Companies Overseas*, Associated Business Press, London

Newfarmer R.S. (1978) 'TNC Takeovers in Brazil: The Uneven Distribution of Benefits in the Market for Firms', *World Development*, 7, 25-43

—— (1979) 'Oligopolistic Tactics to Control Markets and the Growth of TNCs in Brazil's Electrical Industry', *Journal of Development Studies*, 15, 108-40

—— and L.C. Marsh (1981) 'Foreign Ownership, Market Structure and Industrial Performance', *Journal of Development Economics*, 8, 47-75

Northrup, H.R. (1978) 'Why Multinational Bargaining Neither Exists Nor is Desirable', *Labor Law Journal*, 29, 330-42

—— and R.L. Rowan (1974) 'Multinational Collective Bargaining Activity: The Factual Record in Chemicals, Glass and Rubber Tires, Part II', *Columbia Journal of World Business*, 9, 49-63

—— (1979) *Multinational Collective Bargaining Attempts*, University of Pennsylvania Press, Philadelphia

—— and K. Laffer (1977) 'Australian Maritime Unions and the International Transport Workers' Federation', *Journal of Industrial Relations*, 19, 113-32

OECD (1979) *the Impact of the Newly Industrialising Countries on Production and Trade in Manufactures*, OECD, Paris

—— (1981) *Recent International Direct Investment Trends*, OECD, Paris

—— (1982) 'A New Wave of Industrial Exporters', *OECD Observer*, 119, 26-30

—— (1983) *Investment Incentives and Disincentives and the International Investment Process*, OECD, Paris   .

—— (1983b) *Disclosure of Information by Multinational Enterprises: Clarification of the Accounting Terms in the OECD Guidelines*, OECD, Paris

—— (1983c) *Positive Adjustment Policies: Managing Structural Change*, OECD, Paris

Olle, W. and W. Schoeller (1977) 'World Market Competition and Restrictions Upon International Trade Union Policies', *Capital and Class*, 2, 56-74

O'Loughlin, B. and P.N. O'Farrell (1980) 'Foreign Direct Investment in Ireland: Empirical Evidence and Theoretical Implications', *The Economic and Social Review*, 11, 155-85

Oman, C. (1981) 'New North-South Investment Strategies', *OECD Observer*, 112, 13-15

Otterbeck, L. (1981) *The Management of Headquarters – Subsidiary Relationships in Multinational Corporations*, Gower, Aldershot

Ozawa, T. (1982) 'A Newer Type of Foreign Investment in Third World Resource Development', *Rivista Internazionale di Scienze Economiche et Commer-*

ciali, 29, 1133-51

Pack, H. (1979) 'The Substitution of Labour for Capital in Kenyan Manufacturing', *Economic Journal*, 86, 45-58

Palloix, C. (1976) 'The Labour Process: from Fordism to neo-Fordism', *The Labour Process and Class Strategies*, CSE Pamphlet No. 1, Conference of Socialist Economists London

Pastore, J.M.D. (1977) 'Multinational Corporations and Transfer of Technology', in D. Germidis (ed.), *Transfer of Technology by Multinational Corporations*, OECD Development Centre Studies, Vol. 1, Paris

Pavitt, K. (ed.) (1979) *Technical Innovation and British Economic Performance*, Macmillan, London

Peccei, R. and M. Warner (1976) 'Industrial Relations Decision-Making in Multinational Firms', *Journal of General Management*, 4, 66-71

—— (1981) 'Industrial Relations, Strategic Importance and Decision-Making', *Relations Industrielles*, 36, 132-50

Penrose, E.T. (1968) *The Large International Firm in Developing Countries: The International Petroleum Industry*, Allen and Unwin, London

Pichierri, A. (1978) 'Diffusion and Crisis of Scientific Management in European Industry', in S. Giner and M.S. Archer (eds.), *Contemporary Europe*, Routledge and Kegan Paul, London

Plant, R. (1981) *Industries in Trouble*, International Labour Office, Geneva

Plasschaert, S. (1979) *Transfer Pricing and Multinational Corporations*, Gower, Aldershot

Pond, C. (1983) 'Wages Councils, the Unorganised, and the Low Paid', in G.S. Bain (ed.), *Industrial Relations in Britain*, Basil Blackwell, Oxford

Prais, S.J. (1976) *The Evolution of Giant Firms in Britain*, Cambridge University Press, Cambridge

—— (1978) 'The Strike Proneness of Large Plants in Britain', *Journal of the Royal Statistical Society*, A, 141, 368-84

—— (1981) *Productivity and Industrial Structure*, Cambridge University Press, Cambridge

Pratten, C.F. (1976) *Labour Productivity Differentials Within International Companies*, University of Cambridge, Department of Applied Economics, Occasional Paper 50

—— (1977) 'The Efficiency of British Industry', *Lloyds Bank Review*, 123, 19-28

—— and A.G. Atkinson (1976) 'The Use of Manpower in British Manufacturing Industry', *Department of Employment Gazette*, June, 571-6

Preston, L.E. (1980) 'The Manufacturing Environment in the 1980s', in H.A. Juris and M. Roomkin (eds.), *The Shrinking Perimeter*, D.C. Heath, Lexington

Pugel, T.A. (1981) 'The Determinants of Foreign Direct Investment: An Analysis of US Manufacturing Industries', *Managerial and Decision Economics*, 2, 220-8

Radhu, G.M. (1973) 'Some Aspects of Direct Foreign Private Investment in Pakistan', *Pakistan Development Review*, 12, 68-80

Reuber, G.L. *et al.* (1973) *Private Foreign Investment in Development*, Clarendon Press, Oxford

Ricks, D.A. and A. Campagna (1978) 'Job Security in the Foreign-Owned Firm', *Business Horizons*, 21, 73-9

Riedel, J. (1975) 'The Nature and Determinants of Export-Oriented Direct
Foreign Investment in a Developing Country: A Case Study of Taiwan', *Wel-
wirlschaftliches Archiv*, 111, 505-28

Roberts, B.C. (1973) 'Multinational Collective Bargaining: A European Prospect?'
British Journal of Industrial Relations, 9, 1-19

—— and J. May (1974) 'The Response of Multinational Enterprises to International Trade Union Pressures', *British Journal of Industrial Relations*, 12,
403-16

Robinson, J. (1983) *Multinationals and Political Control*, Gower, Aldershot

Root, F. and A.A. Ahmed (1979) 'Empirical Determinants of Manufacturing
Direct Foreign Investment in Developing Countries', *Economic Development
and Cultural Change*, 27, 751-67

Rosenberg, S. (1983) 'Reagan, Social Policy and Labour Force Restructuring',
Cambridge Journal of Economics, 7, 179-96

Rosenbluth, G. (1970) 'The Relation Between Foreign Control and Concentration in Canadian Industry', *Canadian Journal of Economics*, 3, 14-50

Rowan, R.L., H.R. Northrup and R.A. O'Brien (1980) *Multinational Union
Organisations in the Manufacturing Industries*, Industrial Research Unit,
University of Pennsylvania

Rubery, J. and F. Wilkinson (1981) 'Outwork and Segmented Labour Markets', in
F. Wilkinson (ed.), *The Dynamics of Labour Market Segmentation*, Academic
Press, London

Rubin, S.J. (1971) 'Multinational Enterprise and National Sovereignty: A Skeptic's
Analysis', *Law and Policy in International Business*, 3, 1-41

Rubinson, R. (1976) 'The World-Economy and the Distribution of Income Within
States: A Cross-National Study, *American Sociological Review*, 41, 638-59

Rugman, A. (1980) 'A New Theory of the Multinational Enterprise: Internationalisation Versus Internalisation', *Columbia Journal of World Business*,
15, 23-9

—— (1981) *Inside the Multinationals: The Economics of Internal Markets*,
Croom Helm, London

Ruttenberg, S.H. (1971) *Needed: A Constructive Foreign Trade Policy*, Industrial
Union Department, AFL-CIO, Washington, DC

—— (1974) 'The Union View of Multinationals: An Interpretation' in R.J. Flana-
gan and A.R. Weber (eds.), *Bargaining Without Boundaries*, University of Chicago Press, Chicago

Sabolo, Y. and R. Trajtenberg (1976) *The Impact of Transnational Enterprises
on Employment in the Developing Countries*, Internatinal Labour Office,
World Employment Programme, Research Working Paper 6

Sachdev, J.C. (1975) 'Disinvestment: Corporate Strategy or Admission of
Failure?', *Multinational Business*, 4, 12-19

—— (1978) 'Foreign Investment Policies of Developing Host Nations and Multinationals: Interactions and Accommodations', *Management International
Review*, 18, 33-43

Sampson, A. (1973) *The Sovereign State: The Secret History of ITT*, Hodder and
Stoughton, London

Sasaki, N. (1981) *Management and Industrial Structure in Japan*, Pergamon
Press, Oxford

Saul, J.S. (1975) 'The "Labour Aristocracy" Thesis Reconsidered', in R. Sandbrook and R. Cohen (eds.), *The Development of an African Working Class*, Longmans, London

Saunders, C. (1981) *The Political Economy of New and Old Industrial Countries*, Butterworth, London

Sauvant, K.P. (1981) 'The Role of Transnational Enterprises in the Establishment of the NIEO. A Critical View', in J. Lozoya and R. Green (eds.), *International Trade, Industrialisation and the NIEO*, Pergamon Press, London

Scaperlanda A. and R.S. Balough (1983) 'Determinants of US Direct Investment in the EEC: Revisited', *European Economic Review*, 21, 381-90

Schoepfle, G.K. (1982) 'Imports and Domestic Employment: Identifying Affected Industries', *Monthly Labor Review*, 105, 13-25

Sciberras, I.E. (1977) *Multinational Electronic Companies and National Economic Policies*, Contemporary Studies in Economic and Financial Analysis, Vol. 6, JAI Press, Greenwich, Conn

Sekiguchi, S. (1979) *Japanese Direct Foreign Investment*, Macmillan, London

Sewell, J.W. (1978) *Can the Rich Prosper Without Progress by the Poor?*, Overseas Development Council, Washington, DC (mimeographed)

Shah, S.M.S. and J.F.T. Toye (1978) 'Fiscal Incentives For Firms in Some Developing Countries: Survey and Critique', in J.F.T. Toye (ed.), *Taxation and Economic Development*, Frank Cass, London

Sharpston, M. (1975) International Sub-Contracting, *Oxford Economic Papers*, 27, 94-135

Shaw R. and D. Sherk (1976) 'The International Utilization of Labor and the Multinational Corporation in the Pacific Basin', in H.B. Malmgren (ed.) *Pacific Basin Development: The American Interests*, Lexington Books, Lexington, Mass

Shearer, J.C. (1970) 'Manpower Environments Confronting American Firms in Western Europe', in A. Kamin (ed.), *Western European Labor and the American Corporation*, Bureau of National Affairs, Washington

—— (1977) 'Fact and Fiction Concerning Multinational Labor Relations', *Vanderbilt Journal of Transnational Law*, 10, 51-82

Shorey, J. (1980) 'An Analysis of Quits Using Industry Turnover Data', *Economic Journal*, 90, 821-37

Simon, H.A. (1961) *Administrative Behaviour*, Macmillan, London

Singer, H.W. (1970) 'Dualism Revisited: A New Approach to the Problems of the Dual Society in Developing Countries', *Journal of Development Studies*, 7, 60-75

Smith, I.J. (1982) 'The Role of Acquisition in the Spatial Distribution of the Foreign Manufacturing Sector in the United Kingdom', in M. Taylor and N. Thrift (eds.), *The Geography of Multinationals*, Croom Helm, London

Smith, S.K. (1972) 'National Labor Unions v. Multinational Companies: The Dilemma of Unequal Bargaining Power', *Columbia Journal of Transnational Law*, 11, 124-57

Social and Labour Bulletin (1981) 'Egypt: Employment of Nationals in Export Processing Zones', 3, 367

Steuer, M.D. *et al.* (1973) *The Impact of Foreign Direct Investment on the United Kingdom*, Department of Trade and Industry, HMSO, London

—— and J. Gennard (1971) 'Industrial Relations, Labour Disputes and Labour Utilisation in Foreign-Owned Firms in the United Kingdom', in J.H. Dunning (ed.), *The Multinational Enterprise*, Allen and Unwin, London

Stewart, F. (1974) 'Technology and Employment in LDCs', in E.O. Edwards (ed.), *Employment in Developing Nations*, Columbia University Press, New York

Stobaugh, R.B. *et al.* (1976) *Nine Investments Abroad and Their Impact at Home: Case Studies on Multinational Enterprises and the US Economy*, Harvard Business School, Division of Research, Boston

Stoever, W.A. (1979)'Renegotiations: The Cutting Edge of Relations Between MNCs and LDCs', *Columbia Journal of World Business*, 14, 5-13

Stopford, J.M. (1979) *Employment Effects of Multinational Enterprises in the United Kingdom*, International Labour Office, Geneva, Multinational Enterprises Programme, Working Paper 5

Storey, J. (1983) *Managerial Prerogative and the Question of Control*, Routledge and Kegan Paul, London

Strassman, W.P. (1968) *Technological Change and Economic Development: The Manufacturing Experience of Mexico and Peru*, Cornell University Press, Ithaca, New York

Strenger, H.J. (1980) 'The Problems and Pressures on the European Chemical Industry', *Chemistry and Industry*, 6, December 905

Stubenitsky, F. (1970) *American Investment in the Netherlands Industry*, Rotterdam University Press, Rotterdam

Sunkel, O. and E.F. Fuenzalida (1979) 'Transnationalisation and its National Consequences', in J. Villamil (ed.), *Transnational Capitalism*, Harvester Press, Brighton

Svedberg, P. (1982) 'The Profitability of UK Foreign Direct Investment Under Colonialism', *Journal of Development Economics*, 11, 273-86

—— (1983) 'Multinational Enterprise Investment and Import Substitution in Latin America', *Australian Economic Papers*, 21, 321-31

Swords-Isherwood, N. (1979) 'British Management Compared', in K. Pavitt (ed.), *Technical Innovation and British Economic Performance*, Macmillan, London

Szakats, A. (1980) *Trade Unions and Multinational Enterprises*, Victoria University of Wellington, Industrial Relations Centre, Occasional Papers in Industrial Relations, No. 27

Taira, K. and G. Standing (1973) 'Labor Market Effects of Multinational Enterprises in Latin America', *Nebraska Journal of Economics and Business*, 12, 103-17

Takamiya, M. (1981) 'Japanese Multinationals in Europe: Internal Operations and their Public Policy Implications', *Columbia Journal of World Business*, 16, 5-16

Tang, R.Y.W. (1979) *Transfer Pricing Practices in the United States and Japan*, Praeger, New York

—— (1981) *Multinational Transfer Pricing: Canadian and British Perspectives*, Butterworth, Toronto

Taylor, R. (1983) 'Trade Unions' Tory Troubles', *Management Today*, 56-61

Teece, D.J. (1977) *Technology Transfer by Multinational Firms*, Ballinger, Cambridge, Mass

Telesio, P. (1979) *Technology Licensing and Multinational Firms*, Praeger, New York

Tharakan, P.K.M. (1981) *The International Division of Labour and Multinational Companies*, Gower, Farnborough

Thurow, L.C. (1973) *Multinational Companies and the American Distribution of Income*, mimeographed

Torneden, R.L. (1975) *Foreign Disinvestment by US Multinational Corporations*, Praeger, New York

Townsend, A.R. (1983) *The Impact of Recession on Industry Employment and Regions, 1976-1981*, Croom Helm, London

Trades Union Congress (1970) *Report of a Conference on International Corporations*, 21 October, TUC, London

Trajtenberg, R. (1976) *Transnational Enterprises and the Cheap Labour Force in the Less Developed Countries*, International Labour Office, Geneva, World Employment Programme, Research Working Paper 8

Treckel, K.F. (1972) 'The World Auto Councils and Collective Bargaining', *Industrial Relations*, 12, 72-9

Trevor, M. (1983) *Japan's Reluctant Multinationals: Japanese Management at Home and Abroad*, Frances Pinter, London

Tumlir, J. (1974) 'Emergency Protection Against Sharp Increases in Imports', in H. Corbet and R. Jackson (eds.), *In Search of A New World Economic Order*, Croom Helm, London

Turner, H.A., G. Roberts and D. Roberts (1977) *Management Characteristics and Labour Conflict*, Department of Applied Economics, Papers in Industrial Relations and Labour, No. 3, Cambridge University Press, Cambridge

Turner, L., C.I. Bradford, L.G. Franko, N. McMullan and S. Woolcock (1980) *Living With the Newly Industrialising Countries*, Royal Institute of International Affairs, Chatham House Paper No. 7, London

Tyler, W.G. (1974) 'Employment Generation and the Promotion of Manufactured Exports in Less Developed Countries: Some Suggestive Evidence', in H. Giersch (ed.), *The International Division of Labour: Problems and Perspectives*, J.C.B. Mohr, Tubingen

Ulman, L. (1975) 'Multinational Unionism: Incentives, Barriers and Alternatives', *Industrial Relations*, 14, 1-31

UNCTAD (1974) *Major Issues Arising from the Transfer of Technology to Developing Countries*, TD/B/AC 11/10/Rev2, United Nations, New York

—— (1980) *The Set of Multilaterally Agreed Equitable Principles and Rules for the Control of Restrictive Business Practices*, Resolution Adopted 22 April, UNCTAD, New York

—— (1981) *An International Code of Conduct on the Transfer of Technology*, Latest Draft TD/CODE TOT/33, 12 May, UNCTAD, New York

UNESCO (1974) *The Impact of Multinational Corporations on the Development Process and on International Relations: Report of the Group of Eminent Persons*, E/5500/ADDI, UNESCO, New York

—— (1978) *Draft International Agreement to Prevent and Eliminate Illicit Payments in International Commercial Transactions*, UNESCO, New York

United Nations (1978) *Transnational Corporations in World Development: A Re-Examination*, UN Publications, New York

US Senate Committee (1973) *Implications of Multinational Firms for World Trade and Investment and for US Trade and Labor*, Washington, DC, pp. 581-93

US Tariff Commission (1970) *Economic Factors Affecting the Use of Items 807.00 and 806.30 of the Tariff Schedules of the United States*, Washington, DC

—— (1973) *Implications of Multinational Firms for World Trade and Investment and for US Trade and Labor*, Report to the Committee on Finance of the US Senate and its Subcommittee on International Trade, 93rd Congress, 1st Session, Washington, DC

Vaitsos, C. (1974) 'Employment Effects of Foreign Direct Investments in Developing Countries', in E.O. Edwards (ed.), *Employment in Developing Nations*, Columbia University Press, New York

—— (1974b) *Intercountry Income Distribution and Transnational Corporations*, Clarendon Press, Oxford

—— (1976) *Employment Problems and Transnational Enterprises in Developing Countries: Distortions and Inequality*, International Labour Office, Geneva, World Employment Programme, Research Working Paper 11

Van den Bulcke, D. (1983) 'Belgian Industrial Policy and Foreign Multinational Corporations: Objectives Versus Performance', in W.H. Goldberg (ed.), *Governments and Multinationals*, Oelgerschlager, Gunn and Hain, Cambridge, Mass

—— and E. Halsberghe (1979) *Employment Effects of Multinational Enterprises: A Belgian Case Study*, International Labour Office, Geneva, Multinational Enterprises Programme, Working Paper 1

—— et al. (1979) *Investment and Divestment Policies of Multinational Corporations in Europe*, Saxon House, Farnborough

Vaupel, J.W. and J.P. Curhan (1973) *The World's Multinational Enterprises: A Sourcebook of Tables*, Division of Research, Harvard Business School, Boston

Vernon, R. (1966) 'International Investment and International Trade in the Product Cycle', *Quarterly Journal of Economics*, 80, 190-207

—— (1971) *Sovereignty at Bay: the Multinational Spread of US Enterprises*, Basic Books, New York

—— (1974) 'The Location of Economic Activity', in J.H. Dunning (ed.), *Economic Analysis and the Multinational Enterprise*, Allen and Unwin, London

—— (1979) 'The Product Cycle Hypothesis in a New International Environment', *Oxford Bulletin of Economics and Statistics*, 41, 255-68

Vredeling, H. (1983) 'Foreword' to R. Blanpain et al., *The Vredeling Proposal: Information and Consultation of Employees in Multinational Enterprises*, Kluwer, Deventer

Waldmann, R.J. (1980) *Regulating International Business through Codes of Conduct*, American Enterprise Institute for Public Policy Research, Washington, DC

Wall, D. (1976) 'Export Processing Zones', *Journal of World Trade Law*, 10, 478-89

Wallace, D., Jr. (1974) *International Control of Investment: The Dusseldorf Conference on Multinational Corporations*, Praeger, New York

Warner, M. (1976) 'The Comparative Measurement of Industrial Relations in Multinational Firms', in K.P. Tudyka (ed.), *Multinational Corporations and Labour Unions*, SUN, Werkuitgave

Watanabe, S. (1980) *Multinational Enterprises and Employment-Oriented 'Appropriate' Technologies in Developing Countries*, International Labour Office,

Geneva, Multinational Enterprises Programme, Working Paper 14

Watts, H.D. (1980) *The Large Industrial Enterprise: Some Spatial Perspectives*, Croom Helm, London

WCL (1973) *CGT Information* 10, 14

Weinberg, N. (1975a) 'A Labor Approach to International Corporations', in C.F. Bergsten (ed.), *Toward a New World Trade Policy: The Maidenhead Papers*, Lexington Books, Lexington, Mass

—— (1975b) 'The Multinational Corporation and Labor', in A.A. Said and L.R. Simmons (eds.), *The New Sovereigns: Multinational Corporations as World Powers*, Prentice-Hall, New Jersey

Weinberg, P.J. (1978) *European Labor and Multinationals*, Praeger, New York

Welge, M.K. (1931) 'The Effective Design of Headquarters – Subsidiary Relationships in German MNCs', in L. Otterbeck (ed.), *The Management of Headquarters – Subsidiary Relationships in Multinational Corporations*, Gower, Aldershot

Wells, L.T. (1973) 'Economic Man and Engineering Man: Choice of Technology in a Low-Wage Country', *Public Policy*, 21, 319-42

—— (1983) *Third World Multinationals: the Rise of Foreign Investment from Developing Countries*, MIT Press, Cambridge, Mass

White, L.J. (1976) 'Appropriate Technology, X-Inefficiency, and a Competitive Environment', *Quarterly Journal of Economies*, 90, 575-85

White, M. (1981) *Payment Systems in Britain*, Gower/PSI, Aldershot

—— and M. Trevor (1983) *Under Japanese Management: The Experience of British Workers*, Heinemann Educational Books, London

Whitehall, A.M. and S. Takezawa (1978) 'Workplace Harmony: Another Japanese "Miracle"?', *Columbia Journal of World Business*, 13, 25-39

Wilkins, M. (1970) *The Emergence of Multinational Enterprise: American Business Abroad from the Colonial Era to 1914*, Harvard University Press, Cambridge, Mass

Williamson, O.E. (1975) *Markets and Hierarchies, Analysis and Anti-Trust Implications*, The Free Press, New York

Windmuller, J.P. (1980) *The International Trade Union Movement*, Kluwer, Deventer

Wolf, M. (1979) *Adjustment Policies and Problems in Developed Countries*, World Bank Staff Working Paper 349, Washington, DC

Wolter, F. (1976) 'Adjusting to Imports from Developing Countries: the Evidence from a Capital Rich, Human Resource Poor Country', in H. Giersch (ed.), *Reshaping the World Economic Order*, J.C.B. Mohr, Tubingen

Wonnacott, R.J. (1982) 'Controlling Trade and Foreign Investment in the Canadian Economy: Some Proposals', *Canadian Journal of Economics*, 15, 567-85

Wood, S. (1982) 'The Study of Management in British Industrial Relations', *Industrial Relations Journal*, 13, 51-61

—— and J. Kelly (1982) 'Taylorism, Responsible Autonomy and Management Strategy', in S. Wood (ed.), *The Degradation of Work?: Skill, Deskilling and the Labour Process*, Hutchinson, London

Yannopoulos, G.N. and J.H. Dunning (1976) 'Multinational Enterprises and Regional Development: An Explanatory Paper', *Regional Studies*, 10, 389-99

Yeoman, W.A. (1976) *Selection of Production Processes for the Manufacturing*

Subsidiaries of US-Based Multinational Corporations, Arno Press, New York

Zermeno, R., R. Moseley and E. Braun (1980) 'The Robots are Coming Slowly', in T. Forester (ed.), *The Microelectronics Revolution*, Basil Blackwell, Oxford

Ziebura, G. (1982) 'Internationalisation of Capital, International Division of Labour and the Role of the European Community', *Journal of Common Market Studies*, 21, 127-40

INDEX

Addison, J.T. 100, 107
adjustment 159
adjustment assistance *see* trade
    adjustment assistance
Adler, M. 39, 42
'advantages' 28
AFL-CI0 2, 40
Agarwal, J. 56
aggregation problem 45
Aharoni, Y. 3
Ahluwalia, M. 74
Ahmed, A.A. 43
Aho, M.C. 27
Alam, G. 168
Allen, T.W. 17
Aliber, R.Z. 15
'alternative position' 50
alternatives to DFI 166
Andean Code 134, 141
Anell, L. 96, 100
anti-classical case 39, 44, 68
'appropriability problem' 56
appropriate technology 55
appropriation 104
Armstrong, R.B. 99
Arnison, J. 122
Arrighi, G. 70, 89, 90, 103
Arrow, K. 30
Ashcroft, B. 62, 165
Aslegg, R.G. 113
Atkinson, A.G. 80, 126

Baade, H.W. 135
Bacon, R.W. 79
'Badger case' 127, 137
Baerresen, D.W. 49
Bailey, P.J. 41, 99
Balassa, B. 161
Bale, M. 161
Baliga, B.R. 86, 113, 118
Ball, G. 133
Ballance, R.H. 52, 123
Ballmer-Cao, T.H. 101
Balough, T. 43, 129
Baranson, J. 53, 56
Bardhan, P.K. 168
bargaining cartels 152

bargaining disadvantage: of labour
    2, 122; of LDCs 167
'bargaining down' 146
bargaining levels 110
bargaining procedures 111
Barnett, A.H. 107
Barrera, M. 100
barriers to entry 30
Beaumont, P.B. 109
Behrman, J.N. 99
Bellace, J.R. 143
Bello, J.A. 59
Bennett, M.L. 60
Benson, I. 98
Bergsten, C.F. 41, 55, 74, 124, 128
Berthomieu, C. 2, 91
Biersteker, T.J. 47, 56
bilateral investment agreements 130
Blake, D.H. 112, 131, 148, 154
Blam, Y. 19
Blanpain, R. 85, 109, 117, 126, 136
Boddewyn, J.J. 62, 165
Bomers, G.B.J. 93, 113, 123, 146
Booz, Allen and Hamilton 61
Bornschier, V. 2, 73, 101, 173
Bos, H.C. 50
bounded rationality 84
Braun E. 98
Breidenstein, G. 17
Brewer, A. 104
British Leyland 97
Brown, W. 93, 106, 116
Buckley, P.J. 6, 14, 23, 29, 31, 34,
    86, 94, 108, 110, 119, 124, 156,
    166
bureaucratic control 84
Burke-Hartke bill 131, 145, 158
Burton, J. 163
Business and Industry Advisory
    Committee 136
Business International Corporation
    42; 'by-pass option' 143

Cable, V. 66, 160
Calvert, A.L. 28
Campagna, A. 122
capital constraints 39

227